Reading
Workbook

Siegfried Engelmann

Steve Osborn

Jean Osborn

Leslie Zoref

Acknowledgments

Many thanks to the Arthur Academy, Lisa Yates, and her students for field testing this edition of Reading Mastery 5. Thanks also to Lynda Gansel, Crystal Weber, and Chris Gladfelter for their help in preparing the manuscript.

mheducation.com/prek-12

Copyright © 2021 McGraw-Hill Education

All rights reserved. No part of this publication may be reproduced or distributed in any form or by any means, or stored in a database or retrieval system, without the prior written consent of McGraw-Hill Education, including, but not limited to, network storage or transmission, or broadcast for distance learning.

Send all inquiries to:
McGraw-Hill Education
8787 Orion Place
Columbus, OH 43240

ISBN: 978-0-07-905382-4
MHID: 0-07-905382-3

Printed in the United States of America.

5 6 7 8 9 LWI 27 26 25

Name _____

A STORY DETAILS

Work the items.

1. Jess is the ▩ of "The Day I Didn't Go to the Pool."

    a. author   b. illustrator   c. narrator

2. Jess lives in the state of _____ .

3. Jess is _____ years old.

4. How many brothers and sisters does Jess have altogether? _____

5. What is the name of Jess's oldest sister? _____

6. Jess says that his house is like a _____ can.

7. Jess's father once said, "What _____ , _____ ."

8. Jess says the clouds were swirling around like a witch's _____ .

9. Jess was worried because a ▩ was approaching the house.

    a. tornado   b. blizzard   c. hurricane

B CLOZE SENTENCES

Complete each sentence with the correct word.

| issue | quivery | snaked |

1. You could tell that Noah was scared because his voice was _____ .

2. Taka didn't want to be seen, so she got on her stomach and _____ under the bush.

3. The thin branch was too _____ , so the bird flew away.

4. One _____ that everyone talks about is the bad weather.

Lesson 1

C CONTEXT CLUES

For each item, circle the answer that means the same thing as the words in bold type.

1. They cooked beans in a **large metal pot** over the fire.

    a. griddle   b. cauldron   c. sardine can

2. They made pancakes on a **flat cooking surface** in the middle of the stove.

    a. griddle   b. cauldron   c. sardine can

GO TO PART D IN YOUR TEXTBOOK

Name _____

A STORY DETAILS

Work the items.

1. If you're caught outside in a tornado, you need to find the ▓▓▓ spot you can.

    a. highest   b. most secret   c. lowest

2. When the tornado approached, Jess and the others ran toward a drainage _____ .

3. That spot was about one _____ yards from their trailer home.

4. Jess said the funnel was a monster _____ churning through the sky.

5. Jess said Dougie and Lyssa nearly pulled his arms out of their shoulder ▓▓▓ .

    a. sprockets   b. sockets   c. lockets

6. When the tornado hit, the walls of Jess's house exploded ▓▓▓ .

    a. inward   b. outward   c. windward

7. The tornado sucked up everything like a giant _____ cleaner.

8. The storm left chunks of siding and ▓▓▓ of glass.

    a. shards   b. shots   c. ships

9. Jess said that his mom's car was traveling at _____ speed.

B CLOZE SENTENCES

Complete each sentence with the correct word.

| cauldron | issue | pelted |
| griddle | outward | sardine |

1. When Kang turned the box of cereal upside down, the cereal flowed _____ .

2. During the snowstorm, the kids _____ each other with snowballs.

3. Clogging storm drains with litter is a serious _____ .

4. You need a big _____ to make soup for twenty people.

Lesson 2

C CONTEXT CLUES

For each item, circle the answer that means the same thing as the word(s) in bold type.

1. The floor at the window factory was littered with **shards** of glass.

    a. carpets   b. sheets   c. pieces

2. The tiny boat looked like **it couldn't be saved from danger** during the storm.

    a. it was a goner   b. a safe place

    c. it wasn't there

3. The **thrum** of the rain on the windows kept Amelia awake.

    a. sight   b. wetness   c. noise

GO TO PART D IN YOUR TEXTBOOK

Name _____

3

A STORY DETAILS

Work the items.

1. Two of the oldest epics in the world are The _____ and The _____ .

2. About how many years ago do the epics take place?
   a. 30   b. 300   c. 3,000

3. The epic that tells about the Trojan War is called The _____ .

4. In that war, the _____ army fought the Trojan army.

5. The war was fought in and near the walled city of _____ .

6. The main character in the other epic is _____ .

7. That main character came up with the idea of building a hollow wooden _____ to trick the Trojans.

8. The first person to tell the stories was probably a blind poet named _____ .

9. The stories were originally written in the _____ language.

B CLOZE SENTENCES

Complete each sentence with the correct word.

| hinder | outward | shard |
| lyre | prose | translate |

1. Poets write poetry, but novelists write _____ .

2. You have to speak at least two languages to _____ a book from one language to another.

3. Mert cut his foot when he stepped on a _____ of glass.

4. The other team tried to _____ Umi before she scored a goal.

5. The poet played a _____ as she sang the story.

C CHARACTER TRAITS

Complete each sentence with *Zeus*, *Poseidon*, *Hermes*, or *Athena*.

1. _____ was the messenger deity.

2. _____ was the deity of the sea.

3. _____ carried a lightning bolt.

4. _____ protected people who were in danger.

Lesson 3

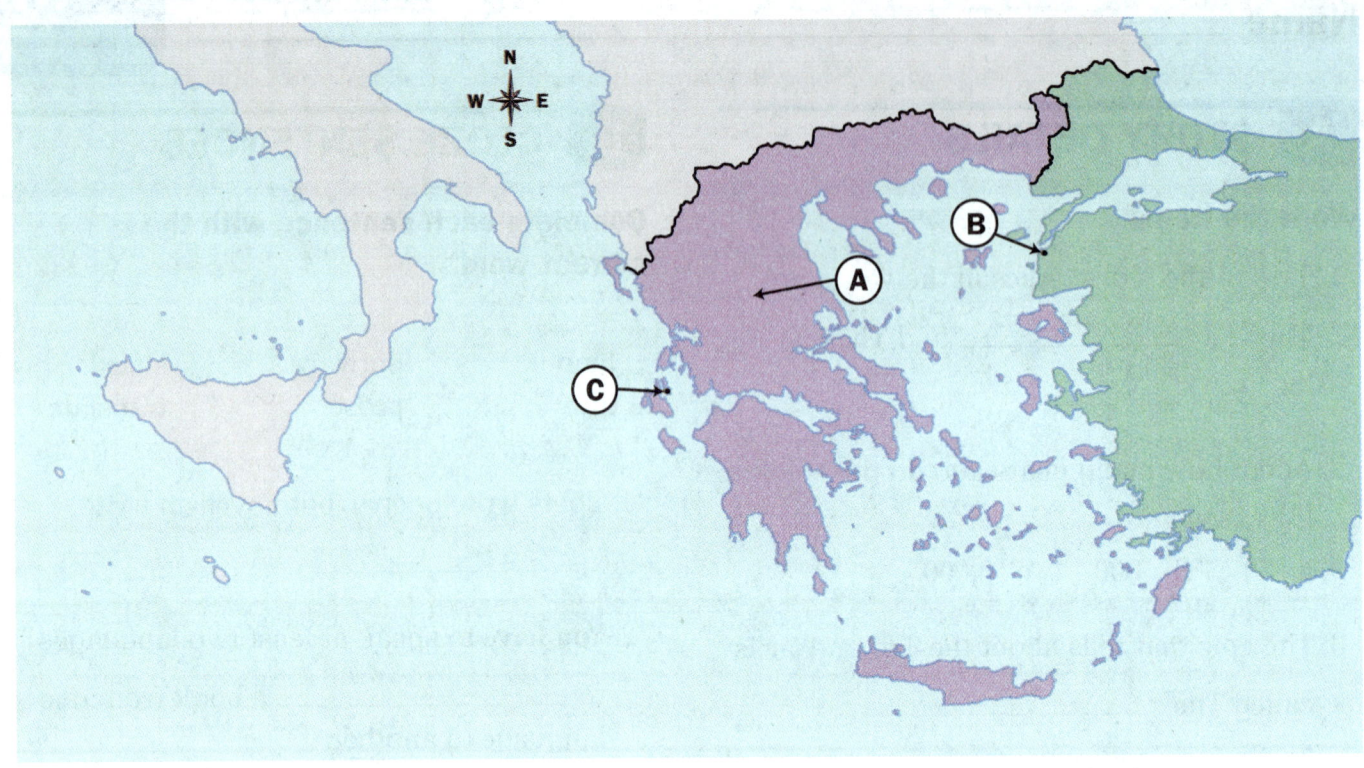

D CONTEXT CLUES

For each item, circle the answer that means the same thing as the word(s) in bold type.

1. You have to be prepared if you **come into contact with** bad weather.

    a. hinder   b. translate   c. encounter

2. People gathered to hear the **long poem that tells the story of a hero.**

    a. epic   b. lyre   c. prose

3. Lily was hard to understand because her voice was **shaking.**

    a. thrumming   b. snaking   c. quivery

E MAPS

Work the items.

1. What is the name of country **A**? _____

2. What language do people speak in that country? _____

3. What is the name of city **B**? _____

4. What were the people who lived in city **B** called? _____

5. What is the name of island **C**? _____

6. Who was the king of island **C**? _____

GO TO PART D IN YOUR TEXTBOOK

Lesson 3

Name _____

4

A STORY DETAILS

Work the items.

1. A Cyclops had one _____ in the middle of his _____.

2. What animals did the Cyclops take care of?
   a. sheep   b. goats   c. cattle

3. Polyphemus used a huge ▓▓▓ to block the opening of his cave.
   a. metal door   b. flagstone   c. boulder

4. Why couldn't Odysseus and his men move that object?
   a. It was too big.
   b. They didn't have the key.
   c. It was electrified.

5. The only god Polyphemus respected was _____.

6. That god was Polyphemus's ▓▓▓.
   a. son   b. father   c. uncle

7. At first, Odysseus told Polyphemus that his name was _____.

8. Odysseus blinded Polyphemus by throwing hot _____ into his eye.

9. Which god began to plot against Odysseus?
   a. Poseidon   b. Zeus   c. Athena

B CLOZE SENTENCES

Complete each sentence with the correct word.

| Cyclops | hinder | prose |
| epic | lyre | troubling |

1. Polyphemus was a _____.

2. The poet sang a long _____ about a mighty hero.

3. The bugs kept _____ the campers all night long.

4. Learning to play the _____ takes a long time.

C RELATED FACTS

Work the items.

1. At the beginning of the epic, Odysseus left the city of _____.

2. He had traveled to that city to fight in the _____ War.

3. How long had he been in that city?
   a. 10 weeks   b. 10 months   c. 10 years

4. Odysseus's home island was named _____.

5. That island was part of the country of _____.

Lesson 4 7

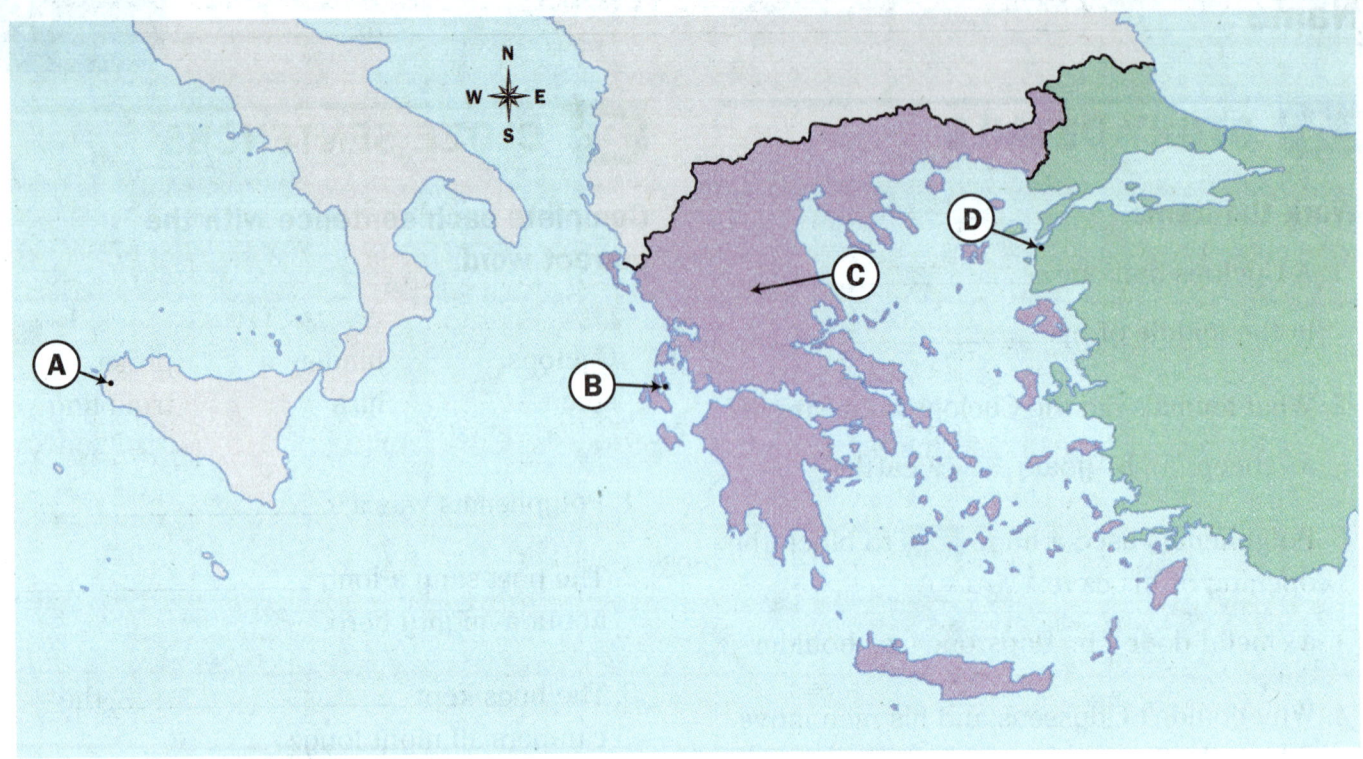

D CONTEXT CLUES

For each item, circle the answer that means the same thing as the words in bold type.

1. The **wool covering a sheep's body** was as white as snow.

   a. blanket   b. cotton   c. fleece

2. The **sheep that was less than a year old** grazed in the pasture.

   a. lamb   b. calf   c. foal

3. Cats love to **travel through an area to learn about it.**

   a. encounter   b. explore   c. pelt

E MAPS

Work the items.

1. Which people lived in place **D**?
   _____

2. What was the name of the Cyclops who lived in place **A**? _____

3. What is the name of country **C**?
   _____

4. What is the name of island **B**?
   _____

5. Draw a line on the map to show Odysseus's journey so far. Put arrows on the line to show the direction he went.

GO TO PART D IN YOUR TEXTBOOK

Name _____

5

A STORY DETAILS

Work the items.

1. The sorceress who lived in a palace was named _____ .

2. She changed the men into _____ and then back to men.

3. Odysseus met the god _____ on his way to the sorceress's palace.

4. The sorceress warned Odysseus not to eat the _____ cattle of _____ on his journey home.

5. The singers Odysseus heard were called the _____ .

6. Odysseus's men didn't hear the singing because ▓▓▓ .
   a. they had wax in their ears
   b. the sea was too loud
   c. they were bound to their seats

7. The singers seemed to offer Odysseus all knowledge and ▓▓▓ .
   a. pleasure   b. power   c. wisdom

8. Why couldn't Odysseus go to the singers' island?
   a. He didn't know how to swim.
   b. The sea was too rough.
   c. He was tied to the mast.

B CLOZE SENTENCES

Complete each sentence with the correct word.

| lyre | sacred | ventured |
| maiden | straws | voyage |

1. Zina was brave, and she often _____ where no one else dared to go.

2. The family had six sons but not even one _____ .

3. Nobody wanted to shovel snow, so they drew _____ to see who would begin.

4. The _____ to the planet Mars took several years.

C CHARACTER TRAITS

Complete each sentence with *Odysseus, Circe, Polyphemus, Poseidon, Sirens,* or *Hermes*.

1. _____ had only one eye.

2. _____ changed men into pigs.

3. _____ was the god of the sea.

4. _____ sang songs that enchanted sailors.

5. _____ loved knowledge and wisdom more than anything else.

Lesson 5

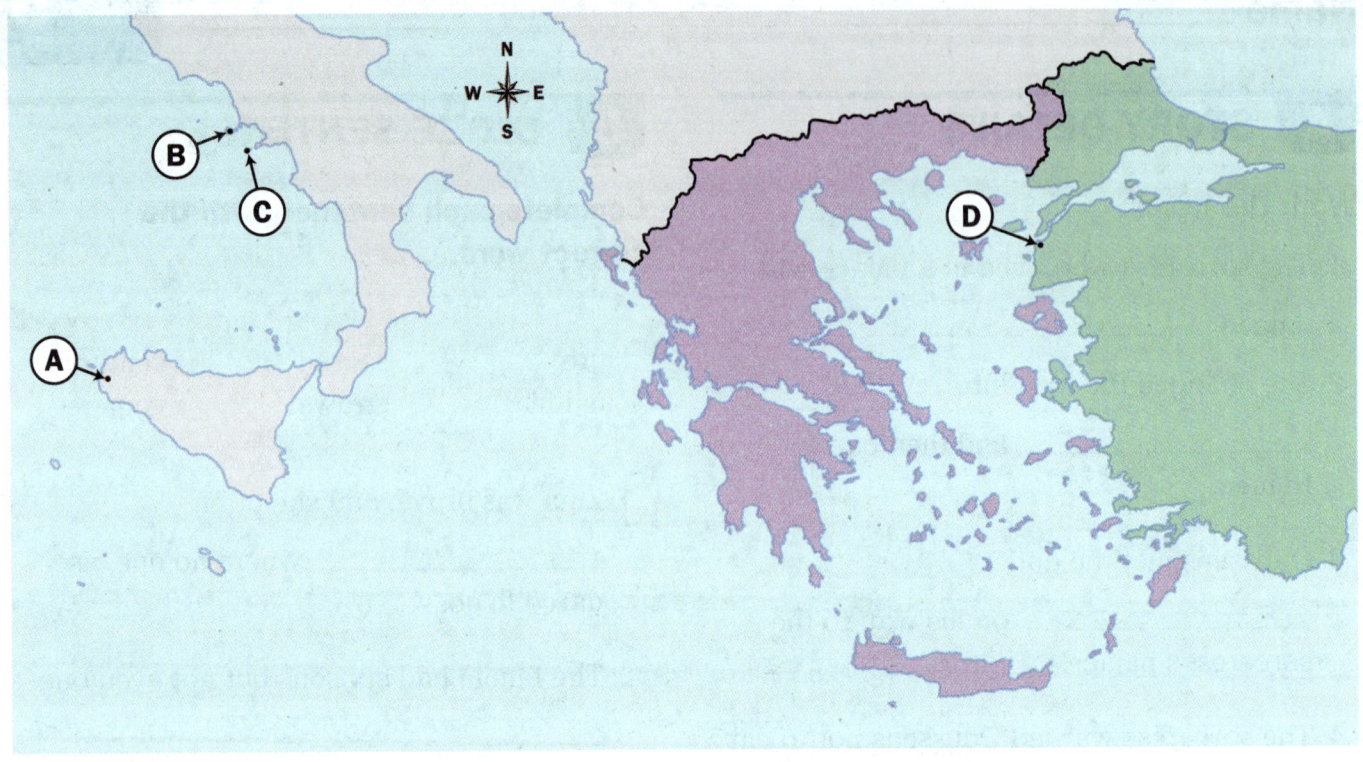

D CONTEXT CLUES

For each item, circle the answer that means the same thing as the word in bold type.

1. Tyler reached down to **pluck** a wildflower from the ground.

    a. quickly pull   b. squash   c. photograph

2. The plane was ready to **depart**, so the passengers fastened their seatbelts.

    a. delay   b. partner   c. leave

3. The hero in the movie had to **slay** a monster to save a group of people.

    a. scare away   b. calm down   c. kill

E MAPS

Work the items.

1. Which sorceress lived at place **B**?
   _____

2. Which people lived at place **D**?
   _____

3. Which creatures lived at place **C**?
   _____

4. Which Cyclops lived at place **A**?
   _____

5. Draw a line with arrows on the map to show Odysseus's journey so far.

GO TO PART E IN YOUR TEXTBOOK

10   Lesson 5

Name _____ 6

A STORY DETAILS

Work the items.

1. What was the name of the creature that lived on the west side of the narrows? _____

2. The east side of the narrows had a dangerous ▨ .
   a. waterfall   b. whirlpool   c. geyser

3. To which god did the cattle on the island belong? _____

4. The men who ate those cattle ▨ .
   a. drowned   b. got sick   c. starved

5. The fairy who found Odysseus on a beach was named _____ .

6. Odysseus stayed on the fairy's island for _____ years.

7. Odysseus's wife was named _____ .

8. Odysseus's son was named _____ .

9. The man who married Odysseus's wife would become ▨ of Ithaca.
   a. king   b. suitor   c. god

B CLOZE SENTENCES

Complete each sentence with the correct word.

| deed | perish | suitor |
| lurked | sheltered | wallow |

1. The rich _____ kept asking Paloma to marry him, but she always said no.

2. The pig loved to _____ around and around in the deep pile of mud.

3. Ghosts _____ behind every door in the haunted house.

4. Rescuing the cat from the burning house was a brave _____ .

Lesson 6   11

C CONTEXT CLUES

For each item, circle the answer that means the same thing as the words in bold type.

1. Medusa's face was so **horrible and disgusting** that it turned people to stone.

   a. troubling   b. hideous

   c. outward   d. quivery

2. It was hard to see down the river because the **cloud of water droplets** was so thick.

   a. mist   b. voyage

   c. fleece   d. prose

3. The hungry lion wanted to **quickly eat** a zebra.

   a. cease   b. slay

   c. pluck   d. devour

D SEQUENCING

Number the events in the correct sequence.

____ A sorceress changed some of Odysseus's men to pigs.

____ Odysseus fought a war at Troy.

____ Odysseus blinded a one-eyed giant.

____ Odysseus heard beautiful singing.

____ Odysseus's men ate a god's cattle.

____ A monster grabbed six men at once.

E CHARACTER TRAITS

Complete each sentence with *Athena*, *Calypso*, *Hermes*, *Odysseus*, *Penelope*, *Poseidon*, *Scylla*, or *Zeus*.

1. _____ was the goddess of wisdom.

2. _____ was a monster with six heads.

3. _____ was the messenger god.

4. _____ was the god of the sea.

5. _____ was Odysseus's wife.

6. _____ was a fairy who lived on her own island.

7. _____ was the only person to survive a shipwreck.

GO TO PART E IN YOUR TEXTBOOK

Name _____

A STORY DETAILS

Work the items.

1. The god that Zeus sent to Calypso's island was named _____ .

2. The woman Odysseus most wanted to see was named _____ .

3. Odysseus left Calypso's island on a ▨ .
   a. sailboat   b. rowboat   c. raft

4. _____ tried to punish Odysseus by creating a storm.

5. The goddess who saved Odysseus from the storm was named _____ .

6. That goddess gave Odysseus a ▨ .
   a. bright cloth   b. brass shield
   c. sharp sword

7. Then Odysseus swam to an island called _____ .

8. The goddess who helped Odysseus after he landed on the island was named _____ .

9. This goddess gave a dream to a ▨ .
   a. princess   b. queen   c. fairy

B CLOZE SENTENCES

Complete each sentence with the correct word.

> backwash   cherished   midst
> breakers   explored   spied

1. Hatsu _____ her little brother and would do anything for him.

2. The _____ from the wave was so strong that it carried the swimmers out to sea.

3. As Pavel walked along the path above the ocean, he could hear the _____ crashing on the rocks below.

4. Sophie _____ a hawk floating high in the sky.

C SEQUENCING

Number the events in the correct sequence.

____ Odysseus heard the Sirens.

____ Odysseus landed on Phaeacia.

____ Odysseus stayed in Calypso's cave.

____ Odysseus blinded Polyphemus.

____ Odysseus sailed past Scylla.

Lesson 7   13

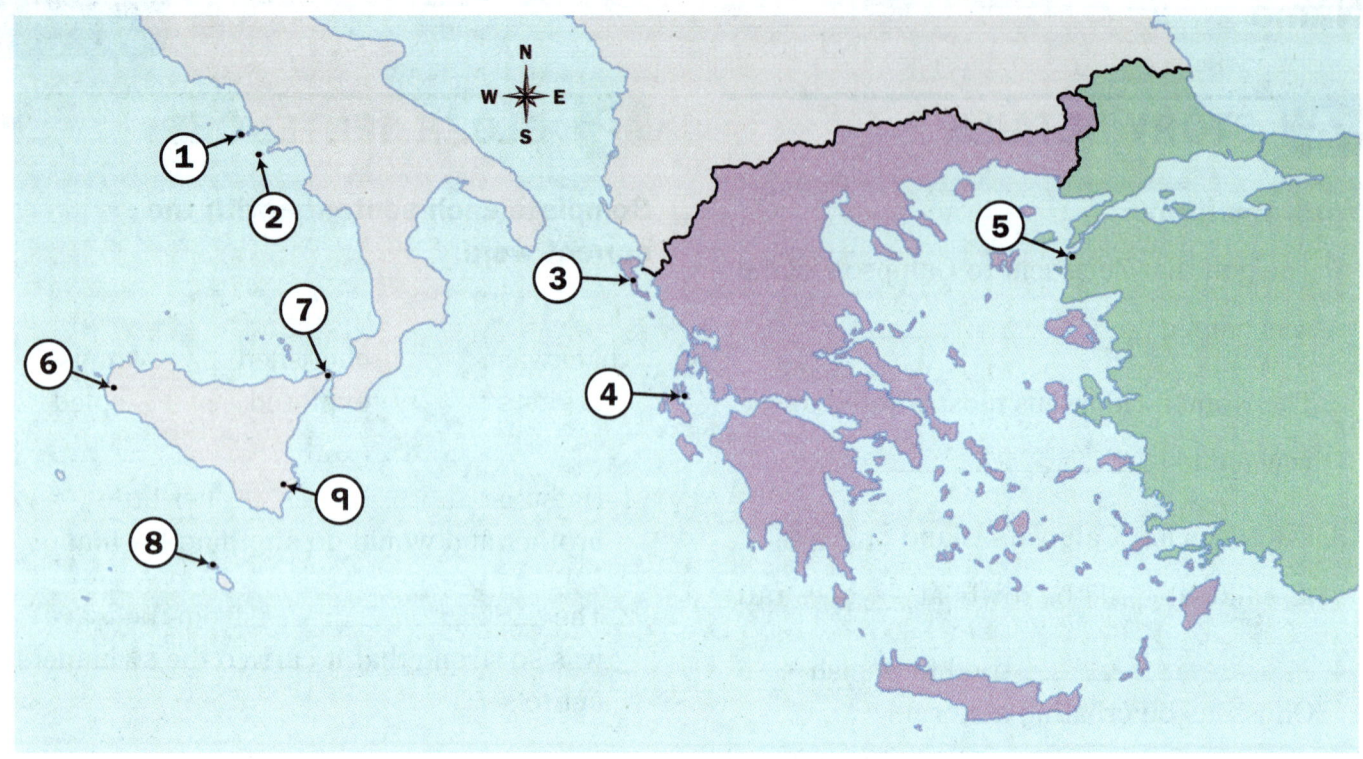

D CONTEXT CLUES

For each item, circle the answer that means the same thing as the word(s) in bold type.

1. Sheets, blankets, and rugs are made on a **device used for weaving cloth.**

   a. lamb b. thrum
   c. loom d. griddle

2. You put yourself in **danger** when you climb a cliff.

   a. peril b. encounter
   c. goner d. issue

3. People thought the lion was a **wild and cruel** beast, but it was really just a pussycat.

   a. savage b. hideous
   c. sheltered d. sacred

E MAPS

Work the items.

1. The animals who lived at place **9** were sacred to the god _____ .

2. Island **3** is named _____ .

3. The fairy who lived on island **8** was named _____ .

4. The six-headed monster who lived at place **7** was named _____ .

5. Draw a line on the map to show Odysseus's journey so far. Put arrows on the line to show which way Odysseus was going.

GO TO PART E IN YOUR TEXTBOOK

A STORY DETAILS

Work the items.

1. After Odysseus washed in the river, he rubbed _____ oil on his skin.

2. After washing, Odysseus put on a dress called a _____ .

3. Athena made Odysseus look ___ .
   a. older   b. stronger   c. taller

4. The princess would like to _____ Odysseus.

5. Which goddess did Odysseus meet when he entered the town? _____

6. The statues in the palace were made of _____ .

7. The queen noticed that Odysseus's clothes were ___ .
   a. dirty   b. from the palace   c. from Ithaca

8. What reason did Odysseus give the queen for not returning to the palace with the princess?
   a. He already knew the way and didn't need the princess's help.
   b. He had to get sandals so he could put them on before he entered the palace.
   c. He didn't think the queen would like to see her daughter with a stranger.

B CLOZE SENTENCES

Complete each sentence with the correct word.

| bronze | devour | sheltered |
| ceased | perished | venture |

1. The unfortunate sailor _____ in the terrible storm.

2. After the war _____ , the soldiers went home.

3. The hero's shield was made of _____ .

4. The wolf wanted to _____ the rabbit for dinner.

C PERSPECTIVES

Complete each sentence with *Penelope, Circe, Siren, Athena,* or *Calypso*.

1. _____ said, "I am waiting for Odysseus to come home."

2. _____ said, "I offered to let Odysseus stay on my island forever."

3. _____ said, "I warned Odysseus about the dangers he would face."

4. _____ said, "I talked about Odysseus with Zeus."

Lesson 8   15

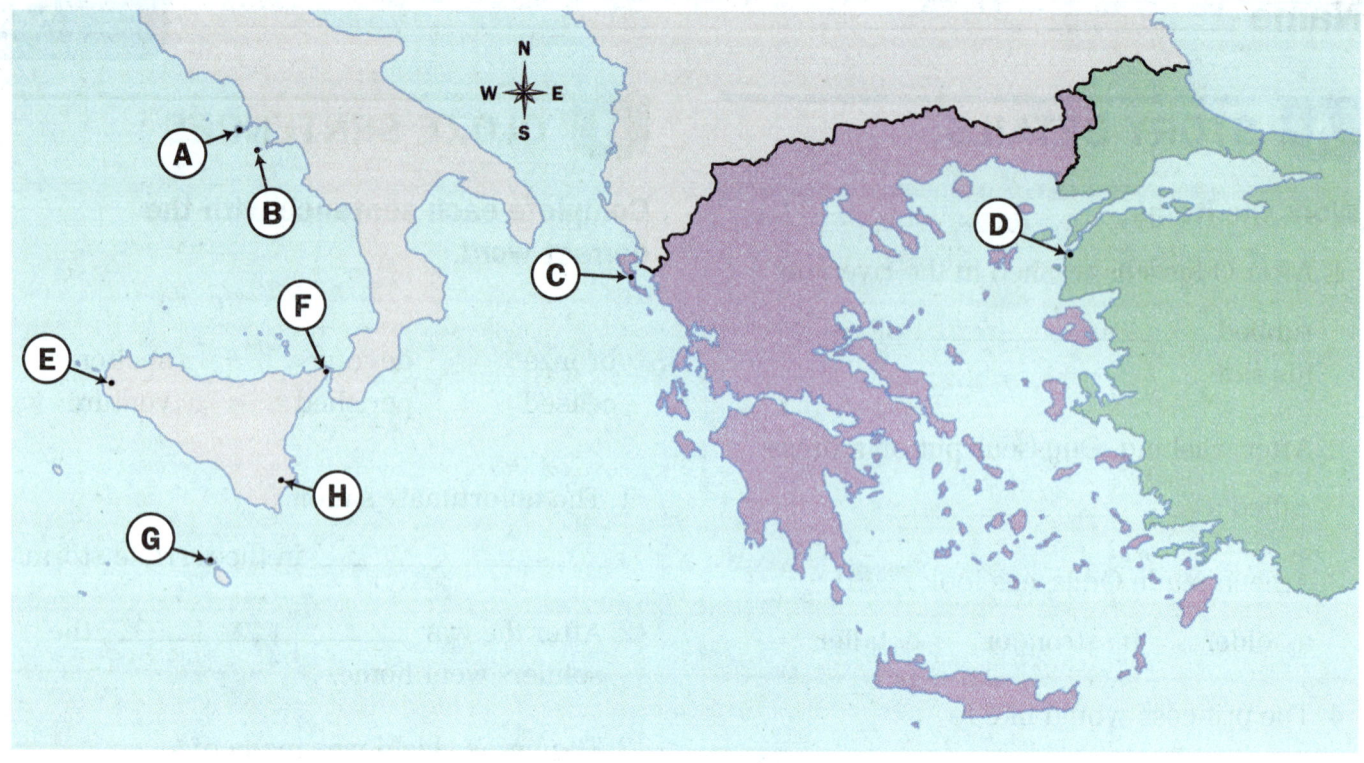

D CONTEXT CLUES

For each item, circle the answer that means the same thing as the word in bold type.

1. Nisha filled a **flask** with water to carry on her hike.

   a. loom   b. backwash

   c. bottle   d. breaker

2. People admire someone who is **noble.**

   a. savage and brutal   b. sacred

   c. maiden   d. brave and wise

3. Odysseus put on a **tunic** after taking a bath.

   a. dress   b. deed

   c. mist   d. suitor

E MAPS

Work the items.

1. The name of island **C** is _____ .

2. The giant who lived at place **E** was named _____ .

3. The singers at place **B** were called _____ .

4. Odysseus's men ate cattle at place ____ .

5. Draw a line on the map to show Odysseus's journey so far. Put arrows on the line to show which way Odysseus was going.

GO TO PART D IN YOUR TEXTBOOK

Lesson 8

Name _____

A STORY DETAILS

Work the items.

1. What did Odysseus do to show his ability at sports?
   a. ran a race
   b. threw a heavy weight
   c. shot arrows at a target

2. Why was the princess sad when she saw Odysseus again?
   a. She was sorry that Odysseus had to leave so soon.
   b. Odysseus didn't give her a parting gift.
   c. She learned that Odysseus was married.

3. Which hero did the minstrel sing about?
   _____

4. Odysseus didn't know where he was when he awoke on Ithaca because the land was hidden by _____ .

5. Which goddess did Odysseus meet on the shore? _____

6. The goddess couldn't help Odysseus on the sea because she couldn't quarrel with _____ .

7. After Odysseus left the goddess, he met a servant named _____ .

8. What kind of animals did that servant herd?
   a. goats   b. pigs   c. sheep

B CLOZE SENTENCES

Complete each sentence with the correct word.

| depart | peril | sportsman |
| faithful | pluck | voyage |

1. Dogs are well known for being _____ animals.

2. The _____ had a shelf filled with racing medals.

3. The sailors had plenty of time to prepare for their _____ across the ocean.

Lesson 9   17

C CONTEXT CLUES

For each item, circle the answer that means the same thing as the word(s) in bold type.

1. The two children began to **quarrel** about who had to do the dishes.

    a. argue   b. spy

    c. lurk   d. wallow

2. The king hired **a person who sings while playing a musical instrument** to entertain guests at the feast.

    a. suitor   b. maiden

    c. minstrel   d. goner

3. Ivan tried to **slay** the fly with a swatter, but he kept missing.

    a. affect   b. cherish

    c. kill   d. devour

D DEDUCTIONS

Work the items.

Once a type, or **species,** of animal becomes extinct, it is gone forever. More than one hundred species of animals have become extinct since the year 1800. In addition to these animals, several hundred species are endangered. An endangered species is one that is nearly extinct.

Sumatran tigers are an endangered species. They used to roam across most of Indonesia. Now they survive only on Sumatra, an island off the coast of Indonesia. Indiana bats, Florida panthers, bighorn sheep, and whooping cranes are other endangered species.

The list of endangered and extinct species will continue to grow until people make the world a better place for all living things. Tigers may not get along well with people, but if we kill all the tigers, we won't ever be able to get them back.

1. What is another word for *type*?

    _____

2. Underline the sentence that helps you answer question 1. Then write 1 next to the sentence.

3. The Indiana bat is an endangered species. Is it nearly extinct? _____

4. Underline the sentence that helps you answer question 3. Then write 3 next to the sentence.

5. Which types of endangered species does the passage mention?

    _____

    _____

    _____

6. Underline the words in the passage that help you answer question 5. Then write 5 next to the words.

GO TO PART D IN YOUR TEXTBOOK

Name _____ 10

A STORY DETAILS

Work the items.

1. How many suitors were at Odysseus's palace?

   a. 18   b. 108   c. 180

2. The suitors left their swords and armor near the palace _____ .

3. When Odysseus walked to the palace, he was disguised as a ▓▓▓ .

   a. merchant   b. shepherd   c. beggar

4. The goat farmer who insulted Odysseus was named _____ .

5. The dog that Odysseus saw outside the palace was named _____ .

6. The dog showed he knew Odysseus by ▓▓▓ .

   a. wagging his tail and dropping his ears
   b. barking joyfully
   c. perking up his ears

7. Odysseus had received a scar on his _____ when hunting with the dog.

8. After the dog made one last effort to stand, he _____ .

   a. stood up   b. wagged his tail   c. died

B CLOZE SENTENCES

Complete each sentence with the correct word.

| doom | minstrel | sportsman |
| faithful | quarrel | unearthly |

1. Everyone was scared by the _____ noises from the flying saucer.

2. It's not a good idea to _____ with a police officer.

3. Carlos had a feeling of _____ when he entered the dark cave.

4. When people get married, they promise to be _____ to each other.

C CHARACTER TRAITS

Write whether *Odysseus* or *Athena* was responsible for each event.

1. Odysseus was disguised so cleverly that no one could recognize him. _____

2. Odysseus told a clever story about how he came to Ithaca with all his riches. _____

3. Odysseus threw a weight farther than any of the Phaeacians. _____

4. Odysseus looked taller and fairer than he really was. _____

Lesson 10   19

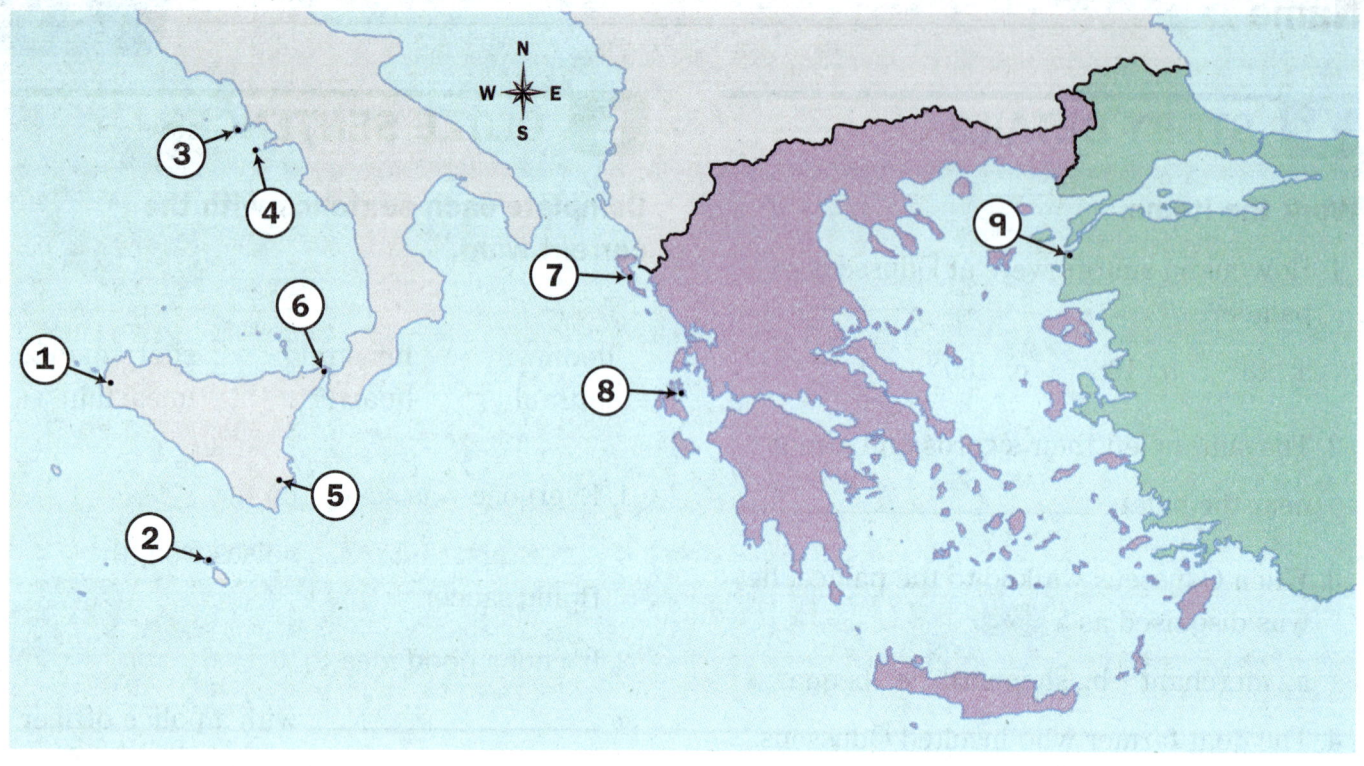

D CONTEXT CLUES

For each item, circle the answer that means the same thing as the word(s) in bold type.

1. The bike was rusty because Tessa **failed to take care of** it.
   a. challenged   b. neglected
   c. disguised   d. cherished

2. The rain finally **ceased**, and the sun began to shine.
   a. shuddered   b. raged
   c. perished   d. stopped

3. Children have to stay home from school when they get **lice** on their heads.
   a. spiders   b. fleece
   c. small insects   d. shards

E MAPS

Work the items.

1. What is the name of island **8**?
   _____

2. Which two directions do you travel to go straight from **7** to **8**?
   a. north and west   b. south and west
   c. south and east

3. Which fairy lived at island **2**?
   _____

4. At which number did Scylla live? _____

5. Draw a line on the map to show Odysseus's journey from beginning to end. Put arrows on the line to show which way Odysseus was going.

GO TO PART D IN YOUR TEXTBOOK

Name _____

A STORY DETAILS

Work the items.

1. The beggar told Penelope that Odysseus wore a ▇▇▇ cloak.

   a. black   b. purple   c. red

2. The nurse saw a long _____ on the beggar's leg.

3. That sight proved to the nurse that the beggar was named _____.

4. The beggar told the nurse to keep silent because he didn't want the _____ to slay him.

5. Penelope planned to _____ the suitor who passed the test with the bow and arrow.

6. To pass the test, a suitor would first have to ▇▇▇ the bow.

   a. find   b. string   c. break

7. Then the suitor would have to shoot an arrow through holes in the ▇▇▇.

   a. wall   b. armor   c. axe blades

8. The next morning, the suitor named _____ threw a cup at the beggar.

9. Telemachus left the hall at the end of the chapter to ▇▇▇.

   a. hide the suitors' weapons
   b. get Penelope
   c. summon the villagers

B CLOZE SENTENCES

Complete each sentence with the correct word.

| bronze | fawn | loom |
| cherish | flask | tunic |

1. When you combine copper and tin, you get _____.

2. The thirsty man drank the entire _____ of water.

3. Both a lamb and a _____ are in their first year of life.

4. Parents _____ their children more than anything.

C CHARACTER TRAITS

Complete each sentence with *Antinous*, *Athena*, *Odysseus*, *Penelope*, *Telemachus*, or *Zeus*.

1. _____ had a scar on one leg.

2. _____ is the son of Odysseus.

3. _____ threw a stool at Odysseus.

4. _____ could make herself invisible.

5. _____ decided to give the suitors a test.

Lesson 11   21

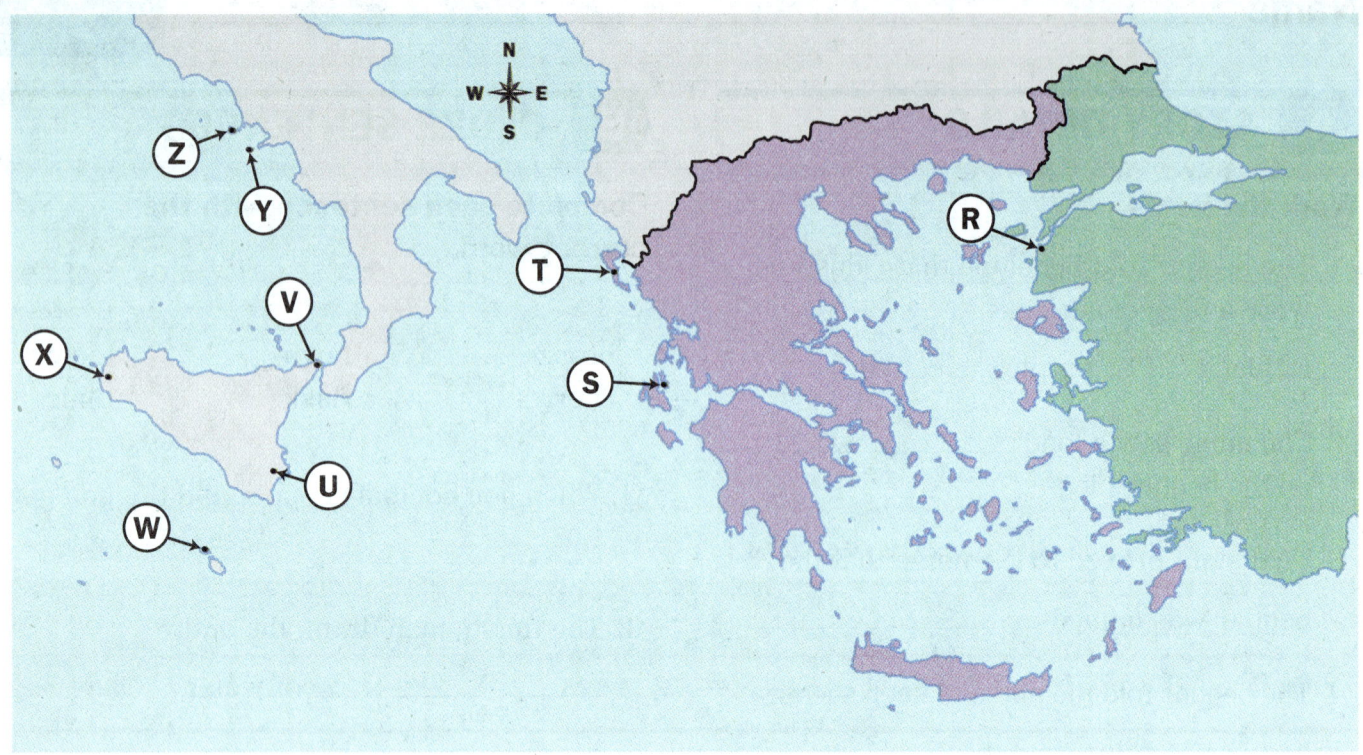

D CONTEXT CLUES

For each item, circle the answer that means the same thing as the word in bold type.

1. People who are **courteous** say *Please* and *Thank you*.
   a. polite
   b. unearthly
   c. faithful
   d. savage

2. The sick man was too **feeble** to get out of bed.
   a. neglected
   b. ragged
   c. hideous
   d. lacking in strength

3. It was hard to see inside the **dusky** cave.
   a. noble
   b. enchanting
   c. somewhat dark
   d. disguised

E MAPS

Work the items.

1. Write the letter of the place that is the farthest north on the map. ____

2. The character who lived at that place was named _____ .

3. The character who lived at place **X** was named _____ .

4. Write the letter of the place that is farthest south. ____

5. The character who lived at that place was named _____ .

GO TO PART D IN YOUR TEXTBOOK

22   Lesson 11

12

A STORY DETAILS

Work the items.

1. Penelope agreed to _____ the suitor who passed the test of the bow and arrow.

2. The character who came close to stringing the bow was named _____ .

3. Odysseus showed Eumaeus the scar ▮ .
   a. so Eumaeus could bandage it up
   b. to prove that he was really Odysseus
   c. to show what the suitors had done to him

4. When Odysseus plucked the bow string, it sounded like a ▮ .
   a. liar   b. lyre   c. lion

5. Odysseus told the suitors to fight or _____ .

6. The suitors couldn't find their weapons because _____ had hidden them.

7. Odysseus told Penelope that she was the fairest and _____ queen alive.

8. Penelope asked the old nurse to move Odysseus's bed _____ the bedroom.

9. The bed couldn't be moved because ▮ .
   a. its legs were nailed to the floor
   b. it was too heavy
   c. the bedpost was made from a standing tree

B CLOZE SENTENCES

Complete each sentence with the correct word.

| lice | nonetheless | uproar |
| midst | reckoning | vain |

1. The nurse used a special comb to get rid of _____ in the students' hair.

2. The _____ was so loud that people covered their ears.

3. The criminal knew his day of _____ had arrived when the jury found him guilty.

4. It was raining hard, but they played the game _____ .

Lesson 12   23

C INFERENCES

Work the items.

Plants and animals need food to survive, but they get their food in different ways. Animals must hunt for their food. Animals that eat plants must hunt for those plants. Animals that eat meat must hunt and kill other animals and eat their meat.

Green plants don't have to hunt for food because they make their own food. The leaves of green plants convert three ingredients—sunlight, water, and carbon dioxide—into food for the entire plant. This process is called **photosynthesis**.

1. Which three ingredients are used by leaves to make food for the entire plant?

   _____

   _____

2. Underline the sentence that helps you answer question 1. Then write 1 next to the sentence.

3. What do we call the process a plant uses to make its own food?

   _____

4. Underline the sentence that helps you answer question 3. Then write 3 next to the sentence.

5. Does a giraffe hunt for food or make its own food?

   _____

6. Underline the first sentence that helps you answer question 5. Then write 5 next to the sentence.

7. Does an elm tree hunt for food or make its own food?

   _____

8. Underline the sentence in the passage that helps you answer question 7. Then write 7 next to the sentence.

D CONTEXT CLUES

For each item, circle the answer that means the same thing as the word in bold type.

1. Willow branches are so **supple** that they can be woven into baskets.

   a. feeble   b. flexible

   c. shadowy   d. scaly

2. The **victorious** skier received a gold medal after the race.

   a. winning   b. second-place

   c. losing   d. serious

3. The archer tried to string another arrow, but her **quiver** was empty.

   a. bow   b. doom

   c. arrowhead   d. arrow container

GO TO PART E IN YOUR TEXTBOOK

Name _____ 13

A STORY DETAILS

Work the items.

1. Lacey says, "The sky flashed with a ghostly light." What is the ghostly light?
   _____

2. Lacey thought the best way to convince Bobby she wasn't afraid was to ▇▇ .
   a. go out into the storm
   b. go back to sleep
   c. make fun of him

3. Lacey thought that storms were sort of like _____ .

4. Mama says that if you _____ , it gives you something to hold on to during life's storms.

5. After her father left, Lacey tried to be ▇▇ that he would return soon.
   a. helpful   b. faithful   c. hopeful

6. When Mama got really quiet, it was like watching her drown in a deep well of ▇▇ .
   a. water   b. memory   c. sadness

7. Mama says that Lacey's bedroom window is full of _____ in a world of uncertainty.

8. The man who lived in the white house on the corner was named Mr. _____ .

9. Lacey and Bobby thought that man was probably waving at _____ .

B CLOZE SENTENCES

Complete each sentence with the correct word.

| courteous | fawn | neglect |
| dusky | feeble | speckle |

1. It's _____ to say "Thank you" when somebody gives you a gift.

2. Odysseus's dog Argos was so _____ that he couldn't stand up.

3. Each _____ on the unusual egg was a different color.

4. If you _____ to water a plant, it will soon die.

Lesson 13

C INFERENCES

Work the items.

Different kinds of animals eat different things. Animals that eat plants are called **herbivores.** Animals that eat herbivores and other animals are called **carnivores.**

Herbivores could not survive without plants. If there were no plants, herbivores would have nothing to eat and would soon become extinct.

Carnivores need plants as much as herbivores do. If there were no plants, there soon wouldn't be any more herbivores to eat. Carnivores would then have to eat each other. Before long, the carnivores would run out of food, and they would become extinct.

Herbivores feed **directly** on green plants. Carnivores feed **indirectly** on green plants because they feed on animals that feed on plants.

1. What are carnivores?

   _____

   _____

2. Underline the sentence that helps you answer question 1. Then write 1 next to the sentence.

3. What are herbivores?

   _____

4. Underline the sentence that helps you answer question 3. Then write 3 next to the sentence.

5. Lions eat other animals, so is a lion a carnivore or an herbivore?

   _____

6. Does a lion feed directly on green plants?

   _____

7. Underline the sentence that helps you answer question 6. Then write 6 next to the sentence.

D CONTEXT CLUES

For each item, circle the answer that means the same thing as the word in bold type.

1. Some parents like to **ruffle** their children's hair.

   a. put ruffs in   b. mess up

   c. comb   d. cut

2. When you're not in a hurry, you can just **amble** down the sidewalk.

   a. walk slowly   b. sprint

   c. freeze   d. roll

3. The weather was cold, but we were **hopeful** that it would warm up.

   a. lacking in hope   b. sure

   c. uncertain   d. full of hope

GO TO PART D IN YOUR TEXTBOOK

26   Lesson 13

Name _____ 14

A STORY DETAILS

Work the items.

1. Bobby and Lacey ran by the gray house because ▓▓▓ .

   a. they were going down a hill

   b. they were having a race

   c. the house was creepy

2. The ladies in the library were gray-haired and ▓▓▓ .

   a. bespectacled   b. bedraggled

   c. becalmed

3. The superintendent of the apartment complex was named

   Mr. _____ .

4. Mama told Lacey that when Daddy went away, a lot of _____ stayed behind.

5. The apartment owner said Mama had to

   _____ , or she had to

   _____ .

6. What did Mama and Lacey agree to keep as a secret?

   a. what Max did at the library

   b. having to move out of their apartment

   c. Daddy leaving the bills behind

7. What did Lacey keep looking for through the special window? _____

B CLOZE SENTENCES

Complete each sentence with the correct word.

| complex | quiver | supple |
| nonetheless | reckoning | unearthly |

1. The team hadn't won all year, but they kept trying _____ .

2. Good dancers have _____ arms and legs.

3. Many people lived in the apartment _____ downtown.

4. Everyone was scared when they heard the _____ sound coming from the flying saucer.

Lesson 14   27

C CONTEXT CLUES

For each item, circle the answer that means the same thing as the word(s) in bold type.

1. The **fastest dog breed in the world** is an impressive animal.
   a. setter
   b. poodle
   c. greyhound
   d. beagle

2. Everyone in the eye doctor's waiting room was **bespectacled.**
   a. a carnivore
   b. an herbivore
   c. wearing glasses
   d. converted

3. Being the **superintendent** of a skyscraper is a hard job.
   a. manager
   b. ingredient
   c. janitor
   d. window cleaner

D DEDUCTIONS

Work the items.

1. Some painters were impressionists. Whistler was a painter.
   - What's the conclusion about Whistler?
   _____
   _____
   _____

2. Vegetarians do not eat meat. Monika is a vegetarian.
   - What's the conclusion about Monika?
   _____
   _____
   _____

3. Kata thought she could get a job if she learned how to fix computers. Kata signed up for a computer class.
   - So, what did Kata believe would happen?
   _____
   _____

GO TO PART D IN YOUR TEXTBOOK

15

Name _____

A STORY DETAILS

Work the items.

1. When Part 3 begins, Lacey and Bobby are in the ____ .
   a. car   b. library   c. apartment

2. Lacey and Bobby saw a blue _____ standing at the water's edge.

3. The other animal Lacey and Bobby saw moving in the water was a ____ .
   a. fish   b. bird   c. mammal

4. Lacey said the park wasn't a playground anymore. It was a _____ .

5. When they lived in their car, Lacey's family went to the _____ to wash their clothes.

6. On which day of the week did Lacey and Bobby return to the library?
   _____

7. What evidence did Mr. Thompson have that something was wrong with Lacey and her family?
   a. Max was tied up outside the library.
   b. Bobby was in the children's department.
   c. He didn't see Lacey on Monday.

8. Lacey was holding a _____ that was heavier than she could bear.

9. Lacey learned that every window in life was a special window full of _____ .

B CLOZE SENTENCES

Complete each sentence with the correct word.

amble	sake	vain
muskrat	uproar	victorious

1. Mama tried to find a home, but her efforts were in _____ .

2. The _____ is a mammal that spends most of its time in water.

3. The students cleaned the classroom for their teacher's _____ .

4. When you walk slowly, you _____ .

Lesson 15   29

C INFERENCES

Work the items.

You have learned that herbivores and carnivores eat different things. Herbivores eat plants, but carnivores eat other animals. Herbivores and carnivores are different in other ways as well.

One difference is the eyes. A carnivore's eyes point straight ahead. When a carnivore focuses on an object, both eyes see almost the same thing.

The eyes of many herbivores work differently. The left eye of a cow, for instance, only sees things on the left side of the cow, while the right eye only sees things on the right side of the cow. When the cow is facing straight ahead, the cow is not really looking straight ahead. Instead, the cow is looking mostly to the right side and the left side. Both eyes can see only a little bit of what is straight ahead.

These eyes help the cow when it is eating grass. If the cow had the same kind of eyes as a carnivore, it would be looking at the ground when it ate, and a predator could sneak up on it. But since the cow has eyes that see to the sides, it can watch out for predators as it eats.

1. What does the left eye of a cow see?

   _____

   _____

2. Underline the sentence that helps you answer question 1. Then write 1 next to the sentence.

3. Would a cow be able to see a bear coming toward the cow's right side?

   _____

4. Underline the sentence that helps you answer question 3. Then write 3 next to the sentence.

5. When a carnivore focuses on an object, what do both eyes see?

   _____

6. Underline the sentence that helps you answer question 5. Then write 5 next to the sentence.

7. If you wanted to hide an object from a cow, would you put the object in front of the cow or to the left of the cow?

   _____

D CONTEXT CLUES

For each item, circle the answer that means the same thing as the word(s) in bold type.

1. Jordan saw a **tall wading bird with long legs and gray-blue wings** flying overhead.

   a. pink flamingo   b. snowy egret

   c. sandhill crane   d. blue heron

2. They looked for couches in the furniture **department** of the big-box store.

   a. factory   b. section

   c. cemetery   d. bedpost

3. If you don't own a washing machine, you can clean your clothes at a **place with washers and dryers.**

   a. windowpane   b. hardware store

   c. laundromat   d. drying shed

GO TO PART D IN YOUR TEXTBOOK

Name _____

A STORY DETAILS

Work the items.

1. Lacey's family became homeless because they ▨ .
   a. damaged their apartment
   b. wanted to live in their car
   c. couldn't pay the rent

2. The rule for affordable rental housing is that you shouldn't spend more than ▨ of your income on rent.
   a. one-third   b. one-half
   c. two-thirds

3. If your income is three thousand dollars per month, you shouldn't spend more than _____ thousand dollars per month on rent.

4. Rental prices keep increasing because the _____ is greater than the _____ .

5. Affordable rental housing is hard to find because people's wages are rising more _____ than the price of rental housing.

6. Cities can help homeless families by ▨ that construction companies build a certain amount of affordable housing.
   a. suggesting   b. requiring
   c. hoping

7. Building houses in factories can cost _____ than building houses in place.

B CLOZE SENTENCES

Complete each sentence with the correct word.

| bespectacled | hopeful | shelter |
| complex | ruffle | speckle |

1. Harley had to live in a homeless _____ because she couldn't afford to rent an apartment.

2. Mohamed was _____ that his wages would go up.

3. More than one hundred people lived in the apartment _____ .

4. The wall was white except for one _____ of red paint.

Lesson 16   31

C CONTEXT CLUES

For each item, circle the answer that means the same thing as the word(s) in bold type.

1. The city needs housing that is **at a price that most people can pay.**

    a. affordable   b. expensive
    c. priceless   d. free

2. When the demand for rental housing is greater than the supply, prices will **increase.**

    a. stay the same   b. go down
    c. go up   d. get creased

3. People closed their umbrellas when the rain began to **decrease.**

    a. get more   b. pour
    c. get smooth d. get less

D DEDUCTIONS

Work the items.

1. Every magazine has an editor. *Teapot* is a magazine.

    • What's the conclusion about *Teapot*?

    _____

    _____

2. Some substances are hard. Silicon is a substance.

    • What's the conclusion about silicon?

    _____

    _____

3. Nasir believed that if he could speak French, he would gain power. Nasir learned to speak French.

    • So, what did Nasir believe would happen?

    _____

    _____

E COMPARING STORIES

Answer each question with one or more of these letters: A, B, C.

A. "The Day I Didn't Go to the Pool"

B. *The Odyssey*

C. "The Secret"

1. The main character was trying to return home. _____

2. The main character's family couldn't pay the rent on their home. _____

3. The main character's home was destroyed. _____

4. The main character's family was together at the end of the story. _____

5. The story is modern. _____

6. The story is an epic. _____

GO TO PART D IN YOUR TEXTBOOK

Name _____

17

A STORY DETAILS

Work the items.

1. Apprentices in the 1300s spent several years ▨ .
   a. completing high school
   b. learning a craft
   c. studying at home

2. Apprentices in the 1300s worked in ▨ .
   a. large factories
   b. medium-sized farms
   c. small shops

3. Apprentices were paid _____ for their work.

4. The average apprenticeship was ▨ years long.
   a. two to four   b. five to seven
   c. eight to ten

5. After the apprenticeship was over, the apprentice became a _____ .

6. A joiner is a type of carpenter who ▨ .
   a. builds houses   b. joins in
   c. makes furniture

7. A miller's job is to ▨ .
   a. bake bread   b. grind grain
   c. grow wheat

8. The machine that turners use to carve wood is called a _____ .

B CLOZE SENTENCES

Complete each sentence with the correct word.

| department | heron | muskrat |
| greyhound | laundromat | superintendent |

1. The young couple met while washing their clothes in the _____ .

2. Devin watched the _____ use its thick tail to swim underwater.

3. None of the other dogs could catch the _____ .

4. Arielle shopped for socks in the clothing _____ .

C CHARACTER TRAITS

Complete each sentence with *apprentice*, *journeyman*, or *master*.

1. The _____ owned the shop.

2. The _____ worked without pay.

3. The _____ earned wages for daily work.

4. The _____ was working on a masterpiece for the guild.

5. The _____ judged masterpieces during guild meetings.

Lesson 17   33

D INFERENCES

Work the items.

You have learned that an herbivore's eyes see to the sides instead of straight ahead. This arrangement helps the herbivore when it is grazing because its eyes can see if a predator is trying to sneak up.

Most farm animals are herbivores. Cows, goats, sheep, and horses get all the food they need by eating grass and other types of plants. All these animals have eyes on the sides of their heads.

Carnivores are different. A carnivore must have a good image of the animal it is hunting. A carnivore needs to see as far forward as possible. Therefore, a carnivore's eyes look straight ahead. When a carnivore sees another animal in the distance, the carnivore focuses both eyes on that animal. And when the carnivore eats, it can see what it's biting into.

1. A puma has eyes that look straight ahead. Is a puma a carnivore or an herbivore? _____

2. Underline the sentence that helps you answer question 1. Then write 1 next to the sentence.

3. A deer has eyes on the sides of its head. Is a deer a carnivore or an herbivore?
   _____

4. Underline the sentence that helps you answer question 3. Then write 3 next to the sentence.

5. What does a carnivore see when it eats?
   _____

6. Underline the sentence in the passage that helps you answer question 5. Then write 5 next to the sentence.

7. How do cows, goats, sheep, and horses get all the food they need?
   _____
   _____

8. Underline the sentence that helps you answer question 7. Then write 7 next to the sentence.

E VOCABULARY IN CONTEXT

For each item, circle the answer that means the same thing as the word(s) in bold type.

1. The **average** temperature in July is hotter than in January.
   a. instance   b. ordinary
   c. dusky   d. hopeful

2. The **person who makes cloth** used many different kinds of thread.
   a. weaver   b. predator
   c. herbivore d. fawn

3. The turner uses a **machine that spins wood** to make chair legs.
   a. speckle   b. quiver
   c. footstool d. lathe

GO TO PART E IN YOUR TEXTBOOK

Name _____

18

A STORY DETAILS

Work the items.

1. The tailor and his sons got _____ from the goat.

2. The goat needed to eat good food so ____ .
   a. she could tell the truth
   b. her meat would taste better
   c. she could make good milk

3. The oldest son brought the goat home because she ____ .
   a. was full   b. needed to eat
   c. was tired

4. Then the son ____ the goat in her stall.
   a. leathered   b. milked
   c. tethered

5. The tailor thought his oldest son was lying because the goat ____ .
   a. was quite thin
   b. said she was hungry
   c. had been inside all day

6. So the tailor made his oldest son ____ .
   a. take the goat out again
   b. leave home
   c. sleep in the barn with the goat

7. Near the end of Part 1, the tailor discovered the goat ____ .
   a. was lying
   b. didn't get enough to eat
   c. had no more milk

8. At the end of Part 1, the goat ____ .
   a. went to sleep
   b. begged for more food
   c. ran away

9. "The Table, the Donkey, and the Stick" is a ____ .
   a. myth   b. realistic story
   c. folktale

B CLOZE SENTENCES

Complete each sentence with the correct word.

average	sake	weaver
lathe	sprouts	wretches

1. The sheep roamed the hills, looking for tender _____ .

2. Those no-good _____ are always getting into trouble.

3. There was nothing unusual about the _____ house.

4. The family kept quiet for the sleeping baby's _____ .

Lesson 18   35

C INFERENCES

Work the items.

You have learned that carnivores and herbivores are different in two ways: they eat different things, and they have different types of eyes. Carnivores eat meat, while herbivores eat plants. Carnivores' eyes see straight ahead, while herbivores' eyes see to the side.

Herbivores and carnivores also have different types of teeth. Herbivores have flat teeth that are designed to grind grass, leaves, and seeds. In contrast, the teeth of carnivores are designed to tear flesh. Carnivores' teeth are pointed and sharp, not flat. Carnivores do not grind food into small pieces. Instead, carnivores tear their food into chunks that are small enough to swallow.

1. Are herbivores' teeth flat or pointed?
   _____

2. Underline the sentence that helps you answer question 1. Then write 1 next to the sentence.

3. Are carnivores' teeth flat or pointed?
   _____

4. Underline the sentence that helps you answer question 3. Then write 3 next to the sentence.

5. A gazelle grinds its food. So is a gazelle an herbivore or a carnivore?
   _____

6. Is question 5 answered by *words in the passage* or by a *deduction*?
   _____

7. A ferret tears its food into chunks. Does a ferret eat plants or meat?
   _____

8. Underline the sentence in the passage that helps you answer question 7. Then write 7 next to the sentence.

D CONTEXT CLUES

For each item, circle the answer that means the same thing as the word in bold type.

1. The farmer **tethered** the cow to the fence.
   a. apprenticed   b. busied
   c. tied   d. ruffled

2. Those people are **fasting** for one day to lose weight.
   a. going faster   b. not weighing
   c. not eating   d. sleeping

3. The man was so full of **wrath** that he shouted and turned red in the face.
   a. greed   b. anger
   c. envy   d. wrong

GO TO PART D IN YOUR TEXTBOOK

Name _____

19

A STORY DETAILS

Work the items.

1. What material does a joiner work with?
   a. stone   b. metal   c. wood

2. At first, the oldest son was ▮▮ joiner.
   a. a master   b. an apprentice
   c. a journeyman

3. Then he became ▮▮ joiner.
   a. a master   b. an apprentice
   c. a journeyman

4. Whenever the joiner wanted to eat and drink, he said "Table, be _____!"

5. The joiner decided to go home because his father's anger had probably ▮▮.
   a. submitted   b. subsided
   c. subscribed

6. The young joiner stayed at an _____ on the last evening of his journey home.

7. The _____ stole the joiner's table.

8. That character thought the table would help his business ▮▮.
   a. prosper   b. prospect
   c. proper

B CLOZE SENTENCES

Complete each sentence with the correct word.

| deprived | sprouts | wrath |
| shelter | tether | wretch |

1. In his _____, Poseidon made a terrible storm.

2. The tired man had been _____ of sleep for days.

3. You need a rope or a chain to _____ an animal.

4. Edwin had no money for a hotel, so he stayed in a free _____.

C SEQUENCING

Number the events in the correct sequence.

____ The oldest son apprenticed with a joiner.

____ The oldest son stayed at an inn.

____ The oldest son became a journeyman.

____ The tailor drove his oldest son from home.

____ The tailor criticized his oldest son's table.

Lesson 19   37

D INFERENCES

Work the items.

You have read about the differences between carnivores and herbivores. Herbivores eat plants, have eyes that look sideways, and have flat teeth. Carnivores eat other animals, have eyes that look straight ahead, and have sharp, pointed teeth.

But what kind of animal is a person? A person has eyes that look straight ahead, so a person might be a carnivore. But a person's teeth are mostly flat, so a person might be an herbivore.

The answer is that a person is neither a carnivore nor an herbivore. A person eats both plants and animals and is called an **omnivore.** *Omni* is a word part that means *all,* so an omnivore is an animal that eats all kinds of things. Other omnivores include bears and pigs.

1. What kind of teeth do herbivores have?

   _____

2. Underline the sentence that helps you answer question 1. Then write 1 next to the sentence.

3. Rats eat both plants and other animals. So what kind of animals are rats?

   _____

4. Underline the sentence that helps you answer question 3. Then write 3 next to the sentence.

5. What does the word part *omni* mean?

   _____

6. Is question 5 answered by *words in the passage* or by a *deduction?*

   _____

E CONTEXT CLUES

For each item, circle the answer that means the same thing as the word in bold type.

1. The baseball players **assembled** on the pitcher's mound.

   a. got together   b. resembled

   c. ambled   d. split apart

2. After the storm, the wind began to **subside.**

   a. succeed   b. increase

   c. settle down   d. convert

3. The **agreeable** sound came from a piano.

   a. particular   b. pleasant

   c. affordable   d. bespectacled

GO TO PART D IN YOUR TEXTBOOK

Lesson 19

Name _____ **20**

A STORY DETAILS

Work the items.

1. What does a miller do for a living?
   a. harvests different grains
   b. grinds flour into grain
   c. grinds grain into flour

2. What was wrong with the donkey?
   a. He would not pull a cart.
   b. He didn't understand commands.
   c. He was too thin.

3. The donkey could spit out pieces of
   _____ .

4. What magic word did the miller use to command the donkey?
   _____

5. On his travels, the miller lived like a  .
   a. journeyman   b. master
   c. king

6. The miller's _____ had already stayed at the inn.

7. The miller went to his donkey in the _____ to get more money.

8. To see what the miller was doing, the innkeeper peeked over a ____ .
   a. door   b. keyhole   c. wall

B CLOZE SENTENCES

Complete each sentence with the correct word.

| average | fasting | supple |
| Bricklebrit | lathe | weaver |

1. The magician put a spell on them by crying "_____!"

2. Jayden used a _____ to make the table legs.

3. Some runners are fast, some are slow, but most are _____ .

4. Some people are _____ because of the holiday.

C CONTEXT CLUES

For each item, circle the answer that means the same thing as the word in bold type.

1. The children **rejoiced** when the holidays arrived.
   a. were successful
   b. became joiners
   c. busied themselves
   d. were full of joy

2. The **remarkable** monkey could add, subtract, divide, and multiply.
   a. truly great   b. wretched
   c. tethered   d. bewildered

Lesson 20   39

D INFERENCES

Work the items.

Some objects will rot, or **decompose,** when they are left in the air. Objects that decompose start out as one material and turn into another material. Leaves, for example, start out as leaves and decompose into a soggy mass that no longer looks like leaves.

Dead animals also decompose. Their flesh becomes rotten, and their bodies shrivel.

Tiny organisms are responsible for much of the change that occurs when matter decomposes. These organisms are called **decomposers.** Decomposers get their food by eating the flesh or waste material of other organisms.

The world would be vastly different if there were no decomposers. Leaves from thousands of years ago would still be piled on the ground, along with the bodies of dead animals. People probably couldn't live in such a world.

1. How do decomposers get their food?
   _____
   _____

2. Underline the sentence that helps you answer question 1. Then write 1 next to the sentence.

3. Do dead birds decompose?
   _____

4. Underline the sentence that helps you answer question 3. Then write 3 next to the sentence.

5. What do leaves turn into when they decompose?
   _____

6. Underline the sentence that helps you answer question 5. Then write 5 next to the sentence.

E CHARACTER DETAILS

Complete each sentence about the 1300s with *joiner, miller, tailor,* or *turner*.

1. The _____ makes a new chair for your kitchen.

2. The _____ repairs your coat.

3. The _____ carves wood for you on a lathe.

4. The _____ sells you flour for baking bread.

5. The _____ makes a living by grinding something.

GO TO PART D IN YOUR TEXTBOOK

Name _____

A STORY DETAILS

Work the items.

1. What does a turner do for a living?
   a. beats people with a stick
   b. joins pieces of wood to make furniture
   c. carves wood on a lathe

2. Why did it take the turner so long to learn his trade?
   a. Turning is difficult.
   b. He was stupid.
   c. He was lazy.

3. What would the stick do to whoever attacked the turner?
   a. pin the attacker to the ground
   b. wave back and forth in front of the attacker
   c. beat the attacker soundly

4. To use the stick, the turner said, "Stick, out of the _____ ."

5. How did the turner find out what had happened to his brothers?
   a. They called him on the phone.
   b. They sent him a letter.
   c. They visited him at the master's house.

6. The innkeeper thought the turner's sack was filled with ▓ .
   a. fancy food   b. precious stones
   c. gold coins

7. When the innkeeper tried to steal the sack, he ▓ .
   a. woke up the turner
   b. tripped and fell
   c. got a beating

8. The innkeeper said, "Make this terrible ▓ go back into the sack."
   a. goblet   b. gobbler   c. goblin

B CLOZE SENTENCES

Complete each sentence with the correct word.

| agreeable | deprive | grisly |
| assemble | goblins | precious |

1. The monster had a disgusting and _____ face.

2. Diamonds and rubies are _____ gems.

3. The magic forest was filled with fairies and _____ .

4. The coach asked the baseball players to _____ at home plate.

Lesson 21   41

C CONTEXT CLUES

For each item, circle the answer that means the same thing as the word in bold type.

1. The rickety tower **collapsed** in the wind.
   - a. decreased
   - b. fell down
   - c. rejoiced
   - d. withstood

2. Being **depressed** is a serious problem.
   - a. remarkable
   - b. wrinkled
   - c. average
   - d. very sad

3. We are going **abroad** on our vacation.
   - a. to our state capital
   - b. across town
   - c. nowhere
   - d. to another country

D CHARACTER STATEMENTS

Complete each sentence with *innkeeper, joiner, miller, tailor,* or *turner*.

1. The _____ said, "My sons are good for nothing."

2. The _____ said, "I wonder what's in that sack?"

3. The _____ said, "I know how to make furniture."

4. The _____ said, "I know how to use a lathe."

5. The _____ said, "That table could really help my business."

6. The _____ said, "How many sacks of flour do you need?"

E RELATED FACTS

Work the items.

1. The epic that tells about Odysseus is called The _____ .

2. The epic that tells about the Trojan War is called The _____ .

3. The poet who first told those stories was named _____ .

4. That poet spoke the _____ language.

5. Odysseus was the king of _____ .

GO TO PART D IN YOUR TEXTBOOK

Name _____

22

A STORY DETAILS

Work the items.

1. What piece of land did the United States purchase in 1803?
   a. Oregon Country
   b. Louisiana Territory
   c. California

2. That purchase ▨ the size of the United States.
   a. decreased   b. tripled   c. doubled

3. Lewis and Clark proved that you can't travel by ▨ from the Missouri River to the Pacific Ocean.
   a. foot   b. horseback   c. boat

4. Lewis and Clark claimed part of ▨ for the United States.
   a. Oregon Country
   b. the Louisiana Territory
   c. the Missouri River

5. Lewis and Clark gathered Western rocks and _____ for American scientists.

6. Which tribe of Native Americans did Sacagawea belong to?
   a. Clatsop   b. Mandan
   c. Shoshone

7. Which body of water do rivers on the west side of the Rockies flow toward?
   a. Atlantic Ocean   b. Pacific Ocean
   c. Mississippi River

B CLOZE SENTENCES

Complete each sentence with the correct word.

| canoe | moccasins | subside |
| journal | recruit | territory |

1. They rode down the river in a _____ .

2. The coach tried to _____ players for the basketball team.

3. The travelers crossed the vast _____ on horseback.

4. Making entries in a _____ every day can help your writing.

C CONTEXT CLUES

For each item, circle the answer that means the same thing as the word(s) in bold type.

1. The road was so **rugged** that cars could not drive over it.
   a. covered with rugs   b. fenced off
   c. rocky and uneven   d. steep

2. You can **accomplish** a lot if you try hard.
   a. ignore   b. finish
   c. attempt d. conduct

3. Members of the **journey with a purpose** made a map of their route.
   a. exhibition   b. excavation
   c. exposition   d. expedition

Lesson 22   43

D MAPS

Work the items.

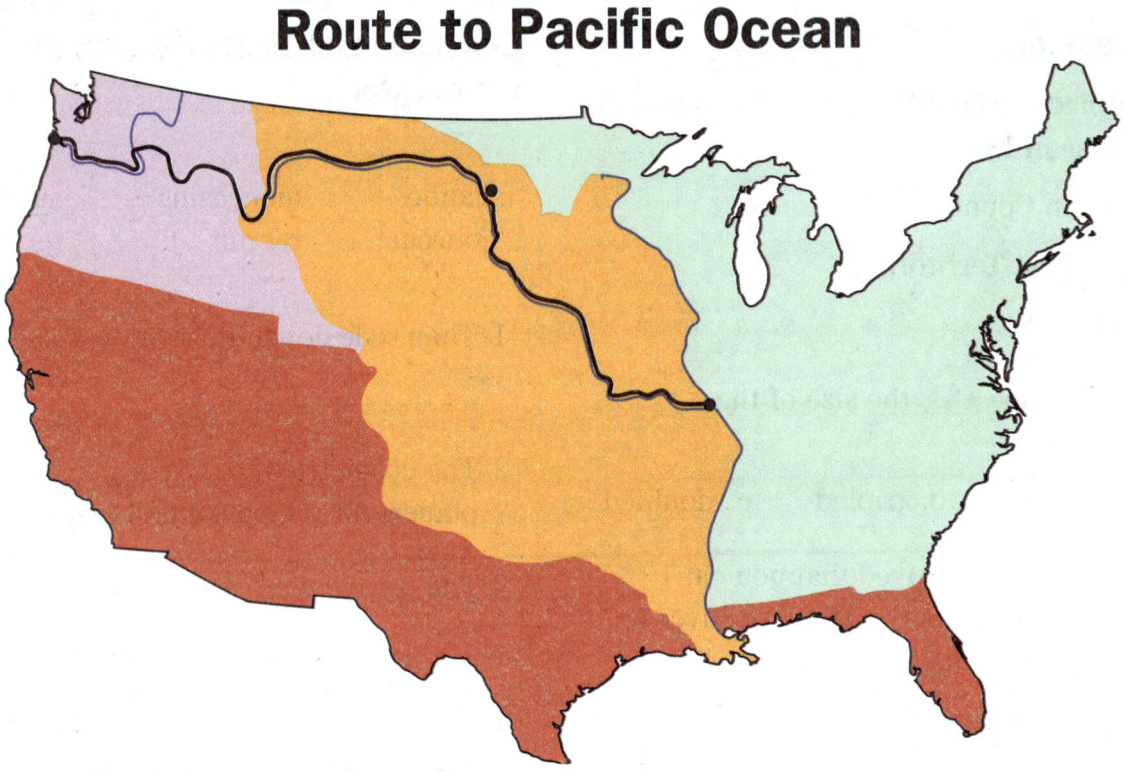

Route to Pacific Ocean

1. What is the name of the purple land in the northwest corner?
   a. Louisiana Territory
   b. Oregon Country
   c. Eastern States

2. What is the name of the gold land in the middle?
   a. Louisiana Territory
   b. Oregon Country
   c. Eastern States

3. Which river flows north to south down the middle of the country?
   a. Columbia River   b. Mississippi River
   c. Missouri River

4. Which river flows into the Pacific Ocean?
   a. Columbia River   b. Mississippi River
   c. Missouri River

5. In which city does the black line begin?
   a. Chicago   b. New Orleans
   c. St. Louis

6. Who traveled from that city to the Pacific Ocean on the black line?
   a. Sacagawea   b. Lewis and Clark
   c. President Jefferson

GO TO PART E IN YOUR TEXTBOOK

Name _____ **23**

A STORY DETAILS

Work the items.

1. What metal was discovered along the Klondike River in 1896?

    a. bronze   b. silver   c. gold

2. The Klondike River is located in the _____ Territory in northwestern _____ .

3. The Irvines live in the village of Glen _____ in the state of _____ .

4. Wolves are colored _____ , but Wolf is colored _____ .

5. When Wolf ran away, what direction did he always go? _____

6. What state borders California on the north? _____

7. The tips of Wolf's ears had been severely _____ .

    a. chewed   b. frozen   c. clipped

8. The man the Irvines met on the path was named _____ .

9. When Wolf rubbed against that man's legs, the dog opened his mouth and _____ .

B CLOZE SENTENCES

Complete each sentence with the correct word.

| abroad | collapsed | goblins |
| bristled | depressed | spring |

1. When the cat _____ , all his fur stood on end.

2. The hikers found a _____ where fresh water came out of the ground.

3. People often dress as witches or _____ for Halloween.

4. When the waiter _____ , all the food fell on the floor.

C CONTEXT CLUES

For each item, circle the answer that means the same thing as the word(s) in bold type.

1. When the tiger yawned, all four of its **fangs** gleamed in the sunlight.

    a. sharp claws   b. long teeth
    c. tooth fillings   d. back teeth

2. The dancer soared **effortlessly** across the stage.

    a. with great effort   b. without effect
    c. without strain   d. like a fortress

3. Only an expert can climb a **steep rock face.**

    a. mountain   b. tunnel   c. cliff

Lesson 23   45

Borders in 1803

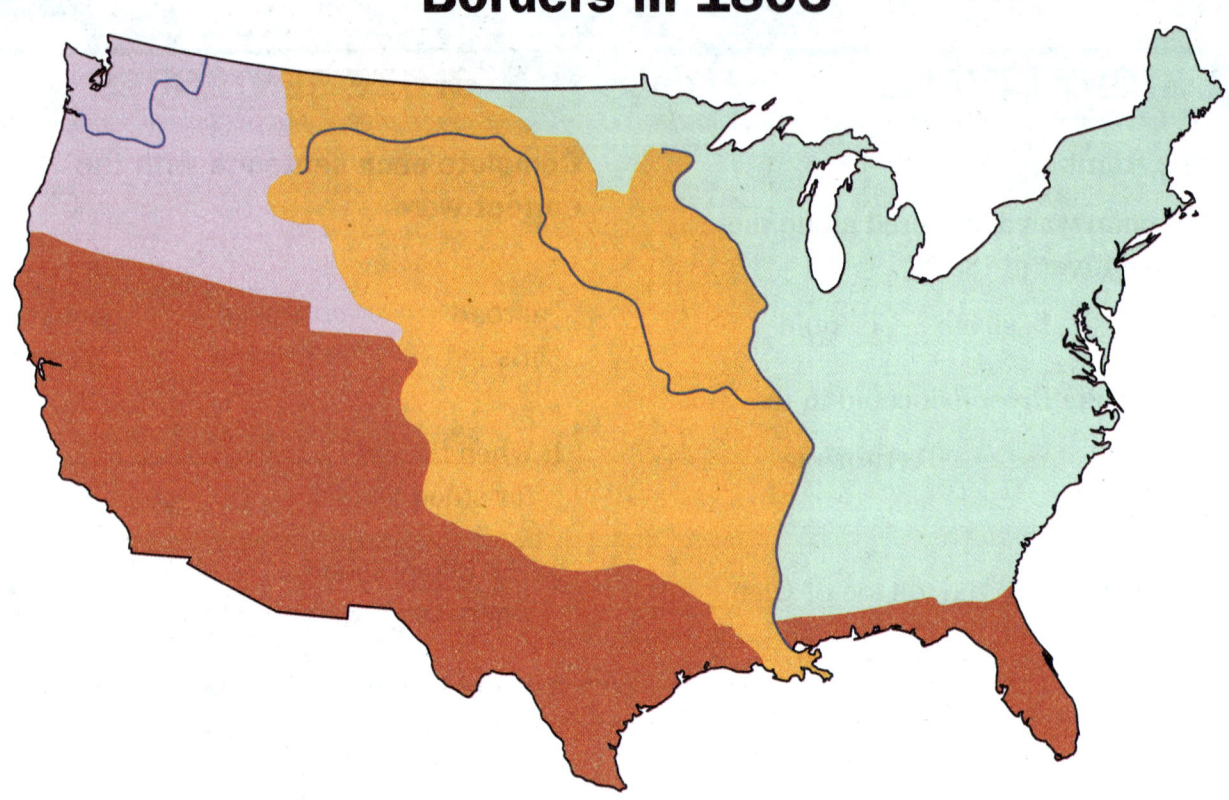

D MAPS

Work the items.

1. What is the name of the green country in the northeast corner of the map?
   a. Canada   b. Oregon Country
   c. United States

2. Who owned the red land in the southwest corner of the map?
   a. Spain   b. United States   c. Oregon

3. The purple land in the northwest corner of the map was called _____ Country.

4. The river that starts in the Rocky Mountains and flows east is called the ▇ River.
   a. Columbia   b. St. Louis   c. Missouri

5. The river on the west side of the Rocky Mountains flows into the _____ Ocean.

GO TO PART E IN YOUR TEXTBOOK

Name _____

24

A STORY DETAILS

Work the items.

1. Skiff Miller said the dog's name is

   _____ .

2. The dog turned to the right when Skiff Miller said, " ▬▬ "

   a. Gee!   b. Haw!   c. Mush on!

3. Madge said the dog will never suffer from ▬▬ in California.

   a. warmth   b. affection   c. hunger

4. Skiff said the dog likes to ▬▬ in the Yukon.

   a. eat too much   b. sleep   c. work

5. Walt said that any sled dog would know the _____ that Skiff gave.

6. Madge told Skiff that he hadn't _____ the dog.

   a. trained   b. considered   c. obeyed

7. Which person walked away at the end of the story?

   _____

8. When the dog got to his feet at the end of the story, his movements were ▬▬ .

   a. decisive   b. uncertain   c. wobbly

B CLOZE SENTENCES

Complete each sentence with the correct word.

| canoe | journal | reappear |
| decisive | moccasin | |

1. Nobody else could make up their mind, but the captain was _____ .

2. It's a good idea to write in a _____ every day.

3. We waited for the sun to _____ after it was covered by a cloud.

C CONTEXT CLUES

For each item, circle the answer that means the same thing as the word in bold type.

1. The travelers kept moving **onward,** no matter what.

   a. northward   b. sideways
   c. on foot   d. forward

2. The judge **reckoned** that the witness was telling the truth.

   a. believed   b. rejoiced
   c. doubted   d. didn't think

3. The boss **demanded** an answer from the frightened worker.

   a. listened to   b. politely requested
   c. insisted on   d. waited for

Lesson 24   47

D CROSSWORD PUZZLE

Use CAPITAL LETTERS to complete the puzzle.

Across

1. When you finish a job, you ▭ the job.
4. Another word for *very sad*.
5. A wicked magic creature.
6. Long, pointed teeth.

Down

1. When you travel to another country, you travel ▭ .
2. When you fall down suddenly, you ▭ .
3. When something has great value, it is ▭ .

GO TO PART E IN YOUR TEXTBOOK

Name _____   25

A RHYME SCHEME

Fill in each blank with the correct word. Then write A, B, C, D, or E at the end of each line, as follows:

- Write **A** if the last word rhymes with *growing*.
- Write **B** if the last word rhymes with *bitter*.
- Write **C** if the last word rhymes with *done*.
- Write **D** if the last word rhymes with *guest*.
- Write **E** if the last word rhymes with *gazing*.

The rooster's _____ , ___

The stream is _____ , ___

The small birds _____ , ___

The lake doth _____ , ___

The green field sleeps in the

_____ ; ___

The oldest and _____ ___

Are at work with the _____ ;

___

The cattle are _____ , ___

Their heads never _____ ; ___

There are forty feeding like

_____ ! ___

B CLOZE SENTENCES

Complete each sentence with the correct word.

| doth | hath | territory |
| expedition | rugged | twittered |

1. Charles doth owe money to the bank, but he _____ none.

2. The knight set forth on an _____ to find the wizard.

3. The birds _____ loudly when the cat walked into the yard.

4. The small plane flew over the vast _____ to look for fires.

C CONTEXT CLUES

For each item, circle the answer that means the same thing as the word(s) in bold type.

1. Say the answer **anon** so everyone can hear it one more time.

   a. louder   b. again

   c. to yourself   d. correctly

2. After a day working in the hot fields, the **plowboy** took a shower.

   a. office assistant   b. doughboy

   c. field-worker   d. smelly boy

3. It was difficult to **prevail over** Juanita in wrestling because of her strength.

   a. lose to   b. defeat

   c. tumble over   d. admire

Lesson 25   49

D MAPS

Borders in 1803

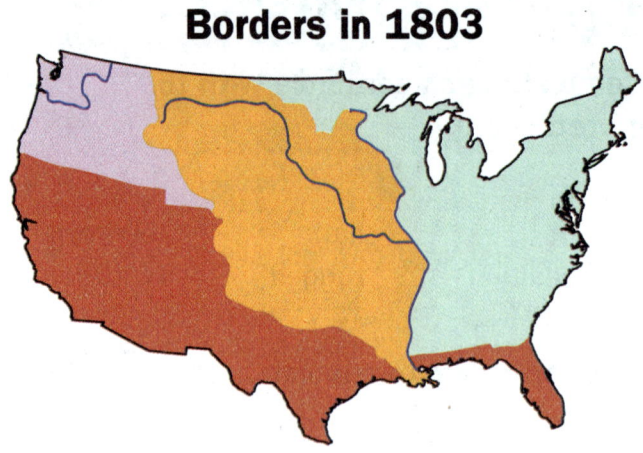

Work the items.

1. The purple land in the northwest corner of the map was called ▇▇▇ Country.

   a. Washington   b. Oregon   c. Idaho

2. The gold land in the middle of the map was called the ▇▇▇ Territory.

   a. Spanish   b. Missouri   c. Louisiana

3. The green land in the northeast corner of the map was called the ▇▇▇ .

   a. Thirteen Colonies   b. United States

   c. Mexican Territory

4. The river that starts in the Rocky Mountains and flows east is called the ▇▇▇ River.

   a. Missouri   b. Mississippi   c. Columbia

5. The river in item 4 flows into the ▇▇▇ River at the edge of the green land.

   a. Missouri   b. Mississippi   c. Columbia

E RELEVANT INFORMATION

Write whether each item is *relevant* or *irrelevant* to the fact.

Fact: The man purchased a needle and thread.

1. He was wearing a green ring.

   _____

2. His shirt was missing a button.

   _____

3. One of his pockets had a hole in it.

   _____

4. His shoes were too tight.

   _____

GO TO PART D IN YOUR TEXTBOOK

50   Lesson 25

Name _____ 26

A STORY DETAILS

Work the items.

1. A single ivy vine can grow up to ▬ feet per year.
   a. 10   b. 100   c. 1,000

2. Ivy can help a brick building during the summer by ▬ .
   a. growing in the gutters
   b. loosening the mortar
   c. shading the walls

3. Boston ivy has ▬ leaves.
   a. one-pointed   b. three-pointed
   c. five-pointed

4. Which type of ivy stays green all year round?
   a. Boston ivy   b. English ivy
   c. Boston ivy and English ivy

5. Why does ivy grow so quickly in the United States?
   a. It doesn't need water.
   b. Farmers plant it in fields.
   c. It has no natural enemies.

6. How can ivy damage brick buildings?
   a. Ivy can loosen the mortar.
   b. Ivy can grow into the bricks.
   c. The weight of the ivy can make the building fall over.

7. The rule about poison ivy and poison oak is *Leaflets three,* _____ .

8. People who touch poison ivy or poison oak can get ▬ .
   a. bitten   b. shocked   c. blisters

9. Poison ivy and poison oak leave a layer of ▬ on whatever they touch.
   a. blisters   b. oil   c. powder

B CLOZE SENTENCES

Complete each sentence with the correct word.

> bristle   effortlessly   gutter
> cliff   gnarled   spring

1. Rain from the roof flowed into the _____ and then the downspout.

2. The _____ old rope was full of knots.

3. People used buckets to gather water from the _____ .

4. Hawks seem to fly through the air _____ .

Lesson 26   51

C CONTEXT CLUES

For each item, circle the answer that means the same thing as the word(s) in bold type.

1. Patients with **pneumonia** cough a lot.
   a. heart disease
   b. moaning fits
   c. stomach aches
   d. lung disease

2. The hiker was careful not to touch the poison oak **leaflet**.
   a. drooping leaf
   b. large leaf
   c. red leaf
   d. small leaf

3. The **person who moved to a new area** built a log cabin on the empty plain.
   a. settler
   b. plowboy
   c. recruit
   d. carpenter

D RELEVANT INFORMATION

Write whether each item is *relevant* or *irrelevant* to the fact.

Fact: The man went to the library.

1. He was looking for a book. _____

2. He was forty-two years old. _____

3. He worked in an office. _____

4. He needed to do research for a report he was writing. _____

5. He was wearing a gray sweater. _____

E RHYME SCHEME

Fill in each blank with the correct word. Then write *A*, *B*, *C*, *D*, or *E* at the end of each line, as follows:

- Write **A** if the last word rhymes with *heated*.
- Write **B** if the last word rhymes with *pill*.
- Write **C** if the last word rhymes with *lawn*.
- Write **D** if the last word is *fountains* or *mountains*.
- Write **E** if the last word rhymes with *trailing*.

Like an army _____, ____

The snow hath _____, ____

And now doth fare _____ ____

On the top of the bare _____; ____

The plowboy is whooping—anon—

_____: ____

There's joy in the _____; ____

There's life in the _____; ____

Small clouds are _____, ____

Blue sky _____; ____

The rain is over and _____! ____

GO TO PART D IN YOUR TEXTBOOK

Lesson 26

Name _____ 27

A STORY DETAILS

Work the items.

1. This story takes place in the _____ Village neighborhood of New York City.

2. What disease stalked the people in the artists' colony that winter?
   _____

3. Which young woman remained healthy?
   _____

4. Which young woman was struck by the disease? _____

5. The doctor said the sick woman's chances of surviving were ____.
   a. one in ten   b. ten to one
   c. fifty percent

6. The doctor subtracted fifty percent of his power for patients who ____.
   a. didn't take their medicine
   b. tried to get out of bed
   c. began thinking of death

7. What type of ivy was growing on the brick wall outside the sick woman's window?
   a. Boston   b. English   c. poison

8. How many ivy leaves were left on the wall at the end of this part?
   a. one   b. four   c. ten

9. The sick woman thought she would die when ____.
   a. pneumonia touched her with his icy fingers
   b. she was very old   c. the last leaf fell

B CLOZE SENTENCES

Complete each sentence with the correct word.

| chance | demanded | studio |
| decisive | prevailing | swaggered |

1. The vain king _____ around his palace, stopping often to admire himself in the mirrors.

2. When you flip a coin, there's one _____ in two that you'll get tails.

3. The walls of the _____ were filled with unfinished paintings.

4. Someone who is good at making decisions is _____ .

Lesson 27

C CONTEXT CLUES

For each item, circle the answer that means the same thing as the word in bold type.

1. You can warm up on a cold day by drinking **broth**.
   a. hot cocoa
   b. clear soup
   c. iced tea
   d. warm milk

2. The two-story house looked **squat** next to the skyscraper.
   a. alternating
   b. short and thick
   c. fast-growing
   d. obedient

3. Cats **stalk** their prey by staying low to the ground.
   a. talk to
   b. race after
   c. quietly follow
   d. suddenly attack

D COMPARING CHARACTERS

Complete each sentence with *Joan, Sue,* or *The doctor*.

1. _____
   had pneumonia.

2. _____
   gave a sick woman one chance in ten of surviving.

3. _____
   thought she would die when the last leaf fell.

4. _____
   drew a picture of a cowboy.

5. _____
   thought she was like a leaf.

GO TO PART E IN YOUR TEXTBOOK

Lesson 27

Name _____ 28

A STORY DETAILS

Work the items.

1. What did Mr. Behrman paint to earn his living?
   a. ivy leaves   b. advertising posters
   c. masterpieces

2. What was the weather like on the night Sue talked to Mr. Behrman?
   a. cold and still
   b. warm and stormy
   c. cold and stormy

3. When Joan looked out the window the next morning, how many leaves did she believe were on the vine?
   a. none   b. one   c. four

4. When the doctor came back, he said Joan's chances had improved to ▇▇▇ .
   a. one in ten   b. fifty-fifty
   c. ten to one

5. What type of disease did Mr. Behrman have?
   a. stomach disease   b. heart disease
   c. lung disease

6. What happened to Mr. Behrman in the hospital?
   a. He died.   b. He got better.
   c. He stayed the same.

7. The ivy leaf painting was Mr. Behrman's _____ .

8. Mr. Behrman painted the leaf after he ▇▇▇ .
   a. went to the hospital
   b. got pneumonia
   c. learned about Joan's belief

B CLOZE SENTENCES

Complete each sentence with the correct word.

| easel | palette | reappeared |
| onward | persistent | twitter |

1. The artist placed her painting on the wooden _____ so she could keep working on it.

2. The _____ cat kept meowing until someone fed it.

3. The magician made the rabbit vanish, but then it _____ in his hat.

4. The artist held a _____ in his left hand and painted with his right.

Lesson 28   55

C CONTEXT CLUES

For each item, circle the answer that means the same thing as the word(s) in bold type.

1. People use **canvas** to paint on, and also for making sails.
   a. thick plastic   b. crushed cans
   c. tough cloth   d. smooth wood

2. Some people **scoff at** modern art.
   a. make fun of   b. are confused by
   c. praise   d. cough at

3. The weaker students had great **contempt** for the mean bully.
   a. respect   b. sympathy
   c. temptation   d. hatred

D CHARACTER STATEMENTS

Complete each sentence with *Joan, Sue,* or *Mr. Behrman.*

1. _____ said, "I am like a leaf."

2. _____ said, "I must get help for my roommate."

3. _____ said, "I have painted a masterpiece."

4. _____ said, "I no longer feel like dying."

5. _____ said, "I know how to save that young woman's life."

E RELEVANT INFORMATION

Write whether each item is *relevant* or *irrelevant* to the fact.

Fact: The girl hammered a nail into a piece of wood.

1. She had yellow hair. _____

2. She was building a doghouse. _____

3. She was putting a roof on the house. _____

4. Her dog was named Spot. _____

GO TO PART D IN YOUR TEXTBOOK

Name _____ 29

A STORY DETAILS

Work the items.

1. Carbonic acid is a combination of water and ▨ .
   a. carbon monoxide   b. carbon dioxide
   c. calcite

2. Carbonic acid can ▨ limestone.
   a. resolve   b. unsolved   c. dissolve

3. Before caves open to the air, they are filled with ▨ .
   a. stalactites   b. water   c. columns

4. Rivers can open up caves by ▨ rock.
   a. cutting through   b. avoiding
   c. melting

5. Rocks that grow up from the floor of a cave are called ▨ .
   a. limestone   b. stalactites
   c. stalagmites

6. Rocks that grow down from the ceiling of a cave are called ▨ .
   a. limestone   b. stalactites
   c. stalagmites

7. Stalactites begin as ▨ .
   a. columns   b. soda straws   c. cones

8. Stalactites and stalagmites are made of ▨ .
   a. frozen water   b. calcite   c. soil

9. What is the world's longest cave?
   a. Mammoth Cave
   b. Carlsbad Caverns
   c. the underworld

B CLOZE SENTENCES

Complete each sentence with the correct word.

| acid | cavern | dissolve |
| calcite | column | vinegar |

1. One part of the roof was held up by a _____ .

2. One type of acid is _____ .

3. A sugar cube will _____ in a glass of water.

4. Each new drop of water leaves a ring of _____ on a stalactite.

Lesson 29   57

C CONTEXT CLUES

For each item, circle the answer that means the same thing as the word(s) in bold type.

1. The bold cowboy **swaggered** into the hotel.
   a. walked confidently
   b. stalked quietly
   c. gnarled
   d. ran quickly

2. The artist's **studio** was filled with pictures.
   a. kitchen
   b. study
   c. workroom
   d. bedroom

3. The **container under the bottom edge of a roof** was filled with leaves.
   a. pneumonia
   b. gutter
   c. settler
   d. leaflet

GO TO PART D IN YOUR TEXTBOOK

Name _____ 30

A STORY DETAILS

Work the items.

1. Demeter ruled over the ▧ .
   a. earth   b. ocean   c. sky

2. The sea nymphs made a necklace of ▧ for Persephone.
   a. flowers   b. pearls   c. shells

3. The sea nymphs would grow faint if they couldn't sniff ▧ .
   a. magnificent flowers   b. rain
   c. a salty breeze

4. What was wrong with the first flowers Persephone saw?
   a. They showed signs of wilting.
   b. They were dead.
   c. They hadn't bloomed yet.

5. Persephone got the most beautiful flowers in the world by ▧ .
   a. picking them off the shrub
   b. cutting down the shrub
   c. pulling the shrub out of the ground

6. The chariot was driven by the god _____ .

7. That god asked Persephone to ▧ .
   a. return to the sea nymphs
   b. put the shrub back in the ground
   c. ride with him

8. Why couldn't Demeter hear Persephone's screams?
   a. There was too much noise.
   b. Demeter was too far away.
   c. Demeter was hard of hearing.

B CLOZE SENTENCES

Complete each sentence with the correct word.

beckoned	contempt	nymph
canvas	easel	wilt

1. The beautiful _____ lived in the ocean.

2. The mother _____ her son by waving her hand.

3. Plants begin to _____ when they don't get enough water.

4. Some artists paint on wood, but others paint on _____ .

Lesson 30   59

C CONTEXT CLUES

For each item, circle the answer that means the same thing as the word in bold type.

1. It would be **prudent** to take your umbrella because a storm is coming.
   a. idiotic
   b. fragile
   c. like a prune
   d. wise

2. The fans cheered loudly for the **triumphant** team.
   a. hard-trying
   b. defeated
   c. victorious
   d. contented

3. The unhappy man was so **sullen** that he never smiled.
   a. gloomy
   b. acidic
   c. regarded
   d. well-mannered

D COMPARING CHARACTERS

Complete each sentence with *Athena, Demeter, Hades, Hermes,* or *Zeus.*

1. _____ was the chief Greek god.

2. _____ often disguised Odysseus.

3. _____ was the messenger god.

4. _____ was the goddess of the earth.

5. _____ was the god of the underworld.

6. _____ controlled thunder and lightning.

GO TO PART E IN YOUR TEXTBOOK

Lesson 30

Name _____

31

A STORY DETAILS

Work the items.

1. Persephone saw the goddess _____ far away in a field of grain.

2. Hades called the underworld his ▮▮▮▮.
   a. dominoes   b. dominions
   c. dominance

3. The dog _____ greeted Hades at entrance to the underworld.

4. How many heads did that dog have? _____

5. In the underworld, the walls had veins of ▮▮▮▮.
   a. blood   b. gold   c. oil

6. The underworld was illuminated by ▮▮▮▮.
   a. electric lamps   b. candle lanterns
   c. precious stones

7. The servants put ▮▮▮▮ water by Persephone's plate.
   a. enchanted   b. boiling   c. mineral

8. Hades hoped that Persephone's ▮▮▮▮ would make his palace more cheerful.
   a. presence   b. absence
   c. confidence

9. Persephone would have been tempted to eat ▮▮▮▮.
   a. chocolate   b. steak   c. fruit

B CLOZE SENTENCES

Complete each sentence with the correct word.

| delicacy | motive | summon |
| morsel | persistent | threshold |

1. Doors that go to the outside often have a _____ made of metal.

2. Sparrows can hold only a _____ of bread in their beak.

3. The cat's _____ for hunting was hunger.

4. Frogs' legs are considered a _____ in France, and restaurants charge a lot for them.

Lesson 31   61

C CONTEXT CLUES

For each item, circle the answer that means the same thing as the word in bold type.

1. No one could move the **massive** rock, which weighed hundreds of tons.
   a. bottomless   b. very large
   c. deep-rooted d. carbonic

2. Some birds build nests on **lofty** branches far above the ground.
   a. crystal   b. violet
   c. low-hanging d. high

3. The candle barely **illuminated** the dark room.
   a. uprooted   b. dissolved
   c. regarded   d. lit up

D CHARACTER TRAITS

Complete each sentence with *Demeter, Hades, Persephone,* or *Zeus.*

1. _____ was the goddess of the earth.

2. _____ was the god of the underworld.

3. _____ wanted a queen for his kingdom.

4. _____ refused to eat sweet or spicy food.

5. _____ was working in a field of grain.

E RELEVANT INFORMATION

Write whether each item is *relevant to fact A, relevant to fact B,* or *irrelevant to both facts.*

Fact A: Odysseus rowed his raft.

Fact B: Odysseus took out his spears.

1. Odysseus was Greek.
   _____

2. Odysseus was fighting the monster Scylla.
   _____

3. Odysseus was trying to cross the sea.
   _____

4. Odysseus wanted to stab someone.
   _____

GO TO PART E IN YOUR TEXTBOOK

Name _____

32

A STORY DETAILS

Work the items.

1. What did Demeter hear when she was working in the field of grain?

    a. the rumbling of thunder

    b. the grain growing

    c. her daughter's shriek

2. After Demeter left the field, the grain looked ▪▪▪ .

    a. ripe   b. magnificent   c. unhealthy

3. Demeter asked the sea _____ if they had seen her daughter.

4. What magic object did Demeter carry?

    a. torch   b. flashlight   c. staff

5. What objects did Demeter discover on the path?

    a. diamonds   b. flowers   c. necklaces

6. Demeter thought those objects were ▪▪▪ .

    a. harmless   b. worthless   c. poisonous

7. On the tenth day, Demeter came to a dark ▪▪▪ .

    a. palace   b. cavern   c. cabin

8. The character inside that place was the witch _____ .

B CLOZE SENTENCES

Complete each sentence with the correct word.

| melancholy | prudent | scoffed |
| nymph | resolve | triumphant |

1. When people are sad, they are _____ .

2. Another word for *victorious* is _____ .

3. If you really want to do something, you _____ to do it.

4. The wild child _____ at the rules and always got in trouble.

Lesson 32   63

C CONTEXT CLUES

For each item, circle the answer that means the same thing as the word in bold type.

1. The leaves on the tree **wilted** before falling to the ground.
   a. withered   b. hastened
   c. exceeded   d. mingled

2. The store owner tried to **entice** customers into her store by lowering prices.
   a. alternate   b. enter
   c. tempt   d. force

3. Jalen **inquired** about the cost of a bus ticket.
   a. was angry   b. didn't know
   c. asked   d. knew

D STORY REVIEW

Work the items.

1. "The Last Leaf" takes place in ▩ Village.
   a. Sandwich   b. Greenwich   c. Granite

2. That village is located in ▩.
   a. New York City   b. Boston   c. Chicago

3. Joan was suffering from ▩.
   a. cancer   b. pneumonia   c. measles

4. What kind of leaves did Joan watch?
   a. oak   b. maple   c. ivy

5. Joan thought she would die when ▩.
   a. the last leaf fell
   b. the storm was over
   c. she finished her painting

6. Mr. Behrman saved Joan's life by ▩.
   a. getting her new medicine
   b. getting her a blanket
   c. painting a leaf

E RELEVANT INFORMATION

Write whether each item is *relevant to fact A*, *relevant to fact B*, or *irrelevant to both facts*.

Fact A: Shani was riding a bicycle.

Fact B: Shani was using a canoe.

1. She used her hands to paddle.
   _____

2. She used her feet to pedal.
   _____

3. She was wearing gray pants.
   _____

4. She used her wrists to shift gears.
   _____

GO TO PART D IN YOUR TEXTBOOK

Name _____

33

A STORY DETAILS

Work the items.

1. Hecate had ____ Persephone, but Hecate hadn't ____ Persephone.
   a. heard / seen   b. seen / heard
   c. smelled / seen

2. Hecate wanted Demeter to ____ .
   a. find Persephone   b. go back home
   c. be miserable

3. Apollo was the god of the ____ .
   a. moon   b. sun   c. stars

4. Apollo had a ____ chariot.
   a. golden   b. silver   c. bronze

5. Apollo held a _____ in his hands.

6. Hades was Apollo's ____ .
   a. father   b. uncle   c. brother

7. Which god was Apollo's father?
   _____

8. Apollo was forbidden to enter the underworld because he would bring _____ .

9. As Demeter continued to search, her face became ____ .
   a. more determined
   b. old and wrinkled
   c. young and smooth

B CLOZE SENTENCES

Complete each sentence with the correct word.

| beckon | indignant | sullen |
| distress | splendor | wilt |

1. From the porch, Hiroshi could enjoy the _____ of the valley below.

2. Kofi became _____ when Kamal insulted him.

3. When people are in _____ , they call for help.

4. The delicate flower began to _____ in the heat of the sun.

C CHARACTER TRAITS

Complete each sentence with *Demeter, Poseidon, Athena, Hades, Zeus,* or *Hermes*.

1. _____ was the chief god.

2. _____ was the father of Polyphemus.

3. _____ ruled the underworld.

4. _____ made plants grow.

5. _____ disguised herself to help Odysseus.

D CONTEXT CLUES

For each item, circle the answer that means the same thing as the word in bold type.

1. It was hard to take Kanya's pointless and **frivolous** remarks seriously.
   - a. massive
   - b. lofty
   - c. unserious
   - d. illuminated

2. The old woman liked to **recollect** her childhood.
   - a. ignore
   - b. criticize
   - c. pursue
   - d. remember

3. Parents buy presents to **gratify** their children.
   - a. satisfy
   - b. punish
   - c. assure
   - d. behold

E RELEVANT INFORMATION

Write whether each item is *relevant to fact A*, *relevant to fact B*, or *irrelevant to both facts*.

Fact A: Dafna was a plumber.
Fact B: Hana was a carpenter.

1. She used a hammer when she worked.

   _____

2. She knew how to fix water heaters.

   _____

3. Electricians can fix bad wiring.

   _____

4. She carried lumber in her truck.

   _____

F VOCABULARY REVIEW

Complete each sentence with the correct word.

| delicacies | motive | sullen |
| morsel | prudent | summoned |

1. The finest or most expensive foods are called _____.

2. When you are gloomy and silent, you are _____.

3. When you are wise and careful, you are _____.

4. Your reason for doing something is your _____ for doing that thing.

GO TO PART D IN YOUR TEXTBOOK

Name _____

34

A STORY DETAILS

Work the items.

1. Persephone had resolved never to ▩ while she was in Hades's dominions.
   a. sleep   b. drink   c. eat

2. Persephone had maintained her resolution for _____ months.

3. Hades thought that ▩ were beautiful.
   a. flowers   b. gems   c. no things

4. Persephone thought that ▩ were beautiful.
   a. flowers   b. gems   c. no things

5. The only fruit the servant found aboveground was a _____ .

6. What condition was that fruit in?
   a. ripe   b. still growing   c. shriveled

7. Which god was concerned about the condition of the earth?
   _____

8. Which god went to Hades's dominions with a message? _____

9. What was the message?
   a. Keep Persephone.
   b. Release Persephone.
   c. Feed Persephone.

B CLOZE SENTENCES

Complete each sentence with the correct word.

| actions | inquire | pomegranate |
| entice | inquiry | resolution |

1. When Elena sliced the _____ in half, she could see the little bits of fruit.

2. It's often true that _____ speak louder than words.

3. Mila's New Year's _____ was to learn Spanish.

4. When you ask a question, you _____ .

C SEQUENCING

Number the events in the correct sequence.

_____ Hermes requested to see Hades.

_____ Hermes leaped over the three-headed dog.

_____ Demeter forbade the plants to grow.

_____ Zeus gave Hermes an order.

_____ Hades gave his servant an order.

Lesson 34   67

D CONTEXT CLUES

For each item, circle the answer that means the same thing as the word(s) in bold type.

1. The lemon was so **shriveled** that it had no juice left.
    a. juicy
    b. shrunken
    c. tasteless
    d. immense

2. It's hard for runners to **continue going at** the same speed during a long race.
    a. maintain
    b. restrain
    c. contain
    d. detain

3. After Brayden crossed the **threshold**, he was inside the house.
    a. bridge
    b. holding tank
    c. threshing machine
    d. bottom of the entry

E RELEVANT INFORMATION

Write whether each item is *relevant to fact A*, *relevant to fact B*, or *irrelevant to both facts*.

Fact A: Vanessa used a ruler.

Fact B: Vanessa used a pair of pliers.

1. She was drawing a chart.
   _____

2. She was making lunch.
   _____

3. She was fixing her bike.
   _____

4. She had to make an exact measurement.
   _____

GO TO PART E IN YOUR TEXTBOOK

Name _____

35

A STORY DETAILS

Work the items.

1. Hades's servant brought a shriveled _____ to Persephone.

2. Persephone had not eaten in _____ months.

3. Which god entered Persephone's room with Hades? _____

4. Hades agreed to ▇ Persephone.
   a. entice   b. detain   c. release

5. When Persephone went aboveground, a ▇ appeared wherever she set her foot.
   a. flower   b. mushroom   c. weed

6. As Persephone approached her home, Demeter's torch ▇ .
   a. began burning brightly
   b. flickered and went out
   c. became too hot to hold

7. What season began when Persephone returned to the underworld?
   a. winter   b. spring   c. summer

8. What season began when Persephone left the underworld?
   a. winter   b. spring   c. summer

B CLOZE SENTENCES

Complete each sentence with the correct word.

| detained | recollect | splendor |
| lush | resolve | withered |

1. After the rain, the fields turned _____ and green.

2. Everyone commented on the _____ of the tall forest.

3. The old man could _____ the time when bread cost only five cents a loaf.

4. The dogcatcher _____ the stray dog until its owner was found.

C CONTEXT CLUES

For each item, circle the answer that means the same thing as the word in bold type.

1. In spring, the bears began to **emerge** from their dens.
   a. grieve   b. illuminate
   c. come out   d. merge into traffic

2. The dog wanted **liberty,** but he was kept in a fenced yard.
   a. dog treats   b. freedom
   c. liver   d. a nap

Lesson 35   69

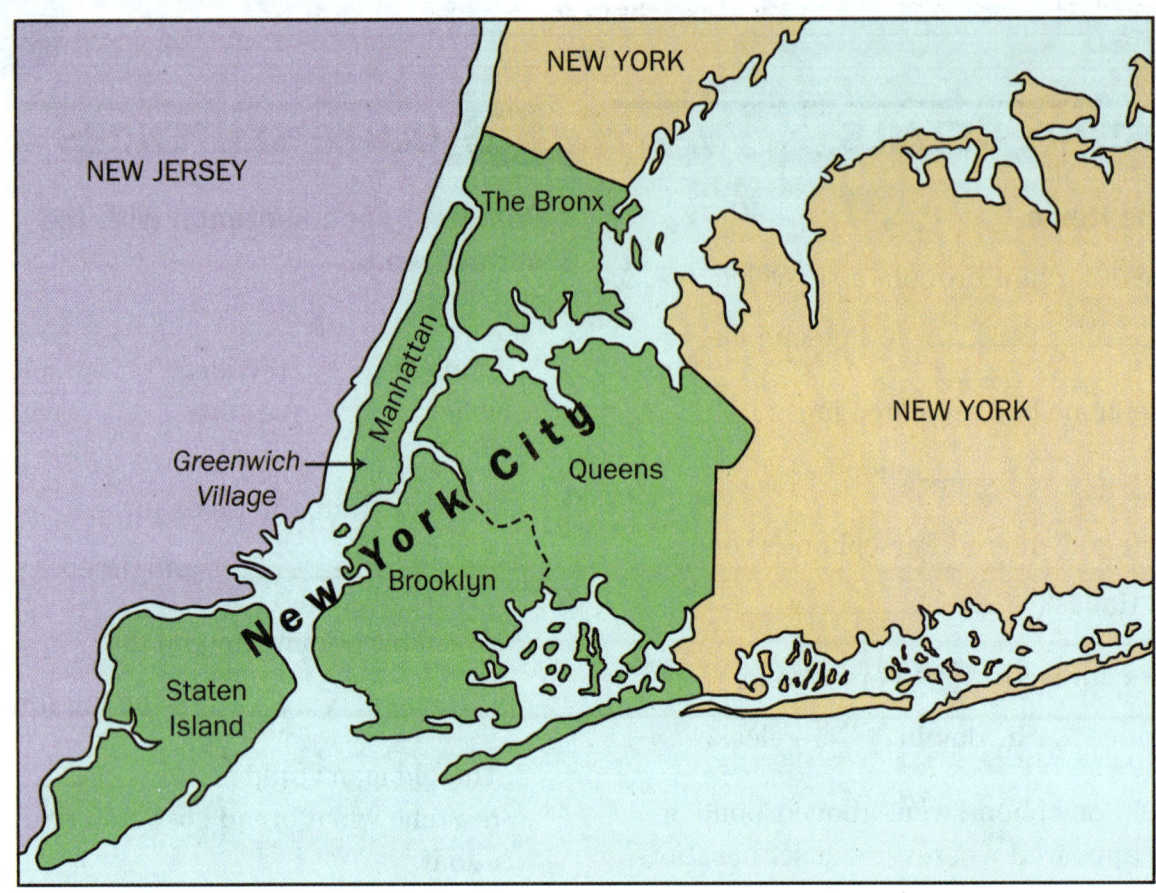

D MAPS

Work the items.

1. Which large city does the map show?
   _____

2. Which state is to the west of the city?
   _____

3. The city has five boroughs. Which borough is farthest north?
   _____

4. Which borough is farthest south?
   _____

5. Which borough covers the largest area?
   _____

E RELEVANT INFORMATION

Write whether each item is *relevant to fact A*, *relevant to fact B*, or *irrelevant to both facts*.

A: Persephone spent six months with Hades.

B: Persephone spent six months with Demeter.

1. The plants no longer grew.
   _____

2. Winter came upon the land.
   _____

3. She was sixteen years old.
   _____

GO TO PART D IN YOUR TEXTBOOK

36

A STORY DETAILS

Work the items.

1. The Mayan god of corn was named Yum  _____ .

2. The Mayan goddess of medicine was named ____ .
   a. Persephone   b. Ixchel   c. Freya

3. The ancient city of Tikal is located in ____ .
   a. Guatemala   b. Mexico
   c. United States

4. A painting made on a wall is called a _____ .

5. The Maya played a ball game called _____ .

6. The soldiers who invaded Mayan cities in the 1500s were from the country of ____ .
   a. France   b. England   c. Spain

7. A *huipil* is a type of ____ .
   a. weapon   b. food   c. clothing

8. During the early 1900s, the government tried to force the Maya to speak ____ .
   a. Mayan   b. Spanish   c. English

B CLOZE SENTENCES

Complete each sentence with the correct word.

| actions | pomegranate | sculpture |
| maintain | resolution | warrior |

1. A statue is a type of _____ .

2. All the players on the team made a _____ to follow the rules.

3. Mechanics are paid to _____ cars and trucks.

4. A soldier is a type of _____ .

Lesson 36   71

C CONTEXT CLUES

For each item, circle the answer that means the same thing as the word in bold type.

1. The army prepared to **invade** another country and start a war.

    a. leave　　b. make peace with

    c. enter　　d. examine

2. Nobody wanted to eat the **shriveled** apple.

    a. delicious　　b. shrunken

    c. wormy　　d. ripe

3. Inside the cave was a **mural** made by an artist thousands of years ago.

    a. painting on canvas　　b. sculpture

    c. drawing on paper　　d. wall painting

D MAPS

Work the items.

1. The seven small countries south of Mexico are part of _____ America.

    a. North　　b. Central　　c. South

2. Which two countries border Costa Rica?

    _____

3. The body of water to the west of Mexico is the _____ Ocean.

4. Mexico and the United States are part of _____ America.

    a. North　　b. Central　　c. South

5. The only country on the map that doesn't border the Pacific Ocean is _____ .

GO TO PART D IN YOUR TEXTBOOK

A STORY DETAILS

Work the items.

1. Tomás wanted to move to ▇▇ City.
   a. Mexico   b. Kansas   c. Guatemala

2. Tomás's village was near Lake ▇▇.
   a. Atitlán   b. Attila   c. Atoll

3. The three volcanoes around the lake were the _____ God's hearth.

4. Tomás's father had "▇▇" during the war.
   a. disappeared   b. appeared
   c. reappeared

5. Tomás's mother said he was now the _____ of the house.

6. Delfina spent her days ▇▇ sun patterns on huipil dresses.
   a. ironing   b. painting   c. embroidering

7. Tourists followed when Grandma Ana visited the sacred Mayan _____ near the market.

8. Tomás knew something was wrong when he saw ▇▇ tracks near the Mayan ruins.
   a. lion   b. tire   c. train

9. The people who plundered the ruins were called _____ poachers.

B CLOZE SENTENCES

Complete each sentence with the correct word.

| embroider | incense | poachers |
| hearth | liberty | thatched |

1. Shane used a needle and thread to _____ his jacket.

2. One problem with _____ roofs is that they can easily catch on fire.

3. The store sold _____ with different types of scents.

4. A game warden's job is to catch _____ who hunt against the law.

Lesson 37

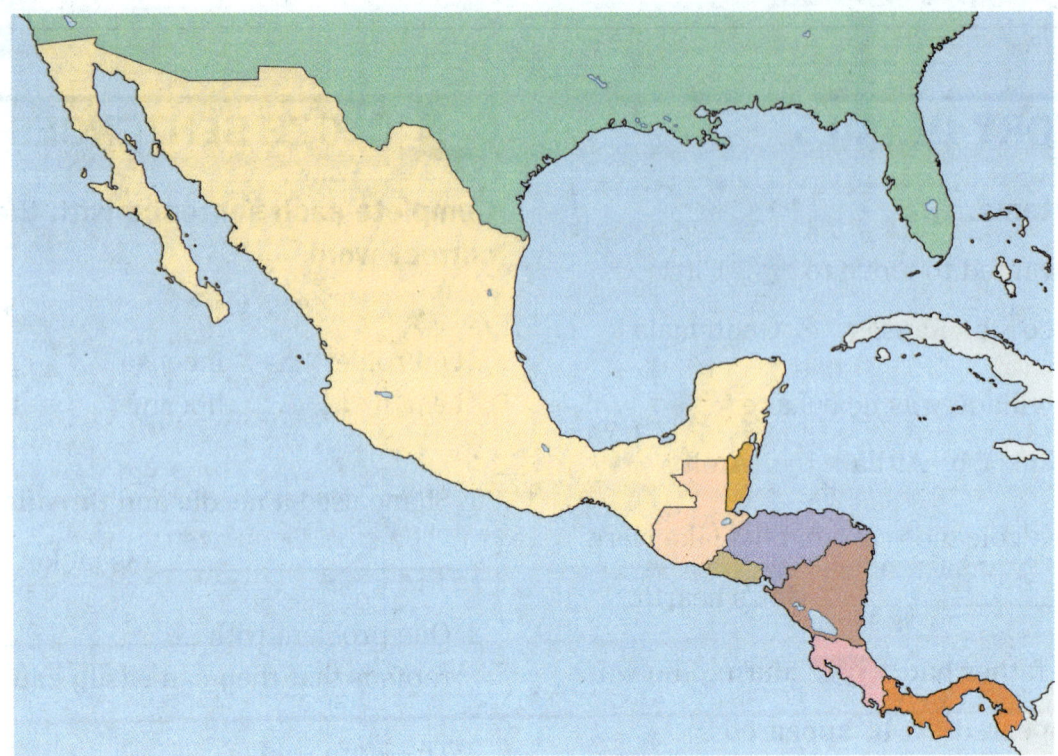

C CONTEXT CLUES

For each item, circle the answer that means the same thing as the word in bold type.

1. The cat waited for the mouse to **emerge** from the hole in the wall.

    a. have an emergency   b. retreat

    c. hold still   d. come out

2. People build jails to **detain** prisoners.

    a. hold   b. detail

    c. release   d. educate

3. A statue of a deity was in the middle of the ancient **shrine.**

    a. culture   b. navel

    c. sacred place   d. plaza

D MAPS

Work the items.

1. The country along the northern edge of the map is the _____ _____ .

2. The large country that starts near the top of the map and goes to the middle of the map is _____ .

3. The small countries in the southeast corner of the map are all part of _____ America.

    a. North   b. Central   c. South

4. The body of water on the west side of the map is the _____ Ocean.

5. One body of water on the east side of the map is the Gulf of _____ .

GO TO PART D IN YOUR TEXTBOOK

Name _____ 38

A STORY DETAILS

Work the items.

1. At first, Tomás thought the underground chamber might be a ▇ .
   a. tourist trap   b. tomb   c. tunnel

2. Tomás tried to escape the chamber by building a ▇ from stones.
   a. pyramid   b. mural   c. thatched roof

3. The character who first saw the wall painting is named _____ .

4. The painting shows Yum Kaax, also known as the _____ God.

5. What color means *birth* and *the rising sun*?
   _____

6. The painting shows Yum Kaax in the _____ , the place of the dead.

7. The two gods who are rescuing Yum Kaax in the painting are called the
   _____
   _____ .

8. Dr. Sanchez was a ▇ at the National Museum in Guatemala City.
   _____

9. The people who will excavate the ruins are called ▇ .
   a. architects   b. archers
   c. archaeologists

B CLOZE SENTENCES

Complete each sentence with the correct word.

| archaeologist | curator | loincloth |
| chisel | jaguar | tomb |

1. The Corn God wore a _____ around his waist.

2. You can tell the big cat is a _____ because it has black spots.

3. The carpenter used a _____ to trim the piece of wood.

4. The sculpture show was organized by a _____ at the art museum.

C CONTEXT CLUES

For each item, circle the answer that means the same thing as the word in bold type.

1. Ariana used a hand shovel to **excavate** the arrowheads.
   a. polish   b. bury   c. dig out   d. sharpen

2. Mateo didn't have any gloves, so his hands were **exposed.**
   a. x-rayed   b. posing
   c. uncovered   d. insulated

3. The lights of the town **glimmered** in the distance.
   a. were glamorous   b. shone faintly
   c. withered   d. resolved

Lesson 38   75

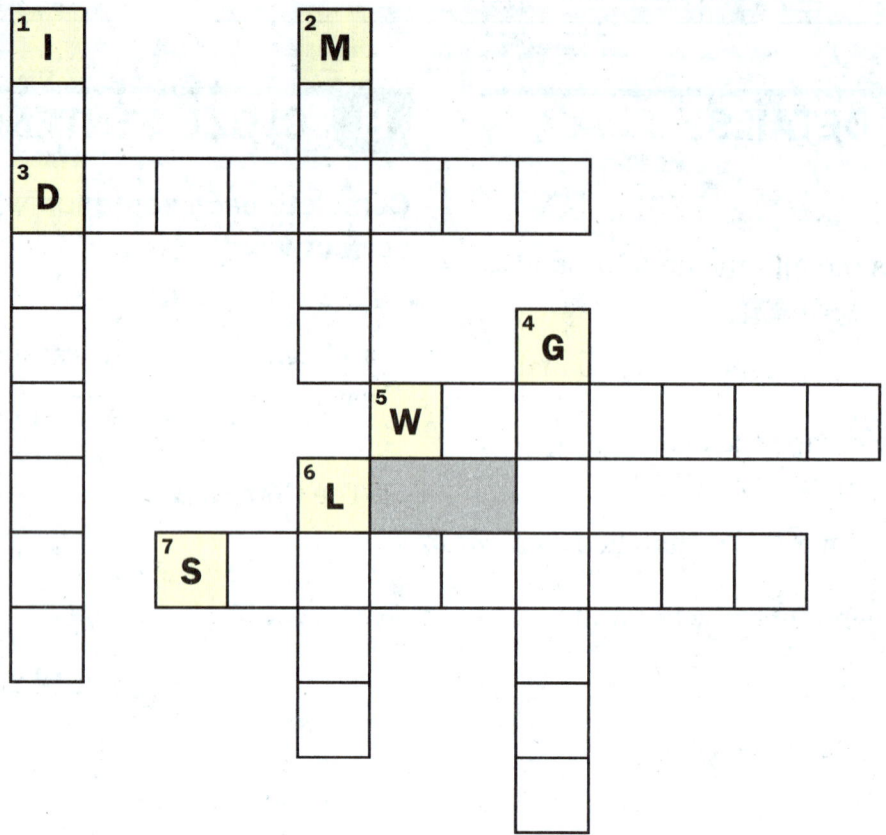

D CROSSWORD PUZZLE

Use CAPITAL LETTERS to complete the puzzle.

Across

3. When you are in great danger, you are in ▨ .

5. Someone who fights in wars.

7. A work of art made of wood, stone, metal, or plaster.

Down

1. When you are angry about being treated unfairly, you are ▨ .

2. Painting made on a wall.

4. Another word for *satisfy*.

6. When plants are growing well and have lots of leaves, they are ▨ .

GO TO PART E IN YOUR TEXTBOOK

76   Lesson 38

39

Name _____

A STORY DETAILS

Work the items.

1. Most of the people in India follow the ▒▒▒ religion.
   a. Christian   b. Hindu   c. Muslim

2. Most of the people in Pakistan follow the ▒▒▒ religion.
   a. Christian   b. Hindu   c. Muslim

3. Between 1757 and 1857, India was ruled by the ▒▒▒.
   a. West India Company
   b. East India Company
   c. Indian government

4. The cartridge for the Enfield rifle insulted both Hindus and Muslims because they thought it was ▒▒▒.
   a. coated with beef fat and pork fat
   b. made of leather and pigskin
   c. made in the United Kingdom

5. In what year did the Indian Rebellion begin?
   a. 1757   b. 1857   c. 1947

6. The two important ideas Gandhi learned in the United Kingdom were nonviolence and ▒▒▒.
   a. blind obedience
   b. violent disobedience
   c. civil disobedience

7. Gandhi first worked as a lawyer in South _____.

8. Gandhi protested the tax by ▒▒▒ salt.
   a. drinking   b. pumping   c. gathering

9. In what year did India become independent?
   a. 1947   b. 1857   c. 1757

B CLOZE SENTENCES

Complete each sentence with the correct word.

| cartridge | hearth | ramrod |
| disposal | incense | shrine |

1. The _____ contained gunpowder and a bullet.

2. You can use all the words at your _____ when you write a story.

3. The soldier used a _____ to load her gun.

4. A fire was blazing in the _____.

Lesson 39   77

C CONTEXT CLUES

For each item, circle the answer that means the same thing as the words in bold type.

1. Gavin used a needle and colored thread to **sew patterns on** a shirt.

    a. detain   b. embroider

    c. excavate   d. expose

2. A game warden's job is to catch **people who hunt against the law.**

    a. archaeologists   b. curators

    c. poachers   d. warriors

3. The ancient village was filled with **straw-roofed** houses.

    a. sculptured   b. lush

    c. frivolous   d. thatched

D SEQUENCING

Number the events from Gandhi's life in the correct order.

____ Gandhi is saddened when India and Pakistan split into two countries.

____ Gandhi works as a lawyer in South Africa.

____ Gandhi leads a march to protest the salt tax.

____ Gandhi returns to India.

____ Gandhi studies law in the United Kingdom

GO TO PART E IN YOUR TEXTBOOK

Lesson 39

Name _____ 40

A STORY DETAILS

Work the items.

1. In which city did Miss Minchin live?
   _____

2. Which country had Sara come from?
   _____

3. The climate in that country was ▇ .
   a. cold   b. mild   c. hot

4. Miss Minchin ran a _____ school for young ladies.

5. Sara was _____ years old when she arrived at Miss Minchin's school.

6. Captain Crewe bought Sara some ▇ clothes.
   a. practical   b. inexpensive
   c. extraordinary

7. Sara's new dresses were made of silk and ▇ .
   a. velvet   b. cotton   c. wool

8. Sara's doll was named _____ .

B CLOZE SENTENCES

Complete each sentence with the correct word.

| bonnet | jaguar | plume |
| chisel | loincloth | wardrobe |

1. The campers found an eagle _____ while walking through the forest.

2. Gabriella wore a _____ to protect her face from the sun.

3. Caleb had a vast _____ with all kinds of wild clothes.

4. The sculptor used a _____ to make a statue from a large rock.

C CONTEXT CLUES

For each item, circle the answer that means the same thing as the word in bold type.

1. The **pupil** was afraid to speak in class.
   a. teacher   b. student
   c. hamster   d. principal

2. Madison was **obliged** to finish the test.
   a. required   b. thatched
   c. exposed   d. unable

3. Jaxon **adored** his cat Lester.
   a. bustled   b. recollected
   c. maintained   d. loved

Lesson 40

D CHARACTER TRAITS

Complete each sentence with *Miss Minchin, Sara Crewe,* or *Captain Crewe.*

1. _____ was an officer in the army.

2. _____ was like a fish.

3. _____'s wife was dead.

4. _____ had an extraordinary wardrobe.

5. _____ ran a school.

E VOCABULARY REVIEW

Complete each sentence with the correct word.

| detain | indignant | recollect |
| emerges | liberty | tomb |

1. When something comes out of a place, it _____ from that place.

2. Another word for *freedom* is _____ .

3. A place used for burying dead people is called a _____ .

4. When you hold somebody against their will, you _____ them.

GO TO PART E IN YOUR TEXTBOOK

Name _____ 41

A STORY DETAILS

Work the items.

1. During Sara's first year at the boarding school, she was a ▓ pupil.
   a. favorite   b. neglected
   c. troublesome

2. Miss Minchin thought that Sara would ▓ her father's fortune.
   a. lose   b. discover   c. inherit

3. Sara was _____ years old when her father died.

4. Why had Captain Crewe lost all his money?
   a. His house was robbed.
   b. His friend had taken it.
   c. He had spent it all on Sara.

5. Why was Sara wearing a black dress when she visited Miss Minchin?
   a. Black was her favorite color.
   b. She was mourning her father's death.
   c. It was the only dress she had.

6. What language would Sara help teach?
   a. French   b. German   c. Hindi

7. If Sara didn't make herself useful, Miss Minchin would send her to ▓.
   a. the attic   b. the street   c. India

8. Sara's room had a ▓ in the ceiling.
   a. chandelier   b. skylight
   c. swing rope

B CLOZE SENTENCES

Complete each sentence with the correct word.

| bedstead | disposal | pupils |
| decked | invade | shrine |

1. For the fancy dinner, everyone was _____ out in their finest clothes.

2. The mattress was soft and supported by a wooden _____ .

3. The _____ hushed when the teacher appeared.

4. The butler said, "I'm at your _____ whenever you need me."

Lesson 41   81

C CONTEXT CLUES

For each item, circle the answer that means the same thing as the word in bold type.

1. Ria had the **determination** she needed to finish the race.

   a. faint glimmer   b. powerful incense

   c. strong will   d. raw courage

2. Everyone respected the **distinguished** judge.

   a. outstanding   b. dishonest

   c. ramrod   d. average

3. Some pens have a **cartridge** that is filled with ink.

   a. sharp tip   b. carrying case

   c. shopping cart   d. small container

D SEQUENCING

Number the events in the correct sequence.

____ Sara refused to thank Miss Minchin.

____ Sara lived in India.

____ Sara moved to the attic.

____ Sara was treated like a favorite pupil.

____ Sara's father died.

E VOCABULARY REVIEW

Complete each sentence with the correct word.

| hearth | invade | resolution |
| incense | poacher | shrine |

1. A person who hunts or fishes when it's against the law is called a

   _____ .

2. The floor of a fireplace and the area in front of a fireplace are called the

   _____ .

3. A sacred place is called a

   _____ .

4. A material that makes a sweet smell when it burns is called _____ .

GO TO PART D IN YOUR TEXTBOOK

A STORY DETAILS

Work the items.

1. Which character did **not** send Sara on errands?
   a. Miss Minchin   b. the cook
   c. a pupil

2. The pupils ▆▆▆ Sara because of her cleverness, her dreary life, and her odd habit of staring people.
   a. admired   b. were violent to
   c. were suspicious of

3. At first, Sara thought that her _____ understood her feelings.

4. Sara had a strong ▆▆▆ .
   a. association   b. imagination   c. arm

5. Emily's face was made of ▆▆▆ .
   a. wax   b. plastic   c. porcelain

6. One night, Sara told Emily, "I am ▆▆▆ !"
   a. satisfied   b. confused
   c. suffering

7. Sara told Emily, "You are nothing but a _____!"

8. While Sara was sobbing, some _____ began fighting inside the wall.

9. Sara told Emily, "You are just being ▆▆▆ ."
   a. yourself   b. unkind   c. aloof

B CLOZE SENTENCES

Complete each sentence with the correct word.

| accustomed | discard | outcast |
| craving | garret | vacant |

1. Please _____ your banana peels in the compost bin.

2. The lonely wolf was an _____ from its wolf pack.

3. The fast runner was _____ to winning races.

4. The poor artist lived in the _____ of a run-down building.

Lesson 42   83

C CONTEXT CLUES

For each item, circle the answer that means the same thing as the word in bold type.

1. Ariel liked her brother, but she **adored** her guinea pig Fluffy.
   a. despised   b. loved
   c. feared   d. adorned

2. The young mother tied a **bonnet** around her baby's head to protect him from the sun.
   a. plume   b. wardrobe
   c. string   d. hat

3. Jordan was **obliged** to wash the dishes before he could play outside.
   a. required b. unable
   c. happy   d. reluctant

D COMPARING CHARACTERS

Complete each sentence with *Captain Crewe, Emily, Miss Minchin,* or *Sara*.

1. _____ said, "Put your doll down!"

2. _____ said, "My doll is all I have."

3. _____ never said anything.

4. _____ said, "I'm cold, I'm wet, and I'm starving to death."

5. _____ said, "Buy whatever clothes you want. The price doesn't matter."

6. _____ said, "If you work hard and make yourself useful, I shall let you stay here."

GO TO PART D IN YOUR TEXTBOOK

Name _____ **43**

A STORY DETAILS

Work the items.

1. How did most of Miss Minchin's pupils feel about reading?
   a. They liked it.
   b. They had no feeling about it.
   c. They did not like it.

2. How did Sara feel about reading?
   a. She liked it.
   b. She had no feeling about it.
   c. She did not like it.

3. Sara read ▉ stories in the maid's magazine.
   a. realistic   b. horror   c. romantic

4. How did Erma's father find out if she had read the books?
   a. She had to write a report on each one.
   b. He asked her questions about them.
   c. He checked with Miss Minchin.

5. Sara made everything sound like a ▉ .
   a. story   b. lecture   c. poem

6. The only friend Sara had besides Erma was named _____ .

7. Sara compared the attic to the _____ .

8. Sara compared Miss Minchin to a _____ .

B CLOZE SENTENCES

Complete each sentence with the correct word.

| Bastille | decked | romantic |
| bedstead | determination | subscribe |

1. Roberto liked _____ movies about people falling in love.

2. It costs money to _____ to a magazine.

3. French kings put prisoners into the _____ .

4. All the soldiers in the parade were _____ out in new uniforms.

Lesson 43   85

C CONTEXT CLUES

For each item, circle the answer that means the same thing as the word in bold type.

1. Shani was **awed** when she saw the lofty peak.
    a. odd
    b. heartbroken
    c. unchildish
    d. amazed

2. The cat made a **dramatic** leap from the roof to the tree.
    a. sudden and exciting
    b. boring and dull
    c. nonviolent
    d. skylight

3. The lost dog looked **forlorn** as it wandered around the neighborhood.
    a. happy and excited
    b. forward
    c. sad and lonely
    d. for Lorne

D CHARACTER TRAITS

Complete each sentence with *Miss Minchin, Erma, Sara,* or *Captain Crewe*.

1. _____ had a strong imagination.

2. _____ needed help with her reading.

3. _____ was compared to a jailer.

4. _____ thought that everything was a story.

5. _____ got books in the mail.

GO TO PART D IN YOUR TEXTBOOK

A STORY DETAILS

Work the items.

1. When Sara wanted to see the sunset, she went to the ▮ window.
   a. kitchen   b. garret   c. classroom

2. From the window, the things happening in the world below seemed ▮.
   a. more real than ever
   b. the same as before
   c. almost unreal

3. During the sunset, Sara and Erma fed ▮.
   a. sparrows   b. pigeons   c. themselves

4. Sara said the attic was so high up it was like a ▮ in a tree.
   a. nest   b. branch   c. leaf

5. Sara couldn't stand up at one end of the attic because the ceiling was ▮.
   a. straight   b. collapsed   c. slanted

6. Sara imagined that ▮ could hang on the wall.
   a. pictures   b. stuffed birds   c. dresses

7. What was the wall really like?
   a. It was smooth and recently painted.
   b. It was the same height all around the room.
   c. It had cracks and broken patches.

8. Sara's bed was covered with a dingy _____.

B CLOZE SENTENCES

Complete each sentence with the correct word.

| awed | dramatic | quilt |
| Bastille | existence | tinged |

1. Hank didn't believe in the _____ of the tooth fairy.

2. The orange towel was _____ with blue.

3. The actress made a _____ gesture with her hands.

4. Elijah and Ava used patches of cloth to make the _____.

C CONTRADICTIONS

Work the items.

Lydia applied for jobs at ten different companies. Nine of the companies said Lydia could not have a job. But the twelfth company gave Lydia a job. She was very happy, and she treated herself to a nice dinner.

1. Underline the statement that you assume is true.

2. Draw a box around the statement that contradicts the true statement.

3. Write an *if-then* statement that explains the contradiction.

_____

_____

_____

Lesson 44   87

D CONTEXT CLUES

For each item, circle the answer that means the same thing as the word in bold type.

1. The crying runner was **evidently** sad about losing the race.
   - a. not very
   - b. obviously
   - c. proudly
   - d. meekly

2. Even **dingy** clothes can get bright and clean in a good washing machine.
   - a. shiny white
   - b. lightly used
   - c. dark and dirty
   - d. new

3. In the field of yellow flowers, the solitary **crimson** rose looked like a drop of blood.
   - a. dark green
   - b. sky blue
   - c. deep red
   - d. dirt brown

E PERSPECTIVES

Complete each sentence with *real* or *pretend*.

1. Sunsets in the west are _____ for Sara.

2. A fire in the stove is _____ for Sara.

3. A hard bed is _____ for Sara.

4. Mountains in the clouds are _____ for Sara.

5. Pictures on the wall are _____ for Sara.

6. A battered footstool is _____ for Sara.

F VOCABULARY REVIEW

Complete each sentence with the correct word.

accustomed	distinguished	pupil
craving	garret	skylight
discard	outcast	vacant

1. An outstanding person is a _____ person.

2. When you have a great desire for something, you have a _____ for that thing.

3. Another word for *empty* is _____ .

4. Somebody who is thrown out of a group is an _____ .

5. When you are used to something, you are _____ to that thing.

6. When you throw something away, you _____ it.

GO TO PART D IN YOUR TEXTBOOK

Name

A STORY DETAILS

Work the items.

1. When Sara first saw the rat, why had he come out of his hole?
   a. He wanted to make friends with Sara.
   b. He had smelled Erma's crumbs.
   c. He wanted to explore Sara's room.

2. Sara had already made friends with birds called _____.

3. The rat came close to Sara so he could ____.
   a. grab a large crumb
   b. get a closer look at Sara
   c. rub up against her feet

4. When the rat came close to her, Sara ____.
   a. sat very still   b. jumped onto the bed
   c. petted him

5. Sara named the rat  _____.

6. Erma thought Sara might be talking to a ____.
   a. teacher   b. rat   c. ghost

7. How did Erma feel when Sara told her about the rat?
   a. interested   b. frightened
   c. thrilled

8. Erma immediately jumped onto the ____.
   a. footstool   b. bed   c. chair

9. What did Erma say when Sara asked if she wanted to see the rat?
   a. nothing   b. yes   c. no

B CLOZE SENTENCES

Complete each sentence with the correct word.

| awed | dramatic | romantic |
| Bastille | forlorn | subscribed |

1. The doctor _____ to medical magazines.

2. The actor gave a very _____ sigh.

3. The bird-watchers were _____ by the size of the eagle.

4. For Valentine's Day, the couple had a _____ dinner in a quiet restaurant.

C CONTEXT CLUES

For each item, circle the answer that means the same thing as the word(s) in bold type.

1. The monster had a **horrid** grin that showed its sharp teeth.
   a. romantic   b. forlorn
   c. horrible   d. dramatic

2. Rajeev had injured his leg, so he had to **shuffle** across the room.
   a. jog slowly   b. skate
   c. play shuffleboard d. walk slowly

3. Logan **was inclined** to have peanut butter sandwiches for lunch.
   a. never wanted   b. tended
   c. rarely wanted d. forgot

D PERSPECTIVES

Complete each sentence with would or wouldn't.

1. Sara _____ try to make friends with a mouse.

2. Sara _____ set traps to catch mice.

3. Sara _____ get angry and hit somebody.

4. Sara _____ look at the bright side of things.

5. Sara _____ try to understand other people.

E CONTRADICTIONS

Work the items.

Many people are changing the way they eat. Rock star Biff Socko says, "I no longer eat any kind of bread. Bread is bad for you and hurts your voice." Every day, Biff has grapes and cucumbers for breakfast. Then he eats a large hamburger bun. He has been eating this way for a long time.

1. Underline the statement that you assume is true.

2. Draw a box around the statement that contradicts the true statement.

3. Write an *if-then* statement that explains the contradiction.

   _____
   _____
   _____

GO TO PART D IN YOUR TEXTBOOK

Name _____ 46

A STORY DETAILS

Work the items.

1. The animal that Sara treated like a person was named _____ .

2. Sara pretended her garret was a real place named the _____ .

3. On the day after Erma met the animal, her father ▮ .
   a. took her to another school
   b. sent her more books
   c. met Sara

4. To lift her spirits, Sara pretended to be a _____ .

5. How did the expression on Sara's face make Miss Minchin feel?
   a. proud   b. angry   c. sad

6. One day, Miss Minchin hurt Sara by ▮ her.
   a. tripping   b. slapping   c. squeezing

7. When that happened, Sara ▮ .
   a. laughed   b. cried   c. hit back

8. Sara said, "I won't apologize for ▮ ."
   a. crying   b. thinking   c. laughing

9. At the end of the chapter, Miss Minchin ordered Sara to ▮ .
   a. run an errand
   b. leave the school forever
   c. go to her room

B CLOZE SENTENCES

Complete each sentence with the correct word.

| challenging | dingy | smarting |
| crimson | evidently | tinged |

1. The catcher's hand was _____ after catching twenty fastballs.

2. Playing an instrument is _____ , but it's also a lot of fun.

3. The girl with the chattering teeth was _____ cold.

C CONTEXT CLUES

For each item, circle the answer that means the same thing as the word in bold type.

1. The loud alarm clock could **rouse** even the deepest sleepers.
   a. soothe   b. ignore
   c. silence   d. awaken

2. It's not a good idea to make **impudent** remarks to a police officer.
   a. rude and bold   b. prudent
   c. calm and polite d. written

3. One thing animals and plants share is **existence.**
   a. extra sense   b. the ability to speak
   c. past tense   d. being alive

Lesson 46   91

D POINT OF VIEW

The way you see or think about someone or something is called your **point of view.**

Here are two points of view about Miss Minchin from two different authors:

Passage A

Miss Minchin was tall and had large, cold, fishy eyes and large, cold hands, which seemed fishy, too, because they were so damp. She touched Sara on the forehead, and chills ran down Sara's back. Miss Minchin repeated, "Yes, she will be a favorite pupil, *quite* a favorite pupil."

Passage B

Miss Minchin was tall and had large eyes and large hands. She touched Sara's forehead and said, "Yes, she will be a favorite pupil."

Work the items.

1. Underline the sentence in passage A that describes Miss Minchin's eyes and hands.

2. Underline the sentence in passage B that describes Miss Minchin's eyes and hands.

3. Draw a box around the sentence in passage A that describes what Sara feels when Miss Minchin touches her.

4. What point of view does passage A present about Miss Minchin?

   _____

5. What point of view does passage B present about Miss Minchin?

   _____

E CONTRADICTIONS

Work the items.

Jan needed a calculator to solve a math problem. She asked several people, but none of them had a calculator. Then she ran into her friend Rosa, who offered to lend her one. Jan said, "That's okay. I can solve this problem in my head."

1. Underline the statement you assume to be true.

2. Draw a box around the contradiction.

3. Write an *if-then* statement that explains the contradiction.

   _____
   _____
   _____
   _____

GO TO PART E IN YOUR TEXTBOOK

Name ______________________________

A STORY DETAILS

Work the items.

1. When Sara went out to do errands, the weather was ____ .
   - a. warm and sunny
   - b. warm and wet
   - c. cold and wet
2. What was the condition of Sara's clothes?
   - a. new and soaked
   - b. shabby and soaked
   - c. shabby and dry
3. Sara found a ____________________penny coin in the street.
4. The beggar girl was sitting on ____ .
   - a. the step of a bakery
   - b. a chair in the bakery
   - c. a bench outside the bakery
5. What did Sara think a princess would do for the girl?
   - a. send her home
   - b. share with her
   - c. give her a job
6. Sara could afford to buy only ____________________ buns.
7. The baker woman gave Sara ____________________ buns.
8. Sara gave the beggar girl ____________________ buns.
9. How many buns did Sara have left for herself? ____________________

B CLOZE SENTENCES

Complete each sentence with the correct word.

bedraggled	dunno	jostled
continuously	inclined	quilt

1. People in the subway ____________________ each other when they got out.
2. His shirt was so ____________________ that it looked like a rag.
3. The bank robber said, "I stole a bunch of money but ____________________ where it all went."

C CONTEXT CLUES

For each item, circle the answer that means the same thing as the word in bold type.

1. The baseball player's shoulder was **smarting** because it was hit by a pitch.
   - a. really smart
   - b. stinging
   - c. feeling great
   - d. shuffled
2. The **impudent** boy was sent to the principal's office after he acted out in class.
   - a. intelligent
   - b. student
   - c. well-behaved
   - d. rude
3. Many people think that cockroaches are **horrid** bugs that need to be killed.
   - a. disgusting
   - b. cuddly
   - c. useful
   - d. horizontal

D POINT OF VIEW

Here are two points of view about Sara from two different authors:

Passage A

Because Sara was mourning for her father, she was wearing a black velvet dress. When she came into the room, she looked like the saddest little figure in the world. The dress was too short and too tight, her face was pale, and her eyes had dark rings around them. She had wrapped her doll, Emily, in a piece of old black velvet, and she held the doll under her arm.

Passage B

Sara wore a black velvet dress that was short and tight. She held a doll wrapped in black velvet under her arm.

Work the items.

1. Underline the sentence in passage A that explains why Sara was wearing a black dress.

2. Does passage B explain why Sara was wearing a black dress? _____

3. Draw a box around the sentence in passage A that describes how the dress fit, and how Sara's face and eyes looked.

4. Draw a box around the sentence in passage B that describes what Sara wore.

5. What point of view does passage A present about Sara?
   _____
   _____

6. What point of view does passage B present about Sara?
   _____
   _____

E CONTRADICTIONS

Work the items.

Angelita loves to read. She spends most of her free time reading, and she hardly ever plays with her friends. Angelita reads only novels. She usually reads at least two novels a week, and sometimes she reads as many as five. When her father calls her to dinner, Angelita says, "I'll be there in a minute. Just let me finish reading this poem."

1. Underline the statement you assume to be true.

2. Draw a box around the contradiction.

3. Write an *if-then* statement that explains the contradiction.
   _____
   _____
   _____

GO TO PART E IN YOUR TEXTBOOK

A STORY DETAILS

Work the items.

1. When the baker woman looked out her window, she saw ▭ eating the buns.
   a. Sara   b. the beggar girl   c. a customer

2. The baker woman told that person to go ▭.
   a. into the shop   b. back to the street
   c. home

3. Sara named the family with many children the _____ Family.

4. To Sara, the most interesting person in the square was the _____ Gentleman.

5. The gentleman lived next door to the ▭.
   a. bakery shop   b. school
   c. family with many children

6. The gentleman had once lived in the country of _____ .

7. A rumor said that the gentleman had a problem with his ▭.
   a. heart   b. kidneys   c. liver

8. Sara called the gentleman's servant the _____ .

9. What could Sara do that surprised the servant?
   a. speak Hindi   b. play with the monkey
   c. pretend about everything

B CLOZE SENTENCES

Complete each sentence with the correct word.

| challenging | lascar | rouse |
| impudent | liver | tropical |

1. Your _____ is one of your most important organs.

2. The _____ brought cakes and tea to his employer.

3. Bananas grow easily in _____ climates.

4. The rooster's job is to _____ the farm every morning.

C CHARACTER TRAITS

Complete each sentence with *Sara*, *Miss Minchin*, *The Indian Gentleman*, or *The lascar*.

1. _____ was surprised to hear Sara speak his own language.

2. _____ had a problem with his liver.

3. _____ liked to imagine things about people.

4. _____ was very rich.

5. _____ served a gentleman.

Lesson 48

D CONTEXT CLUES

For each item, circle the answer that means the same thing as the word in bold type.

1. The expensive car had **luxurious** seats made of real leather.

   a. cheap and sticky   b. reclining

   c. fine and elegant   d. smarting

2. Crying sounds came from the **stroller** as the father pushed it through the park.

   a. lawnmower   b. sports car

   c. trailer   d. baby carriage

3. The student had to **ponder** the question before answering the teacher.

   a. think about   b. forget about

   c. repeat   d. ignore

E RELEVANT INFORMATION

Write whether each item is *relevant to fact A*, *relevant to fact B*, or *irrelevant to both facts*.

Fact A: Sara pretended to be a princess.

Fact B: Sara pretended her doll was alive.

1. Sara needed someone to talk to.
   _____

2. Sara wanted to feel like a royal person.
   _____

3. Sara had black hair.
   _____

4. Sara lived in London.
   _____

GO TO PART D IN YOUR TEXTBOOK

Name _____ 49

A STORY DETAILS

Work the items.

1. Why was Miss Minchin angry when Sara came back to the school?
   a. Sara had forgotten to buy meat for the cook.
   b. Sara's room had been improved.
   c. Sara had been out for hours.

2. All Sara received for supper was a piece of _____ .

3. Why did it take Sara so long to climb the stairs to her room?
   a. She was tired.
   b. She had hurt her leg.
   c. She was lazy.

4. The kettle on Sara's stove was made of ▨ .
   a. iron   b. steel   c. brass

5. The robe on Sara's bed was made of ▨ .
   a. cotton   b. silk   c. wool

6. One plate had toast and the other had _____ .

7. At first, Sara thought her room was ▨ .
   a. bedraggled   b. becalmed
   c. bewitched

8. The note to Sara was inside ▨ .
   a. an envelope   b. a book   c. a package

9. Sara thought these gifts had been given to her by ▨ .
   a. a friend   b. her father
   c. Miss Minchin

B CLOZE SENTENCES

Complete each sentence with the correct word.

| bedraggled | continuously | vent |
| bewitched | dunno | |

1. The golfer liked to _____ her anger by throwing her golf club.

2. The marble sculpture began to move because it was _____ .

3. Pablo said, "My hat is missing and _____ where it is."

4. After the children played in the puddle, their clothes were _____ .

Lesson 49   97

C CONTEXT CLUES

For each item, circle the answer that means the same thing as the word(s) in bold type.

1. The cake was so **luscious** that everyone wanted a piece.
   a. burned   b. delicious
   c. expensive   d. lush

2. Janelle put **her purchases** into a canvas bag.
   a. her purses
   b. the things she was giving away
   c. cat toys
   d. the things she bought

3. The crowd **jostled** for position in the long line.
   a. pushed and shoved   b. drew straws
   c. did nothing   d. argued loudly

D SEQUENCING

Number the events in the correct sequence.

____ Sara could not believe what she saw.

____ Sara gave some buns to a beggar girl.

____ Sara made friends with a rat.

____ Sara had a hard time climbing the stairs.

____ Sara was warm and comfortable.

E POINT OF VIEW

Sara believed that a princess would do some things but not others.

Complete each sentence with would or wouldn't.

1. A princess _____ get angry when people scold her.

2. A princess _____ help someone who is worse off than she is.

3. A princess _____ give people gifts.

4. A princess _____ look the other way when she sees a beggar.

5. A princess _____ complain about being hungry.

GO TO PART D IN YOUR TEXTBOOK

Name _____ 50

A STORY DETAILS

Work the items.

1. When the attic changed, Sara thought she was living in a _____ tale.

2. The comforts Sara enjoyed were making her ▨ .
   a. more obedient   b. smarter
   c. stronger

3. Who were the parcels addressed to?
   a. The Girl in the Attic
   b. Sara Crewe   c. Miss Minchin

4. What did the parcels contain?
   a. food   b. books   c. clothing

5. Miss Minchin was quite ▨ when Sara received the parcels.
   a. elated   b. irritated   c. elevated

6. Miss Minchin thought Sara might have a powerful friend in the ▨ .
   a. foreground   b. background
   c. underground

7. Miss Minchin told Sara to put on the new clothes so she would look ▨ .
   a. respectable   b. incapable
   c. detectable

8. One girl thought Sara had ▨ a fortune.
   a. inherited   b. squandered
   c. purchased

B CLOZE SENTENCES

Complete each sentence with the correct word.

| draperies | luscious | respectable |
| incident | purchases | vent |

1. Getting a medal was a big _____ in Waylon's life.

2. Iris wanted to _____ her emotions, but she kept still.

3. The man looked well dressed and _____ , but he was really a criminal.

4. The windows were covered with _____ to block the light.

C MOTIVES

Complete each sentence with *well* or *poorly*.

1. When Captain Crewe was alive, Sara had a lot of money, so Miss Minchin treated her _____ .

2. Captain Crewe lost all his money, so Miss Minchin treated Sara _____ .

3. Sara had no friends or family, so Miss Minchin treated her _____ .

4. Somebody powerful might be interested in Sara, so Miss Minchin treated Sara _____ .

Lesson 50   99

D CONTEXT CLUES

For each item, circle the answer that means the same thing as the word in bold type.

1. Delilah closed the **parcel** with tape and mailed it.
   a. parsley   b. paper
   c. package   d. painting

2. There was **scant** water for the plants, so they began to die.
   a. not enough   b. too much
   c. flavored   d. scarlet

3. Xavier was **irritated** by the loud music, so he covered his ears.
   a. bewitched   b. annoyed
   c. overjoyed   d. attracted

E VOCABULARY REVIEW

Complete each sentence with the correct word.

| discarded | inclined | pondered |
| impudent | luxurious | tropical |

1. Cats are _____ to sleep on chairs and couches.

2. It's almost always warm in _____ climates.

3. The students _____ the riddle for a long time but finally solved it.

4. Their _____ living room had thick carpets and comfortable chairs.

F CONTRADICTIONS

Work the items.

Loretta lived about two hundred miles from Kansas City. The town she lived in was quite small. Loretta would often go into Kansas City to visit her uncle. She would drive into the city in her red sports car. She always drove fifty miles an hour, and the trip usually took about an hour. Once she got to Kansas City, she would stay for a few hours and then return home.

1. Underline the statement you assume to be true.

2. Draw a box around the contradiction.

3. Write an if-then statement that explains the contradiction.

   _____
   _____
   _____
   _____

GO TO PART D IN YOUR TEXTBOOK

Name _____

A STORY DETAILS

Work the items.

1. What did Sara write to her unknown friend?
   a. diary entry   b. thank-you note
   c. set of instructions

2. When the monkey was in Sara's room, he had a ▭ look on his face.
   a. forlorn   b. forbidden   c. forgotten

3. When Sara went up to the monkey, he put out his ▭ little hands.
   a. dwarfish   b. selfish   c. elfish

4. Why did the monkey give a little scream of anger before he left Sara's room?
   a. He was angry at Sara for not giving him more cake.
   b. He didn't want to leave the room.
   c. He was mad at Miss Minchin.

5. What language did Sara use when she spoke to the lascar at the Indian Gentleman's door?
   a. English   b. French   c. Hindi

6. The Indian Gentleman's face was ▭ .
   a. pale   b. red   c. blue

7. The Indian Gentleman was Captain Crewe's ▭ .
   a. enemy   b. friend   c. brother

8. Why had Sara's father lost all his money?
   a. He gambled the money away.
   b. He put the money in a bag and lost the bag.
   c. He gave the money to a friend and the friend lost it.

B CLOZE SENTENCES

Complete each sentence with the correct word.

| agitated | caress | luscious |
| bewitched | frightfully | purchases |

1. The child was so _____ that he screamed and yelled.

2. Cats purr when you _____ their head and neck.

3. Prices in the jewelry store are _____ high.

4. They topped the ice cream with _____ strawberries.

Lesson 51   101

C CONTEXT CLUES

For each item, circle the answer that means the same thing as the word in bold type.

1. The coach **addressed** the players before the big game.
   - a. glimpsed
   - b. bedraggled
   - c. spoke to
   - d. listened to

2. The electric company made a **miscalculation** on the bill.
   - a. new calculation
   - b. tax
   - c. higher charge
   - d. mistake

3. The weather can be **frightfully** bad during the winter.
   - a. very
   - b. frighteningly
   - c. scary
   - d. a little

D COMPARING CHARACTERS

Complete each sentence with *The Indian Gentleman, Captain Crewe, Sara,* or *The lascar.*

1. _____ thought all his money had been lost.

2. _____ died in India.

3. _____ had hollow eyes.

4. _____ took care of a sick man.

5. _____ discovered who Sara really was.

E VOCABULARY REVIEW

Complete each sentence with the correct word.

| lascar | stroller |
| liver | vent |

1. A small carriage for babies and young children is called a _____.

2. An organ in your body that keeps your blood healthy is called your _____.

3. When you let your emotions show, you _____.

GO TO PART D IN YOUR TEXTBOOK

102   Lesson 51

52

Name _____

A STORY DETAILS

Work the items.

1. The Indian Gentleman's real name was

   Mr. _____ .

2. The lawyer's name was

   Mr. _____ .

3. One of Captain Crewe's ▇▇▇ had doubled his fortune.

   a. divestments   b. assessments

   c. investments

4. Ram had brought the gifts to Sara's room.

5. The real name of the Large Family was

   the _____ family.

6. Sara told the Large Family the story of the night she was too tired to suppose she

   was a _____ .

7. On that night, Sara's room turned into ▇▇▇ .

   a. Fairyland   b. the Bastille

   c. a classroom

8. After Sara left the Large Family, she

   moved in with Mr. _____ .

B CLOZE SENTENCES

Complete each sentence with the correct word.

| draperies | irritated | respectable |
| investments | parcels | scant |

1. You can make a lot of money if you make

   wise _____ .

2. The post office has to handle millions of

   _____ during the holidays.

3. Gemma grew _____ when the dog kept barking.

4. A judge has to be a _____ person in the courtroom.

C CONTEXT CLUES

For each item, circle the answer that means the same thing as the word in bold type.

1. Mr. Corbin's children loved him because he was **devoted** to them.
   a. mournful   b. wolfish
   c. impolite   d. loyal

2. Almost all the players were at the practice, but one was **absent.**
   a. grumbling   b. not present
   c. roughened   d. enraged

3. The big fire was an **incident** that's hard to forget.
   a. event   b. impudent
   c. outpouring   d. enjoyment

D RELEVANT INFORMATION

Write whether each item is *relevant to fact A, relevant to fact B,* or *irrelevant to both facts.*

Fact A: Miss Minchin thought Sara was poor.

Fact B: Miss Minchin thought Sara might have a rich friend.

1. Miss Minchin ran a boarding school.
   _____

2. Miss Minchin treated Sara like a servant.
   _____

3. Miss Minchin made Sara sleep in the attic.
   _____

4. Miss Minchin started to treat Sara better.
   _____

E PERSPECTIVES

Complete each sentence with *Ram Dass, Miss Minchin, Sara, Captain Crewe,* or *Mr. Carrisford.*

1. _____ said, "This must be a dream."

2. _____ said, "I must find my friend's daughter."

3. _____ said, "I will take advantage of her by making her teach French."

4. _____ said, "Now is a good time to creep through the window."

5. _____ said, "I will never forget opening the attic door."

GO TO PART D IN YOUR TEXTBOOK

Name _____ 53

A STORY DETAILS

Work the items.

1. Sara called Mr. Carrisford a ▓ .
   a. magician   b. musician   c. mechanic

2. Miss Minchin thought she had made a serious mistake with Sara from a ▓ point of view.
   a. third-person   b. second-person
   c. business

3. What reason did Sara have for refusing to stay with Miss Minchin?
   a. Sara was too old for Miss Minchin's school.
   b. Sara couldn't afford Miss Minchin's school.
   c. Sara remembered how Miss Minchin had treated her.

4. What type of document did Miss Minchin send to Mr. Carrisford?
   a. friendly letter   b. bill
   c. thank-you note

5. What child did Sara remember one night?
   a. Erma   b. the beggar girl
   c. one of the Carmichael children

6. Sara had given that child five _____ and kept one for herself.

7. Sara knew what it was like to be ▓ .
   a. wicked   b. arrogant   c. hungry

8. Sara asked the baker woman to give hungry children ▓ .
   a. money   b. food   c. housing

9. The beggar girl was named _____ .

B CLOZE SENTENCES

Complete each sentence with the correct word.

| address | appeal | fortunes |
| agitated | caress | frightfully |

1. The novel told about the main character's _____ during her long life.

2. When people are _____ , they can't think clearly.

3. The food bank made a widespread _____ for donations during the disaster.

4. People like to _____ their pets.

Lesson 53   105

C CONTEXT CLUES

For each item, circle the answer that means the same thing as the word in bold type.

1. Hiroshi enjoyed the **companionship** of his fellow students.
   a. friendship   b. miscalculation
   c. likeness   d. resentment

2. The city council discussed the mayor's **proposal** to build more sidewalks.
   a. order   b. refusal
   c. plan   d. agreement

3. The soccer fans felt **desolate** after their team lost the World Cup final.
   a. annoyed   b. heavenly
   c. miserable d. respectable

D CHARACTER TRAITS

Complete each sentence about Sara Crewe with *would* or *wouldn't*.

1. Sara _____ give money to the poor.

2. Sara _____ get bored with books.

3. Sara _____ forget to thank somebody.

4. Sara _____ speak to someone in French, German, or Hindi.

5. Sara _____ like people just because they dress well.

E VOCABULARY REVIEW

Complete each sentence with the correct word.

| incident | luxurious | scant |
| luscious | ponder | tropical |

1. The queen's room was filled with _____ furniture.

2. Everyone wanted to eat the _____ cake.

3. The banana is a _____ fruit.

4. The victims remember the _____ as if it happened yesterday.

GO TO PART D IN YOUR TEXTBOOK

Name _____ 54

A CLOZE SENTENCES

Complete each sentence with the correct word.

absent	curlew	investment
agitated	hostler	nevermore

1. As Magnus left the wretched town, he said, "I shall _____ return."

2. At the ocean, we saw a gull and a _____ flying over the beach.

3. Courtney got a job as a _____ at a stable.

4. The sick student was _____ from class for a week.

B CONTEXT CLUES

For each item, circle the answer that means the same thing as the word in bold type.

1. The child tried to **efface** the crayon marks on the floor.
   a. deepen   b. caress
   c. irritate   d. erase

2. The rider put her foot in the stirrup and mounted the **steed.**
   a. stage   b. horse
   c. cow   d. step

3. Dogs can be quite **devoted** to their owners.
   a. loyal   b. fatherly
   c. elfish   d. unkindly

C CHARACTER TRAITS

Complete each sentence with *A person* or *The sea*.

1. _____ does something only once.

2. _____ does things again and again.

3. _____ does the same thing during the day and the night.

4. _____ does one thing during the day and another thing during the night.

5. _____ leaves signs that last for a short time.

6. _____ erases signs left by somebody else.

Lesson 54   107

D RHYME SCHEME

Fill in each blank with the correct word. Then add *A*, *B*, *C*, or *D* at the end of each line, as follows:

- Add **A** if the line rhymes with **halls**.
- Add **B** if the line rhymes with **gown**.
- Add **C** if the line rhymes with **lands**.
- Add **D** if the line rhymes with **tore**.

The first line has been done for you.

The tide rises, the tide <u>falls</u>, **A**

The twilight darkens, the curlew
_____ ; ___

Along the sea-sands damp and
_____ ___

The traveler hastens toward the
_____ , ___

   And the tide rises, the tide
_____ . ___

Darkness settles on roofs and
_____ , ___

But the sea, the sea in the darkness
_____ ; ___

The little waves, with their soft, white
_____ , ___

Efface the footprints in the
_____ , ___

   And the tide rises, the tide
_____ . ___

The morning breaks; the steeds in their
_____ ___

Stamp and neigh, as the hostler
_____ ; ___

The day returns, but
_____ ___

Returns the traveler to the
_____ , ___

   And the tide rises, the tide
_____ . ___

GO TO PART E IN YOUR TEXTBOOK

108   Lesson 54

Name _____ 55

A STORY DETAILS

Work the items.

1. Every diamond that has been tested for its age is more than 500 ▨ years old.

   a. million   b. billion   c. trillion

2. Diamonds are harder than any ▨ natural substance.

   a. super   b. known   c. unknown

3. Diamonds are made of ▨ .

   a. carbon   b. coal   c. fullerite

4. The best place to find diamonds is ▨ .

   a. under the ocean
   b. inside volcanoes   c. in fields

5. Rough diamonds usually come in an eight-sided shape called an ▨ .

   a. ocarina   b. octopus   c. octahedron

6. Carats measure the ▨ of diamonds.

   a. size   b. weight   c. brightness

7. True or false: Most diamonds are used for jewelry.

   a. true   b. false

8. The most expensive diamond colors are the ▨ ones.

   a. most common   b. clearest   c. rarest

B CLOZE SENTENCES

Complete each sentence with the correct word.

| appeal | erupt | fullerite |
| carat | fortunes | octahedron |

1. A dead volcano will never _____ again.

2. The diamond weighed less than one _____ , but it was worth thousands of dollars.

3. The _____ had eight sides.

4. A new material harder than diamonds is _____ .

Lesson 55   109

C CONTEXT CLUES

For each item, circle the answer that means the same thing as the word in bold type.

1. The jeweler carefully placed a **gemstone** in the wedding ring.
   a. piece of gold   b. jewelry stone
   c. button   d. piece of magma

2. Dogs are valued for their **companionship** and loyalty.
   a. proposal   b. barking
   c. worship   d. friendship

3. Everyone felt **desolate** during the flood.
   a. delighted   b. wet
   c. miserable   d. very late

D CHARACTER TRAITS

Complete each sentence about "The Tide Rises, the Tide Falls" with *A person* or *The sea*.

1. _____ leaves footprints that last for a short time.

2. _____ effaces footprints.

3. _____ hurries toward the town.

4. _____ does the same thing over and over again.

5. _____ does something only once.

E VOCABULARY REVIEW

Complete each sentence with the correct word.

| absent | devoted | investment |
| address | frightfully | miscalculation |

1. Someone who is loyal is _____ .

2. An attempt to make a profit by spending money is called an _____ .

3. An old-fashioned word for *very* is _____ .

4. When you speak to somebody, you _____ them.

5. An error or mistake is sometimes called a _____ .

GO TO PART D IN YOUR TEXTBOOK

Name _____

56

A STORY DETAILS

Work the items.

1. The author of "The Necklace" is _____ de Maupassant.

2. Mr. Loisel worked as a _____ for the government.

3. One day Mr. Loisel brought home an _____ to the Governor's Grand Ball.

4. What did Matilda say she needed after she bought a dress?
   a. natural flowers   b. jewels
   c. new shoes

5. Matilda visited her friend Mrs. _____ to get what she needed.

6. At her friend's house, Matilda borrowed a _____ made of _____ .

7. At the ball, Matilda was in a cloud of ▪▪▪ .
   a. smoke   b. steam   c. happiness

8. After the ball, the Loisels tried to find a _____ on the street.

9. Why did Matilda utter a cry at the end of this part?
   a. She was sorry the ball was over.
   b. Her dress was torn.
   c. Something was missing.

B CLOZE SENTENCES

Complete each sentence with the correct word.

| contrasted | franc | modest |
| curlew | hostler | nevermore |

1. Lorenzo was so _____ that he almost never spoke.

2. A _____ is a unit of money.

3. The colorful parrot _____ with the colorless sparrow.

4. The _____ made sure all the horses in the barn were fed.

C CONTEXT CLUES

For each item, circle the answer that means the same thing as the word in bold type.

1. The loss was so **humiliating** that all the players on the team looked at the ground.
   a. suitable   b. effaced
   c. embarrassing   d. bewitched

2. Alina tried to escape her **drab** apartment by playing outside.
   a. noisy   b. desirable
   c. rosy   d. dull

3. The cowgirl leaped on her trusty **steed** and galloped away.
   a. cow   b. horse
   c. donkey   d. mule

Lesson 56   111

D PERSPECTIVES

Complete each sentence with *dream* or *reality*.

1. Real silverware was Matilda's _____.

2. Worn tablecloths were Matilda's _____.

3. Ugly curtains were Matilda's _____.

4. Trout for dinner was Matilda's _____.

5. Stew for dinner was Matilda's _____.

6. Golden plates were Matilda's _____.

E VOCABULARY REVIEW

Complete each sentence with the correct word.

> appeal　　　　desolate　　　proposal
> companionship　　fortunes

1. Daisy's _____ in life improved when she started working harder in school.

2. The drowning man made a desperate _____ for help.

3. The builder made a _____ to construct a new apartment complex.

4. Dogs offer _____ to lonely people.

GO TO PART E IN YOUR TEXTBOOK

A STORY DETAILS

Work the items.

1. Matilda told Mrs. Forester that she had broken the _____ of the necklace and was having it mended.

2. The Loisels paid ____ francs for a new necklace.

   a. 500   b. 36,000   c. 40,000

3. How did the Loisels pay for the new necklace?

   a. They charged it to their credit card.

   b. They sold their apartment.

   c. They went into debt.

4. To save money, the Loisels moved into a ____ .

   a. hotel   b. house   c. garret

5. Matilda worked as a _____ after the Loisels moved.

6. The Loisels repaid their loans after ____ years.

   a. five   b. ten   c. twenty

7. At the end of that time, Matilda had become a woman of ____ .

   a. poverty   b. leisure   c. wealth

8. At the end of the story, Mrs. Forester told Matilda that the necklace was _____ .

B CLOZE SENTENCES

Complete each sentence with the correct word.

| carat | Fahrenheit | lobby |
| debt | gemstones | octahedron |

1. After Mr. Lopez bought the fancy car, he had a large _____ to pay.

2. When you walk through the front door of a large building, you enter the _____ .

3. Water freezes at 32 degrees _____ .

4. Diamonds, emeralds, and rubies are all _____ .

Lesson 57

C CONTEXT CLUES

For each item, circle the answer that means the same thing as the word in bold type.

1. Dogs can **detect** smells much better than people can.
   a. notice   b. erupt
   c. apply   d. hasten

2. Poloma was in deep **anguish** after her cat died.
   a. water   b. woods
   c. sorrow   d. debt

3. Matilda claimed that she broke the **clasp** of the necklace.
   a. diamonds   b. connector
   c. front   d. neck

D PERSPECTIVES

Complete each sentence with *Matilda, Mr. Loisel,* or *Mrs. Forester.*

1. _____ said, "I have to work as a maid."

2. _____ said, "Ten years after the ball, I still look young and beautiful."

3. _____ said, "I like to eat simple stew."

4. _____ said, "Some of my jewelry is fake."

5. _____ said, "I have to bargain with the grocer."

E VOCABULARY REVIEW

Complete each sentence with the correct word.

| curlew | hostler | purchases |
| effaced | nevermore | steed |

1. The _____ flew over the waves.

2. Weston's old _____ needed a new saddle.

3. The _____ held the horse by its bridle.

4. The rain _____ the chalk marks on the sidewalk.

GO TO PART D IN YOUR TEXTBOOK

Name ____

A STORY DETAILS

1. Wool socks, cotton shirts, and blue jeans are all made of ____ .

   a. cotton b. wool c. thread d. leather

2. Bolls are used to make

   ____________________ thread.

3. The fur of sheep is used to make

   ____________________ .

4. Bolls and sheep fur are made of thousands of short pieces called ____ .

   a. thread b. fibers c. straw d. blades

5. Cloth that is made by weaving is called

   ____________________ cloth.

6. The two kinds of threads used for weaving are called warp threads and

   ____________________ threads.

7. Threads of ____________________ go right and left.

8. A machine that weaves cloth is called a

   ____________________ .

9. When you knit, you use a thread called

   ____________________ .

B CLOZE SENTENCES

Complete each sentence with the correct word.

drab	modest	suitable
fiber	shear	yarn

1. The farmer used a special clipper to

   ____________________ her sheep.

2. The warm sweater was made of thick blue

   ____________________ .

3. Cotton bolls are made of short pieces of

   ____________________ .

4. A warm coat is not ____________________ for hot weather.

C CONTEXT CLUES

For each item, circle the answer that means the same thing as the word in bold type.

1. The wool sweater began to **unravel** after it was torn.

   a. come together b. darken

   c. fall apart d. contrast

2. The metal wire was stored on a **spool.**

   a. franc b. warp

   c. drab d. container

3. The actor was **humiliated** when she forgot her lines.

   a. embarrassed b. thunderstruck

   c. rare d. supposing

D RELATED FACTS

Tell whether each statement refers to *spinning*, *weaving*, or *knitting*.

1. You do it on a loom. _____

2. You do it with two needles and a ball of yarn. _____

3. You combine warp thread and weft thread. _____

4. You pull and twist fibers at the same time. _____

5. You use a wheel to store thread on a spool. _____

6. You create a space between every other warp thread. _____

7. You can make a scarf from one long piece of yarn. _____

E DIAGRAMS

Study the diagram and work the items.

1. Vertical threads 1–5 are called _____ threads.

2. The horizontal thread is called a _____ thread.

3. Which vertical threads will the horizontal thread go **under** in the top row? List the numbers in order. _____

4. Which vertical threads will the horizontal thread go **over** in the top row? List the numbers in order. _____

5. Which type of cloth making does the diagram show?
   a. knitting   b. shearing
   c. spinning   d. weaving

GO TO PART D IN YOUR TEXTBOOK

59

A STORY DETAILS

1. Male sheep are called
   _____ , and female sheep
   are called _____ .

2. All sheep less than one year old are called
   _____ .

3. Most kinds of sheep are covered with
   _____ .

4. Sheep farmers use two types of dogs:
   _____ dogs and
   _____ dogs.

5. Which kind of fencing can hurt sheep?
   a. wooden   b. mesh   c. barbed-wire

6. When are lambs fully weaned?
   a. when they're born
   b. when they start to eat grass
   c. when they no longer need their mother's milk

7. Sheep farmers often hire a
   _____ to shave the wool
   off their sheep.

8. A sheep usually has ▓ pounds of wool.
   a. 1–5   b. 5–10
   c. 10–15   d. 15–20

B CLOZE SENTENCES

Complete each sentence with the correct word.

| anguish | debt | mastiff |
| clasp | lobby | octahedron |

1. The sheep were guarded by a large
   _____ with a loud bark.

2. When Ezra entered the Empire State Building, he walked into the
   _____ .

3. Most people go into _____
   when they buy a house.

4. His weeping was filled with
   _____ .

Lesson 59

C CONTEXT CLUES

For each item, circle the answer that means the same thing as the word in bold type.

1. The **collie** helped drive the sheep into the upper pasture.
   - a. herding dog
   - b. guard dog
   - c. lap dog
   - d. bus

2. Last year the **ewe** gave birth to a beautiful lamb.
   - a. male sheep
   - b. female goat
   - c. female sheep
   - d. cow

3. You need sharp eyes to **detect** shapes in the dark.
   - a. apply
   - b. bump into
   - c. notice
   - d. ignore

D DIAGRAMS

Study the diagram and work the items.

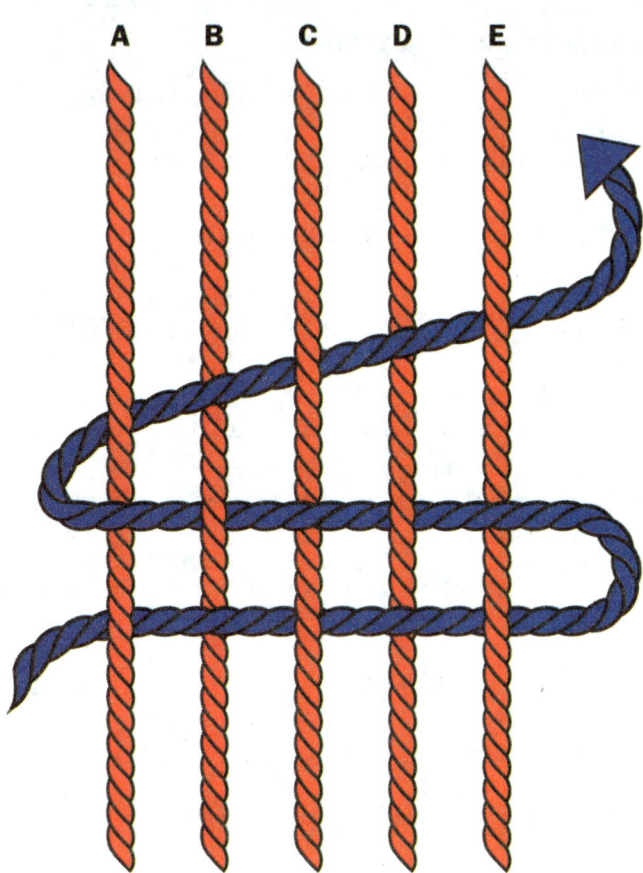

1. What color are the warp threads in the diagram? _____

2. What color are the weft threads in the diagram? _____

3. Which red thread will the blue thread go **over** next? Write **A, B, C, D,** or **E**. ____

4. What is the first red thread the blue thread will go **under**? ____

5. The machine that uses warp and weft threads to make cloth is called a _____.

GO TO PART D IN YOUR TEXTBOOK

118   Lesson 59

Name ______________________________

A STORY DETAILS

1. April Rose got irritated when her mother said, "Goodness, you're getting so __________________."

2. April Rose showed she was irritated by ______.
   a. throwing a fit b. rolling her eyes
   c. yelling d. stomping off

3. The two guard dogs were called Rufus and __________________.

4. The two herding dogs were called Lucky and __________________.

5. The best shepherd April Rose knows is her __________________.

6. Old Ma felt ______ when April Rose scratched between her ears and horns.
   a. blah b. irritated
   c. scratchy d. bliss

7. April Rose noticed an __________________ dark cloud scudding over the horizon.

8. April Rose went back to the house to drop off the ______.
   a. binoculars b. cell phone
   c. lambs d. guard dogs

9. April Rose tried to sound ______ when she called her mother.
   a. worried b. irritated
   c. casual d. frantic

B CLOZE SENTENCES

Complete each sentence with the correct word.

bliss	fiber	spool
documents	ominous	yarn

1. Some people put diplomas and other important __________________ in picture frames.

2. The electric wire was stored on a __________________.

3. Sleeping late on the weekends is pure __________________.

4. The huge wave racing toward the beach looked __________________.

C CONTEXT CLUES

For each item, circle the answer that means the same thing as the word in bold type.

1. The wool scarf began to **unravel** after somebody poked a hole in it.
   - a. warm up
   - b. roost
   - c. humiliate
   - d. fall apart

2. Luca often **mused** about becoming an actor.
   - a. thought
   - b. laughed
   - c. talked
   - d. worried

3. The children were **dismayed** that the ice cream had melted in the cooler.
   - a. detected
   - b. disturbed
   - c. erupted
   - d. tortured

D EXAGGERATION

Work the items.

Exaggeration A

The steak was tougher than a rubber tire.

1. How tough does exaggeration A say the steak was?

   _____

   _____

2. Write an accurate statement that tells how tough the steak was.

   _____

   _____

Exaggeration B

The baseball player hit the ball a mile.

3. How far does exaggeration B say the player hit the ball?

   _____

4. Write an accurate statement that tells how far the baseball player hit the ball.

   _____

   _____

GO TO PART D IN YOUR TEXTBOOK

Name _____

A STORY DETAILS

1. The little voice in April Rose's head said that she should _____ shut the walk-through gate.

2. The first sheep that April Rose moved into the barn was named Old _____ .

3. When trees flash the undersides of their leaves, it's a ▒▒ sign of a bad storm.
   a. flashflood   b. surefire
   c. possible   d. light-headed

4. The ▒▒ always hung out in the farthest corner of the field.
   a. rams   b. ewes   c. lambs

5. The dog that herded the rams was named _____ .

6. The ewes were swept up in the rams' ▒▒ and followed them down the hill.
   a. wagon   b. grazing
   c. momentum   d. horns

7. The dog that kept Big Mae from turning back was named _____ .

8. Big Mae was trying to turn back because she couldn't find her _____ .

9. The dog that was trying to tell April Rose something was named _____ .

B CLOZE SENTENCES

Complete each sentence with the correct word.

> ewe   momentum
> mastiff   straddle

1. The runaway truck gained _____ as it rolled down the steep road.

2. You need long legs to _____ a horse and hang on.

3. The huge _____ protected the house from robbers.

Lesson 61

C CONTEXT CLUES

For each item, circle the answer that means the same thing as the word(s) in bold type.

1. The mayor **advised** staying inside during the major snowstorm.
   a. prevented   b. recommended
   c. preferred   d. permitted

2. The horses **loped** down the dirt road as fast as they could.
   a. trotted with high steps
   b. trudged
   c. walked unsteadily
   d. ran with long strides

3. You need to **redouble your efforts** when you fall behind in a race.
   a. try much harder
   b. go twice as slowly
   c. restart your efforts
   d. give up

D FIGURATIVE LANGUAGE

Write whether each item is a *simile* or an *exaggeration*.

1. Her face was as pale as a distant star. _____

2. The apartment was like a prison. _____

3. The sports car zoomed down the freeway at about a thousand miles an hour. _____

4. The road went up and down like a roller coaster. _____

5. The bag of potatoes weighed a ton. _____

GO TO PART D IN YOUR TEXTBOOK

Name _____

A STORY DETAILS

Work the items.

1. The senior guard dog was named _____.

2. April Rose said that she jumped a _____ when lightning jagged across the sky.

3. The lamb that April Rose found was stuck in a ▓▓ .
   a. ditch   b. clump of barbed wire
   c. mudhole   d. thicket

4. April Rose freed the lamb by ▓▓ a barbed cane.
   a. cutting   b. waggling
   c. tearing   d. digging up

5. April Rose said that lightning lit the field like a ▓▓ carnival scene.
   a. garage   b. dimly lit
   c. garish   d. cheap

6. April Rose knew where she was when she felt the _____ of the bridge under her feet.

7. While April Rose was crossing the bridge, the water rose ▓▓ .
   a. up to her ankles   b. up to her knees
   c. above her knees   d. above her waist

8. The lamb that April Rose rescued belong to _____ .

9. Where was the little voice coming from at the end of the story?
   a. April Rose's mother   b. Rufus
   c. April Rose's sister   d. April Rose

B CLOZE SENTENCES

Complete each sentence with the correct word.

| bliss | enliven | thicket |
| document | muse | whicker |

1. The rabbit hid in the _____ until the hunters went away.

2. The host tried to _____ the party by playing loud music.

3. Some people like to scratch their chin when they _____ about a difficult problem.

4. The mother horse liked to _____ when her foal snuggled up to her.

Lesson 62   123

C CONTEXT CLUES

For each item, circle the answer that means the same thing as the word in bold type.

1. Everything got wet in last night's **deluge**.
   a. luge contest   b. powerful rain
   c. freezing cold   d. roost

2. The outfielder tried to **gauge** where the speeding baseball was headed.
   a. figure out   b. dismay
   c. run to   d. engage

3. The clown always wore **garish** clothes.
   a. torn and tattered
   b. garage-sale
   c. dark and ominous
   d. bright and colorful

D METAPHORS

Work the items.

Metaphor A

The injured woman roared with pain.

1. Which animals roar?
   _____

2. Use accurate language to tell how the sound the woman and those animals make could be the same.
   _____
   _____

Metaphor B

Odysseus swooped down on the lazy suitors.

3. Which types of birds swoop down from the sky?
   _____

4. Use accurate language to tell how Odysseus and those animals could be the same.
   _____
   _____

GO TO PART D IN YOUR TEXTBOOK

Name _____

63

A STORY DETAILS

Work the items.

1. "Hans in Luck" is a type of story called a ▩ .

   a. myth   b. folktale
   c. novel   d. realistic short story

2. Hans's master gave him a lump of gold as big as his _____ .

3. First, Hans traded the lump of gold for a _____ .

4. Second, Hans traded his _____ for a _____ .

5. Third, Hans traded his _____ for a _____ .

6. Fourth, Hans traded his _____ for a _____ .

7. Fifth, Hans traded his _____ for a grinding stone and a rock.

8. Hans's last trade happened when he knocked the stone and the rock down a _____ .

9. At the end of the story, Hans said that he was the ▩ man under the sun.

   a. dumbest   b. strongest
   c. luckiest   d. smartest

B CLOZE SENTENCES

Complete each sentence with the correct word.

| fend | slaughter | trudge |
| lope | straddle | |

1. The baby fawn was too young to _____ for itself in the forest.

2. You need to _____ a horse before you can ride it.

3. The mule was carrying so much weight that it could only _____ along the path.

4. The farmer decided to _____ one of her chickens for a special meal.

Lesson 63   **125**

C CONTEXT CLUES

For each item, circle the answer that means the same thing as the word in bold type.

1. Olive was **vexed** by the pebble in her shoe.
   a. advised   b. pleased
   c. annoyed   d. redoubled

2. One **remedy** for aching feet is to soak them in water.
   a. solution   b. momentum
   c. plank   d. underside

3. The backpack was such a **burden** that Jaiden took it off.
   a. fine handiwork   b. powerful torrent
   c. crowded roost   d. heavy weight

D FIGURATIVE LANGUAGE

Write whether each statement is a *metaphor* or an *exaggeration*.

1. The day lasted forever.
   _____

2. The sound floated across the water.
   _____

3. Her cheeks were roses.
   _____

4. The dog vacuumed up the food under the table. _____

5. The ball left the bat at the speed of light.
   _____

E STORY STRUCTURE

Work the items.

1. In many stories, the first section introduces the main character and is called the _____.

2. In the next section of these stories, the main character faces a ▓▓▓▓.
   a. solution   b. comparison
   c. sequence   d. problem

3. In the last section of these stories, the main character comes up with a ▓▓▓▓.
   a. solution   b. comparison
   c. sequence   d. problem

4. What happens in the setup for "Hans in Luck"?
   a. Hans trades his cow for a pig.
   b. Hans gets freedom from care.
   c. Hans gets a lump of gold.
   d. Hans gets thrown from a horse.

GO TO PART D IN YOUR TEXTBOOK

Name _____

A STORY DETAILS

Work the items.

1. Herons and egrets belong to the same ▭ of birds.
   a. species   b. genus
   c. family   d. subspecies

2. Herons and egrets hunt for fish in ▭ water.
   a. shallow   b. deep
   c. mineral   d. distilled

3. True or false: Herons and egrets in the United States migrate north in the winter.
   a. true
   b. false
   c. both true and false
   d. neither true nor false

4. In the spring, herons gather in large groups called _____.

5. The most common heron in North America is the _____ heron.

6. When they fly, herons hold their neck in an _____ shape, but swans hold their neck _____.

7. Geese and ducks are members of the ▭ family of birds.
   a. heron   b. swan
   c. hawk   d. seagull

8. Great egrets have black legs, but great white herons have _____ legs.

9. Egrets were threatened with extinction in the 1890s because of the demand for women's hats with _____ .

B CLOZE SENTENCES

Complete each sentence with the correct word.

| enliven | recover | whicker |
| gauge | thicket | wingspan |

1. The _____ of the airplane was more than 100 feet long.

2. Carlotta needed several weeks to _____ from her injuries.

3. The robin disappeared into the _____ when the cat strolled by.

4. You can use a tape measure to _____ the size of a room.

Differences Between Ducks and Egrets

	Ducks	Egrets
1		
2		
3		
4		

C COMPARE AND CONTRAST

Complete the table above.

1. In row 1, tell which bird family each one belongs to.

2. In row 2, name two other types of birds that belong to the same family.

3. In row 3, tell what shape each bird's neck has when the bird flies.

4. In row 4, tell whether each bird's legs are long or short.

D FIGURATIVE LANGUAGE

Write whether each statement is a *simile* or an *exaggeration*.

1. The engine purred like a cat.
   _____

2. The dog's barking shattered my eardrums.
   _____

3. The basketball player was taller than a skyscraper. _____

4. Tatum's smile was as bright as a sunny day. _____

E CONTEXT CLUES

For each item, circle the answer that means the same thing as the word in bold type.

1. Dozens of egrets lived in a **colony** next to the lake.
   a. large nest   b. skyscraper
   c. group   d. state

2. All our lawn furniture was swept away by the **deluge.**
   a. street cleaners   b. big broom
   c. wind   d. flood

3. The store used **garish** lighting to attract customers.
   a. bright and colorful
   b. dim
   c. dark but colorful
   d. black-and-white

GO TO PART D IN YOUR TEXTBOOK

Name _____

65

A STORY DETAILS

Work the items.

1. Sylvia had found the cow hiding behind a ▓▓▓ bush.
   a. blueberry   b. huckleberry
   c. thicket   d. mulberry

2. The ▓▓▓ made Sylvia feel as if she were a part of the gray shadows and the moving leaves.
   a. young man   b. cow
   c. moths   d. darkness

3. Sylvia thought she had never been ▓▓▓ at all before coming to the farm.
   a. scared   b. successful
   c. alive   d. punished

4. How long had Sylvia been living on the farm?

   _____

5. The children in town used to chase and ▓▓▓ Sylvia.
   a. frighten   b. hit
   c. tackle   d. run from

6. The young man said he was hunting for some _____ .

7. Which **two** of these words describe Sylvia?
   a. bold   b. talkative
   c. quiet   d. shy

8. The person who owned the farm was named Mrs. _____ .

9. That person was Sylvia's ▓▓▓ .
   a. employer   b. mother
   c. foster parent d. aunt

B CLOZE SENTENCES

Complete each sentence with the correct word.

| fend | huckleberry | trio |
| foster | slaughter | trudge |

1. The Three Stooges were a famous _____ of actors.

2. After Fernando moved out of his parents' house, he had to _____ for himself.

3. Serena was an orphan who lived with a _____ parent.

4. After Nasir finished eating, there was just one _____ left in the bowl.

Lesson 65   129

C CONTEXT CLUES

For each item, circle the answer that means the same thing as the word in bold type.

1. Everyone admired the **gallant** hero.
   a. stupid and cowardly
   b. shifty and dishonest
   c. brave and noble
   d. vexed

2. Julio used a slingshot to hunt for **game**.
   a. chessboards
   b. wild animals
   c. remedies
   d. burdens

3. They found **lodging** at a lonely inn.
   a. a place to work
   b. a place to swim
   c. a place to buy
   d. a place to sleep

D SARCASM

Work the items.

Felicia was at a fast-food restaurant. She said, "The food in this place is simply marvelous. The hamburger buns taste like cardboard, and the patties are as big as postage stamps. This place really goes all out to please its customers."

1. Underline the statement that Felicia later contradicts.

2. Draw a wavy line under the statement that contradicts the underlined statement.

E CHARACTER TRAITS

Complete each sentence with *Sylvia*, *Mrs. Tilley*, or *The stranger*.

1. _____ was very shy and quiet.

2. _____ whistled loudly while walking through the forest.

3. _____ had lived on the farm for only a year.

4. _____ owned a farm deep in the country.

5. _____ felt like a part of the woods.

6. _____ used a gun to kill birds.

GO TO PART D IN YOUR TEXTBOOK

130 Lesson 65

Name _____ 66

A STORY DETAILS

Work the items.

1. Mrs. Tilley's only relative was named _____.

2. That relative was living in the state of _____.

3. Which one of these animals had Sylvia **not** tamed?
   a. squirrels   b. jaybirds   c. herons

4. The birds in the young man's collection were ▇▇▇ .
   a. painted   b. caged   c. stuffed

5. The young man was looking for a white _____.

6. How much money did the young man offer for information about the bird?
   _____

7. The landmark half a mile from Sylvia's house was a ▇▇▇ tree.
   a. maple   b. pine   c. huckleberry

8. Sylvia believed that whoever climbed to the top of that landmark could see the _____.

9. Sylvia planned to climb the landmark at _____.

B CLOZE SENTENCES

Complete each sentence with the correct word or phrase.

| colony | maple | wilderness |
| England | recover | wingspan |

1. An area where few people live is called a _____.

2. Maine, Vermont, and New Hampshire are states in New _____ .

3. The _____ of a bald eagle can be more than seven feet long.

4. Farmers tap _____ trees for sap in late winter or early spring.

Lesson 66   131

C CONTEXT CLUES

For each item, circle the answer that means the same thing as the word(s) in bold type.

1. An orange is **vastly** different from an apple.
   a. somewhat   b. really
   c. never   d. a little

2. The **easily recognized feature** could be seen for miles.
   a. landfill   b. landslide
   c. landlord   d. landmark

3. Angelica sighed when she finally lifted the **burden** off her shoulder.
   a. bird den   b. scarf
   c. heavy weight   d. light purse

D SARCASM

Work the items.

Noriko went to a baseball game with a friend. She said, "That Kirk McDermott is probably the finest player on the team. He has the speed of a snail, the power of a lamb, and the grace of an elephant. No wonder they traded half the team to get him."

1. Underline the statement that Noriko later contradicts.

2. Draw a wavy line under the statement that contradicts the underlined statement.

E CAUSE AND EFFECT

Complete each sentence with *finds* or *doesn't find*.

1. Sylvia will get a hundred dollars if she _____ the heron.

2. The heron will live if Sylvia _____ it.

3. The heron will be stuffed if Sylvia _____ it.

4. The young man will reward Sylvia if she _____ the heron.

5. The young man will go away empty-handed if Sylvia _____ the heron.

GO TO PART D IN YOUR TEXTBOOK

Name _____ 67

A STORY DETAILS

Work the items.

1. Sylvia climbed the pine tree to ▓▓ .
   a. see the ocean
   b. find out where the heron lived
   c. see how far up she could go
   d. get away from the hunter

2. As Sylvia climbed the tree, the pine ▓▓ made her fingers clumsy and stiff.
   a. twigs   b. needles
   c. branches   d. pitch

3. Sylvia reached the top of the pine tree at ▓▓ .
   a. sunset   b. sunrise
   c. noon   d. midnight

4. Which direction did Sylvia look to see the sunrise? _____

5. The white heron flew up from a ▓▓ tree.
   a. birch   b. pine
   c. hemlock   d. maple

6. The hunter wanted Sylvia to ▓▓ her secret.
   a. reveal   b. reseal
   c. redeal   d. repeal

7. True or false: When Sylvia answered the hunter, she looked him straight in the eye.
   a. true   b. false

8. What did Sylvia give up to save the life of the bird?

   _____

9. Sylvia wondered if the heron was a better _____ than the hunter might have been.

B CLOZE SENTENCES

Complete each sentence with the correct word.

| gallant | lodging | trio |
| huckleberry | pitch | waver |

1. Birds who glide through the air often _____ .

2. Bears love to eat the fruit from _____ bushes.

3. Pine _____ can get really sticky during the summer.

4. The baseball team had a _____ of outfielders in left, center, and right.

Lesson 67 133

C CONTEXT CLUES

For each item, circle the answer that means the same thing as the word in bold type.

1. Birds bend their necks when they **plume** their feathers.
   a. foster   b. lodge
   c. clean   d. garish

2. Everyone waited for the judge to **reveal** the winner.
   a. tell about   b. attract
   c. recover   d. redouble

3. You need to pull a rope to ring the bells inside the **steeple**.
   a. organ   b. game
   c. tower   d. gallant

D RELEVANT INFORMATION

For each item, write *relevant to fact A*, *relevant to fact B*, or *irrelevant*.

Fact A: Sylvia lived on a farm with her foster mother.

Fact B: Sylvia wanted to save the heron's life.

1. Sylvia made friends with the heron.
   _____

2. Sylvia brought the cow home.
   _____

3. Sylvia didn't tell anybody about the nest.
   _____

4. Sylvia was quite shy.
   _____

E PERSPECTIVES

Complete each sentence with *Sylvia* or *The hunter*.

1. _____ said, "I think a bird's life is more important than money."

2. _____ said, "I need some stuffed birds to add to my collection."

3. _____ said, "I think it's all right to kill animals."

4. _____ said, "I could use a hundred dollars."

5. _____ said, "I can see for miles and miles."

6. _____ said, "I have shared precious moments with a bird."

GO TO PART D IN YOUR TEXTBOOK

Name _____ 68

A STORY DETAILS

Work the items.

1. Geese make their ▓▓ in the fall and in the spring.
   a. nation   b. carnation
   c. migration   d. separation

2. Geese know how to ▓▓ their comings and goings.
   a. debate   b. calibrate
   c. congregate   d. record

3. In the poem, cold weather is the time for the kill of _____ .

4. Geese fly in a ____ formation.

5. Geese make that formation by ▓▓ .
   a. collaborating b. debating
   c. contemplating d. dating

6. When flying, geese take their turn to follow and to _____ .

7. Geese congregate at edge of _____ .

8. Geese contemplate the great _____ .

9. When geese in North America migrate in the fall, they fly toward ▓▓ places.
   a. northerly   b. southerly
   c. easterly   d. westerly

B CLOZE SENTENCES

Complete each sentence with the correct word.

| choreography | landmark | orchestrate |
| debate | navigate | wilderness |

1. The sailor used a compass to _____ northward.

2. The team had a huge _____ over who should be the captain.

3. When composers _____ a symphony, they write parts for every instrument in the orchestra.

4. The dance company was famous for its vastly beautiful _____ .

Lesson 68   135

C CONTEXT CLUES

For each item, circle the answer that means the same thing as the word in bold type.

1. The chess player needed lots of time to **contemplate** her next move.
   a. slaughter b. squelch
   c. think about d. forget

2. You can use a tree's shadow to **calibrate** the height of the tree.
   a. figure out b. celebrate
   c. guess d. maple

3. The whole class decided to **collaborate** on the teacher's birthday party.
   a. fend b. argue
   c. elaborate d. work together

D COMPARING CHARACTERS

Complete each sentence with *The hunter*, *Sylvia*, or *Both*.

1. _____ thought stuffed birds were better than live birds.

2. _____ did not have much money.

3. _____ did not like to kill animals.

4. _____ was only interested in collecting animals.

5. _____ looked for the white heron.

E POEM STRUCTURE

Fill in the first blank at the end of each line. In the second blank, write a capital letter to show the rhyme scheme, starting with A.

We are the _____ : ___

We _____ — ___

Not too _____ , ___

Not too _____ — ___

To make our _____ ___

We _____ ___

Our comings and _____ ___

To match the _____ ___

Of air, the _____ ___

Of leaf; the _____ . ___

We are the _____ : ___

We do not get _____ . ___

GO TO PART E IN YOUR TEXTBOOK

Lesson 68

Name _____

A STORY DETAILS

1. What is Jack London's best-known novel?
   a. *The Iron Heel*
   b. *White Fang*
   c. *The Call of the Wild*
   d. *The Sea-Wolf*

2. London was born in ▭ .
   a. San Francisco   b. Oakland
   c. San Jose   d. Santa Cruz

3. When London was a pirate, he stole _____ .

4. London sailed a fast boat called a ▭ .
   a. speedboat   b. schooner
   c. tanker   d. sloop

5. London's life changed when he read a story in the Oakland _____ .

6. In 1897, London quit college to join the ▭ Gold Rush.
   a. Alaska   b. Midas
   c. Klondike   d. California

B CLOZE SENTENCES

Complete each sentence with the correct word.

| lighthouse | reveal | strait |
| plume | steeple | waver |

1. The captain guided the oil tanker carefully through the narrow _____ .

2. The cook lifted the lid off the pot to _____ the delicious soup.

3. The sailors were almost blinded by the glare from the _____ .

4. The church was short, but its _____ was quite tall.

Lesson 69

C CONTEXT CLUES

For each item, circle the answer that means the same thing as the word(s) in bold type.

1. Once Sam began working **in earnest,** he finished the job.
   a. slowly   b. while earning more
   c. inside   d. seriously

2. The wind blew the tiny **sloop** far out into the bay.
   a. ferry   b. sailboat
   c. ocean liner   d. motorboat

3. Anika barbecued the **oyster** for about ten minutes and then took off the shell.
   a. pine pitch   b. hamburger
   c. chicken   d. shellfish

D COMPARING CHARACTERS

Complete each item with *Demeter, Matilda, Sara Crewe,* or *Sylvia.*

1. _____ lost a fake necklace.

2. _____ chose between a bird and a reward.

3. _____ forced plants to stop growing.

4. _____ pretended to be a princess.

5. _____ lived in Paris, France.

E MAPS

Work the items.

1. Which city touches the southern end of San Francisco Bay?
   _____

2. Which island is north of San Francisco?
   _____

3. Which body of water connects the Pacific Ocean and San Francisco Bay?
   _____

4. Which islands are west of San Francisco?
   _____

5. Which direction is Oakland from San Francisco?
   _____

6. Pretend you are in Santa Cruz and can travel across land or water at the same speed. The quickest way to San Jose is by ▨ .
   a. land   b. water   c. land and water

GO TO PART D IN YOUR TEXTBOOK

138   Lesson 69

Name _____

70

A STORY DETAILS

Work the items.

1. The *Dazzler* is a type of sailboat called a ▓▓▓ .

   a. sloop   b. skiff   c. schooner

2. Which boy is an experienced sailor?

   _____
   _____

3. Which boy is a newcomer to sailing?

   _____
   _____

4. The newcomer is _____ years old.

5. The captain of the *Dazzler* is named

   _____
   _____
   _____.

6. The newcomer said he would like to go to sea in the forecastle. How did he pronounce that word?

   a. **fore** castle   b. **foke** sull

   c. **foke** castle

7. *Forecastle* is a compound word. The first part shows that the forecastle is located near the ▓▓▓ of a ship.

   a. front   b. back   c. middle

8. One character warned another to "keep his tongue between his teeth." What does that phrase mean?

   a. try to whistle   b. not breathe

   c. keep his mouth shut

B CLOZE SENTENCES

Complete each sentence with the correct word.

> acquaintance   navigate   suppress
> choreography   porthole

1. I made the _____ of a spider while crawling under the bed.

2. We could see clouds through the _____ of our plane.

3. The woman had to _____ a scream when she saw her husband's new haircut.

Lesson 70   139

C CONTEXT CLUES

For each item, circle the answer that means the same thing as the word(s) in bold type.

1. The irritated mother told her laughing son to wipe the **smirk** off his face.
   a. ugly frown   b. smug smile
   c. fresh dirt   d. debate

2. It was hard to see the **skiff** sailing across the bay, but the huge oil tanker couldn't be missed.
   a. small car   b. shore bird
   c. small plane d. small boat

3. When people **work together,** they can accomplish great things.
   a. collaborate b. contemplate
   c. calibrate   d. orchestrate

D MAPS

Work the items.

1. What is the name of city **D**?
   _____

2. Which letter shows Angel Island? ____

3. The strait that connects the ocean and the bay is called the _____ _____ .

4. What is the name of city **B**?
   _____

5. Which letter shows Santa Cruz? ____

GO TO PART F IN YOUR TEXTBOOK

Name _____ 71

A STORY DETAILS

Work the items.

1. How many boats did Joe and the others take on shore? _____

2. The men began stealing pieces of scrap _____.

3. Joe heard a ▨ sound coming from the beach.
   a. screaming   b. whispering
   c. hooting   d. guitar

4. Which person got into the wrong boat? _____

5. Why did Joe and Frisco Kid throw that person overboard?
   a. They wanted to play a trick on him.
   b. His weight was making the lifeboat sink.
   c. They wanted to make some noise.

6. The lifeboat ▨ as it approached the *Dazzler*.
   a. sank   b. overturned   c. split apart

7. Joe realized that Pete and the others were ▨.
   a. fishermen   b. iron workers   c. pirates

8. Because of his ▨, Joe didn't understand about the men at first.
   a. ignorance   b. intelligence
   c. poor eyesight

B CLOZE SENTENCES

Complete each sentence with the correct word.

| earnest | lighthouse | pier |
| ignorance | oysters | strait |

1. Your _____ of a law is no excuse for breaking that law.

2. The divers looked for _____ that contained pearls.

3. Several large boats were tied to the _____.

4. Odysseus had sailed through a narrow _____ with a monster on one side and a whirlpool on the other.

Lesson 71   141

C CONTEXT CLUES

For each item, circle the answer that means the same thing as the word(s) in bold type.

1. Her plans for the future were **vague** and uncertain.
   a. sloop   b. well known
   c. unclear   d. disgusted

2. The two football players **collided with** each other in the end zone.
   a. ran into   b. ran by
   c. avoided   d. outraced

3. The children **floundered** in the deep snow when they played in the yard.
   a. dove   b. collaborated
   c. ran clumsily   d. walked quickly

D ANAPHORS

For each item, circle the word(s) that the anaphor in bold type refers to.

1. Nathan lived in a dangerous building. **It** had many broken windows, and the roof leaked.

2. Nathan's mother and father were poor, and **they** could not afford to leave the building.

3. Nathan said, "This building gives me the creeps. I can't stand living **here**."

4. His father told Nathan, "**You** might get your wish sometime soon."

E COMPARING CHARACTERS

Complete each sentence with the name of a character from *The Cruise of the Dazzler*.

1. _____ was the only character Joe could trust.

2. _____ was just learning how to sail.

3. _____ was the captain of the *Dazzler*.

4. _____ decided to escape from the *Dazzler*.

5. _____ spoke with a French accent.

GO TO PART D IN YOUR TEXTBOOK

Name _____

72

A STORY DETAILS

Work the items.

1. Joe was afraid of Frisco Kid because Frisco Kid was a ▉ .
   a. sailor   b. criminal
   c. teacher   d. friend

2. Frisco Kid treated Joe ▉ .
   a. badly   b. indifferently
   c. kindly   d. with contempt

3. Joe tried to pull the ▉ closer to the sloop.
   a. lifeboat b. skiff
   c. anchor   d. canoe

4. As Joe was pulling, the ▉ slipped out of his hand.
   a. towrope   b. sail
   c. mast   d. rudder

5. Frisco Kid operated the _____ at the back of the sloop.

6. To the south, the boys saw the lights of San _____ stretching for miles.

7. The boys passed a naval training station on _____ Island.

8. Frisco Kid planned to anchor near _____ Island.

B CLOZE SENTENCES

Complete each sentence with the correct word.

| acquaintance | bungle | porthole |
| adjust | forecastle | ticklish |

1. Doing surgery is _____ work for a doctor.

2. You need a pump to _____ the air pressure in a bike tire.

3. If you work too fast, you can easily _____ a job.

C CONTEXT CLUES

For each item, circle the answer that means the same thing as the word in bold type.

1. The crafty pitcher could **outwit** any batter with his curveballs and sliders.
   a. outrun   b. skiff
   c. outsmart d. smirk

2. In a small town, the courthouse is often the **principal** building.
   a. most important   b. prince's
   c. school chief's   d. tallest

3. A person looks **puny** next to a giant redwood tree.
   a. suppressed   b. punishing
   c. dark green   d. small and weak

Lesson 72   143

D ANAPHORS

Write which people or objects the anaphor in bold type refers to.

1. Effie and her friend Norma were on their way to the movie theater. **They** were riding bikes.
   _____

2. "I wonder if **it** will be a good one," Effie said.
   _____

3. "Oh, I don't know. It's just another one of those monster movies. **They** are all alike."
   _____

4. "Are **you** sure you want to go?" Effie asked.
   _____

5. "Why not? There's nothing better to do," **her friend** answered.
   _____

E VISUAL INFORMATION

Write whether each boat will go *left*, *right*, or *straight*.

1. _____

2. _____

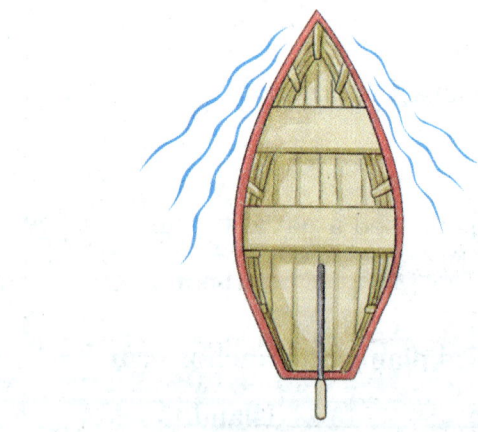

3. _____

GO TO PART E IN YOUR TEXTBOOK

A STORY DETAILS

Work the items.

1. Joe's thought of his companions ▨ the beauty of the day.
   a. marred   b. perplexed   c. unmoved

2. Joe was ▨ by the harsh reality of the pirates' lives.
   a. impressed   b. not surprised
   c. shocked

3. Joe resolved to be ▨ and strong.
   a. clean   b. cunning   c. vicious

4. What disease was coming in on the ships?
   _____

5. The last person to catch a fish had to _____ the fish.

6. Joe tried to escape to _____ Island.

7. Joe escaped in the ▨ .
   a. sloop   b. lifeboat   c. skiff

8. As Joe approached the shore, the _____ shouted at him.

9. That character was pointing his _____ at Joe.

B CLOZE SENTENCES

Complete each sentence with the correct word.

ignorance	pier	smallpox
mar	quarantine	vague

1. Jamil didn't want anything to _____ or wrinkle his new shirt.

2. The vet had to _____ the dog until the disease went away.

3. One serious disease that spreads easily from person to person is called _____ .

4. The sloop was tied up at the end of a long _____ .

C CONTEXT CLUES

For each item, circle the answer that means the same thing as the word in bold type.

1. The carpenter brought a **keg** of nails to work.
   a. woodbox
   b. flounder
   c. small barrel
   d. small bag

2. Kelvin erased his mistakes with **vigor**.
   a. hazy
   b. energy
   c. handling
   d. vitamins

3. It's hard to **persuade** a donkey to move.
   a. collide
   b. surge
   c. suppress
   d. convince

D FIGURATIVE LANGUAGE

Work the items.

Here's a statement: *The sails began to snarl loudly.*

1. Which type of figurative language does that statement use?
   a. exaggeration
   b. metaphor
   c. simile

2. Which two things does that statement compare?
   _____
   _____

E POINT OF VIEW

Tell which point of view each story has.

1. Wee Willie Winkie runs through the town, upstairs and downstairs, in his nightgown. Rapping at the window, crying through the lock, "Are the children in their beds? Now it's eight o'clock."
   a. first person
   b. third person limited
   c. third person unlimited

2. In my younger years, my father gave me some advice that I've been turning over in my mind ever since.
   a. first person
   b. third person limited
   c. third person unlimited

3. The seven dwarves told Snow White to be careful before they left their cottage for work. Far away from the cottage, the queen looked in her mirror and asked who was the fairest one of all.
   a. first person
   b. third person limited
   c. third person unlimited

4. The sound ripped through the air and jerked me awake. I covered my ears and curled my body into a tight ball, trying to hide from the noise exploding around me.
   a. first person
   b. third person limited
   c. third person unlimited

GO TO PART D IN YOUR TEXTBOOK

A STORY DETAILS

Work the items.

1. Joe couldn't land on Angel Island because it was a _____ station.

2. Which disease did people on Angel Island have?
   a. measles   b. mumps
   c. smallpox   d. chicken pox

3. Joe threatened to send Pete to ▨ .
   a. San Francisco   b. the army
   c. prison   d. Angel Island

4. Joe might also go to that place because he ▨ .
   a. helped steal the scrap iron
   b. ran away from home
   c. tried to land on Angel Island

5. Pete threatened to hit Joe with ▨ .
   a. his fist   b. an oar   c. his rifle

6. Which character prevented a fight?
   _____

7. Pete asked Joe to ▨ and forget.
   a. rob   b. forgive   c. escape

8. Pete ordered the sloop down to ▨ Point.
   a. Golden's   b. Goat's
   c. Angel's   d. Hunter's

B CLOZE SENTENCES

Complete each sentence with the correct word.

bungle	puny	taunt
cove	spunk	ticklish

1. The basketball player was short, but she had a lot of _____ .

2. The water in the ocean was rough and wild, but it was calm inside the _____ .

3. The mean student liked to _____ the other students, but they ignored him.

4. The gigantic redwood tree towered over the _____ sapling.

C CONTEXT CLUES

For each item, circle the answer that means the same thing as the word in bold type.

1. Firefighting is a dangerous **occupation**.
   a. principal   b. job
   c. ellipsis   d. orderly

2. Kama tried not to **wince** when the doctor gave him a shot.
   a. whine   b. ease
   c. flounder   d. tense up

3. No one dared to **defy** the general's orders.
   a. outwit   b. adjust
   c. challenge   d. startle

D SARCASM

Work the items.

Louise went to the Roxy Movie Palace. She said, "Wow, this is really a great place. My feet are stuck to the floor because of the chewing gum. Somebody from the balcony threw popcorn in my hair. And the best part is that the people behind me talked all through the movie."

1. Underline the statement that Louise later contradicts.

2. Draw a wavy line below the sentences that contradict Louise's statement.

E MAPS

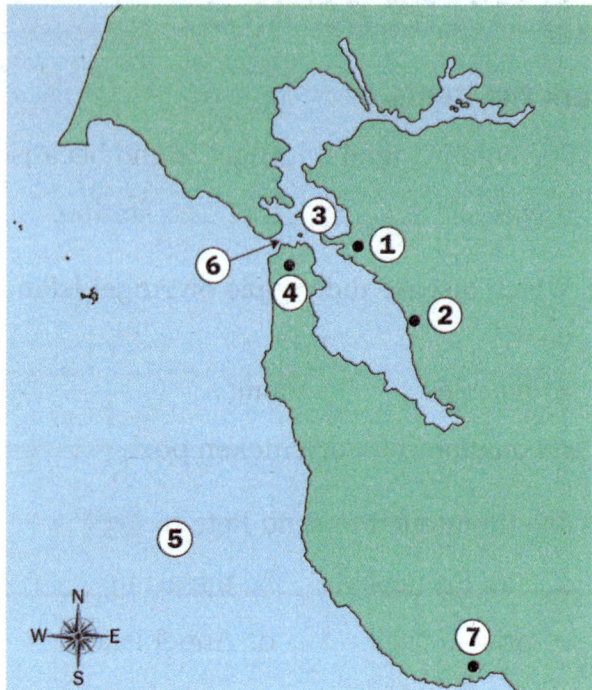

Work the items.

1. Which city does circle **1** show?
   _____

2. What kind of metal did the pirates try to steal at circle **2**?
   _____

3. Circle **3** shows an island where Joe tried to escape. What is the name of that island?
   _____

4. Which city does circle **4** show?
   _____

5. Which ocean does circle **5** show?
   _____

6. Which strait does circle **6** show?
   _____

GO TO PART D IN YOUR TEXTBOOK

A STORY DETAILS

Work the items.

1. Joe saw rows of people on the ▭ .
   a. docks   b. ferryboat   c. ocean liner

2. Where would Joe rather have been: with the people or on the *Dazzler*?
   _____

3. The *Dazzler* met a sloop called the
   _____ .

4. Which direction had the *Dazzler* sailed to meet that sloop?
   a. north   b. south
   c. east   d. west

5. The captain of that sloop was
   _____ Nelson.

6. Which of the two sloops was faster?
   _____

7. Frisco Kid said he liked the *Dazzler* but not the ▭ .
   a. food   b. fishing   c. stealing

8. Frisco Kid was afraid of going to ▭ school.
   a. high   b. reform   c. elementary

B CLOZE SENTENCES

Complete each sentence with the correct word.

| account | defy | reform |
| adjust | persuade | skirt |

1. The travelers used a side road to _____ the small town.

2. Ads try to _____ people to buy products.

3. The young pickpocket was sent to _____ school.

4. Don't turn up the heat on my _____ .

Lesson 75

C CONTEXT CLUES

For each item, circle the answer that means the same thing as the word in bold type.

1. You can **hail** a taxi by raising your hand and shouting.

    a. ignore   b. overtake

    c. mar   d. summon

2. Danica's desk was so **untidy** that she couldn't find anything inside it.

    a. quarantined   b. disordered

    c. shipshape   d. downturned

3. Vance shook the towel with **vigor** to get all the sand out.

    a. energy   b. standstill

    c. smallpox   d. disgust

D ELLIPSIS

Show each place words are left out by inserting a ^ mark. Then write the missing words above the ^ mark.

1. Norma's voice was louder than Odessa's.

2. The sloop's sail was torn, but the schooner's wasn't.

3. The wife disagreed, but the husband agreed with the plan.

E COMPARING CHARACTERS

Complete each sentence with *Joe*, *Frisco Kid*, or *Both*.

1. _____ did not trust Pete.

2. _____ had a home in the city.

3. _____ knew all about sailing.

4. _____ did not like the stealing.

5. _____ was an orphan.

GO TO PART D IN YOUR TEXTBOOK

Name

A STORY DETAILS

Work the items.

1. Frisco Kid had a picture of a _____ sitting together.

2. After Frisco Kid saw the picture, he realized he was ▭ .
   a. free   b. a bad person   c. lonely

3. Frisco Kid knew the picture was make-believe, but when he looked at it, he thought it was ▭ .
   a. out of focus   b. real   c. not realistic

4. Frisco Kid found out that pirating was wrong after he ▭ .
   a. learned to read   b. went to prison
   c. talked to Joe

5. After the boys stopped talking about the picture, Joe's ▭ suddenly became important to him.
   a. family   b. adventures   c. sailing skills

6. Epont Nelson was captain of the _____ .

7. Pete asked the boys to raise the mainsail and pull up the _____ .

8. Who had taught Frisco Kid how to sail?
   _____
   _____

B CLOZE SENTENCES

Complete each sentence with the correct word.

| cove | sic | taunt |
| occupation | spunk | wince |

1. Police officers sometimes _____ their dogs on criminals.

2. The bully tried to _____ the children by calling them names.

3. The small cat showed _____ when it hissed at the big dog.

4. Fighting fires is a dangerous _____ .

Lesson 76

C CONTEXT CLUES

For each item, circle the answer that means the same thing as the word in bold type.

1. We really **appreciate** all the gifts you've given us.
   - a. dislike
   - b. are grateful for
   - c. admire
   - d. are ashamed by

2. Interrupting someone when they're speaking is **downright** rude.
   - a. downturned
   - b. dangerously
   - c. somewhat
   - d. completely

3. Gandhi used civil disobedience to **defy** the law.
   - a. define
   - b. challenge
   - c. obey
   - d. strengthen

D ELLIPSIS

Show each place words are left out by inserting a ^ mark. Then write the missing words above the ^ mark.

1. Anita's hair was red, but Loretta's wasn't red.

2. Tito could run faster than Kevin.

E CONTRADICTIONS

Work the items.

   Jesse lived in a one-story house in a row of other one-story houses in one of the drabbest suburbs of a drab city. Jesse's life was as drab as his house. Every morning, he trudged out to his drab car and drove downtown to his drab job. Every evening he fixed himself a drab hamburger and watched television. When he got tired, he slowly climbed the stairs to his drab bedroom. Then he fell asleep and dreamed drab dreams.

1. Underline the statement you assume to be true.

2. Draw a wavy line under the contradiction.

3. Write an *if-then* statement that explains the contradiction.

   _____
   _____
   _____

GO TO PART D IN YOUR TEXTBOOK

Name _____

A STORY DETAILS

Work the items.

1. When the men went to shore, their faces had a _____ seriousness.

2. Before Pete left, he buckled on his _____ belt.

3. The boys planned to escape by ____ .
   a. sailing away on the *Dazzler*
   b. paddling away on a skiff
   c. swimming to shore

4. Frisco Kid escaped from the pirates during the _____ season.

5. Frisco Kid was arrested for being a ____ .
   a. sailor   b. farmhand   c. tramp

6. After Frisco Kid was arrested, he was sent to _____ school.

7. The only thing that Frisco Kid liked in that place was the ____ .
   a. food   b. mattresses   c. books

8. A type of pistol called a _____ made a loud sound at the end of the chapter.

B CLOZE SENTENCES

Complete each sentence with the correct word.

| account | revolver | untidy |
| blotted | strained | wharf |

1. The students felt _____ while waiting for their test scores.

2. A pistol with a rotating bullet container is called a _____ .

3. Cars stopped because the fog _____ out the road.

4. Fifty boats were docked at the busy _____ .

C SETTINGS

Complete each item with *country*, *reform school*, or *bay*.

1. Frisco Kid did a lot of reading in the _____ .

2. Frisco Kid could not find any work in the _____ .

3. Frisco Kid became tired of stealing on the _____ .

4. People sicced their dogs on Frisco Kid in the _____ .

Lesson 77

D CONTEXT CLUES

For each item, circle the answer that means the same thing as the word in bold type.

1. Even though the robbers **muffled** their voices, the dog could still hear them talking.

    a. raised   b. silenced

    c. quieted d. hailed

2. Dimitri took time to **survey** the city from atop the skyscraper.

    a. look completely at

    b. completely ignore

    c. reform

    d. carefully listen to

3. Cars used the freeway to **skirt** the crowded downtown area.

    a. drive into   b. go around the edge of

    c. clothe   d. overtake

E ELLIPSIS

Show each place words are left out by inserting a ^ mark. Then write the missing words above the ^ mark.

1. Although Nora has blue eyes, her sister doesn't.

2. Four sea nymphs sat on the rocks near the shore, but two were still in the sea.

F ANAPHORS

Write which words the anaphors in bold type refer to.

1. The people gathered their ropes. **They** were old and had been tied together where they had broken.

   _____

2. Sue was standing on a ladder, and Linda was below her on the ground. **She** said, "Hand the paint brush up to me."

   _____

3. The rabbits quickly went into their holes. **They** huddled there and waited for the fox to leave.

   _____

4. They performed dances at their celebrations. One of **these** was the pearl dance.

   _____

5. The people bought large pots. **They** were made of black metal.

   _____

GO TO PART E IN YOUR TEXTBOOK

Name

A STORY DETAILS

Work the items.

1. The pirates stole an office _____ when they were on shore.

2. The pirates put the object on the sloop named the _____.

3. The pirates planned to sail all the way to _____.
   a. Canada   b. Mexico
   c. South America

4. The *Dazzler* was heading toward the _____ Ocean.

5. To get to the ocean, the *Dazzler* had to sail through the _____ _____.

6. The safe belonged to a company named _____ and Tate.

7. Why was that company important to Joe?
   a. It was the biggest company in San Francisco.
   b. It was owned by his father and a partner.
   c. He used to work for the company.

8. Joe thought the battle between people and _____ was magnificent.

B CLOZE SENTENCES

Complete each sentence with the correct word.

| appreciate | incorporated | sic |
| downright | rover | steamer |

1. The _____ moved slowly into port with lots of cargo.

2. The company became legal after it was _____.

3. Robbing other ships is what a _____ does.

4. Riding on a roller coaster can be _____ scary.

C POINT OF VIEW

Some parts of Joe's new life please him, but others disgust him.

Complete each sentence with *pleases* or *disgusts*.

1. Looking at the bay from Angel Island _____ Joe.

2. Stealing scrap iron from a factory _____ Joe.

3. Helping the *Dazzler* escape from the police _____ Joe.

4. Fishing for rock cod with Frisco Kid _____ Joe.

Lesson 78   155

D CONTEXT CLUES

For each item, circle the answer that means the same thing as the word in bold type.

1. The crew had to take down the sails during the **gale.**
   a. hailstorm
   b. wide fairway
   c. long waterfront
   d. heavy wind

2. Arden rode her bike toward the **destination.**
   a. dusty nation
   b. bike path
   c. place she was going
   d. place she left

3. Brendan sweated as he **heaved** the heavy suitcase up the stairs.
   a. lifted
   b. left
   c. rolled
   d. eased

E MAPS

Work the items.

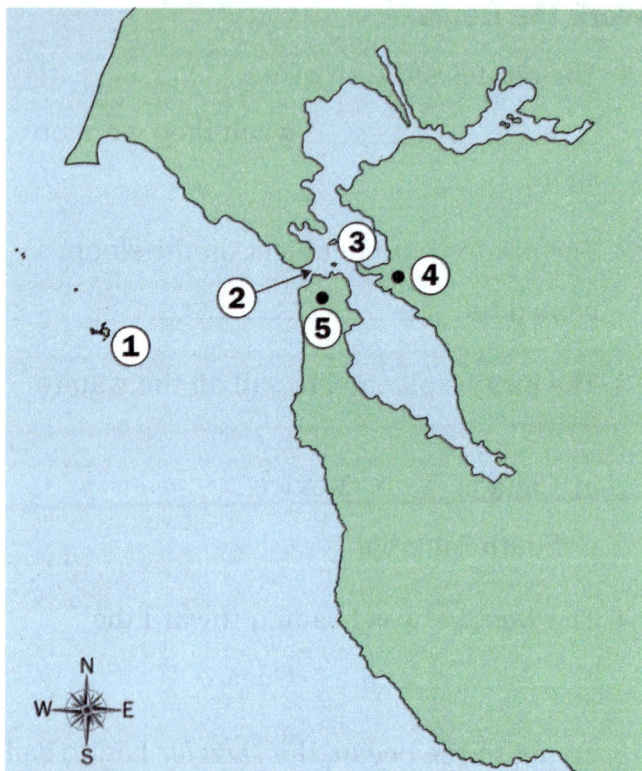

1. Circle **1** shows the _____ Islands.

2. Circle **2** shows the _____ Gate.

3. Circle **3** shows _____ Island.

4. Circle **4** shows the city of _____.

5. Circle **5** shows the city of _____.

GO TO PART D IN YOUR TEXTBOOK

Name

A STORY DETAILS

Work the items.

1. Whose future did Joe feel responsible for?

   _____

2. Joe wanted to protect his

   _____ property.

3. As the *Dazzler* went through the Golden Gate, the police boat ▓▓▓ .

   a. gave chase   b. stayed behind

   c. started their engine

4. When the sloops left the Farallon Islands, they headed ▓▓▓ to Mexico.

   a. north   b. south   c. east   d. west

5. Pete planned to stay ▓▓▓ sight of the land during the day.

   a. within   b. beyond   c. above

6. After lunch, the wind turned into a ▓▓▓ .

   a. breeze   b. hurricane   c. gale

7. Pete tried to launch a

   _____ anchor to slow down the *Dazzler*.

8. As Pete tried to launch the device, what happened to the mast and the mainsail?

   a. They fell overboard.

   b. They bent but did not break.

   c. They stayed where they were.

B CLOZE SENTENCES

Complete each sentence with the correct word.

blot	property	revolver
crest	responsibility	survey

1. Kama has a _____ to take care of his baby sister.

2. It's wrong to take _____ that doesn't belong to you.

3. The foamy _____ of the wave loomed above their tiny rowboat.

4. You need a telescope to _____ the surface of the moon.

Lesson 79

C CONTEXT CLUES

For each item, circle the answer that means the same thing as the word in bold type.

1. The view from the **summit** of the hill is magnificent.

    a. pistol   b. top

    c. base   d. cove

2. The bird was **poised** on the thin branch before flying off.

    a. muffled   b. strained

    c. persuaded   d. balanced

3. Waves crashed over the **wharf** during the gale, but nothing broke.

    a. dock   b. cloud

    c. taunt   d. ellipsis

D SEQUENCING

Number the events in the correct sequence.

____ Frisco Kid showed Joe a picture of a family.

____ Joe tried to row to a quarantine station.

____ Pete tried to launch the sea anchor.

____ The pirates stole an office safe.

____ The *Dazzler* sailed through the Golden Gate.

E ELLIPSIS

Write whether *Juan* or *Leroy* says each numbered statement.

"Look over there, Juan," Leroy said. "What is that thing?" [1]

"Gee, I don't know. It sure is strange looking." [2] Juan looked more closely for a moment and then said, "Maybe it's a flying saucer." [3]

The younger boy looked at Juan. "Do you really think it's a flying saucer?" he asked. [4]

"Anything is possible," the elder boy said with a stuffy tone in his voice. [5] "When you've lived as long as I have," he continued, "you'll know what I mean." [6]

"If anything is possible, it's possible you're wrong." [7]

"All right, smart guy, let's find out." [8]

1. _____
2. _____
3. _____
4. _____
5. _____
6. _____
7. _____
8. _____

GO TO PART D IN YOUR TEXTBOOK

Name _____

80

A STORY DETAILS

Work the items.

1. Which word does the story use to refer to the *Reindeer*?
   a. he   b. she   c. it   d. they

2. The huge ▆▆ made it difficult for the *Reindeer* to come alongside the *Dazzler*.
   a. waves   b. mountain
   c. distance   d. sail

3. The story says that Joe felt sorrow for the way in which Nelson used his ▆▆.
   a. intelligence   b. courage
   c. boat   d. cowardice

4. The only person who jumped from the *Dazzler* to the *Reindeer* was
   _____ .

5. What was the fate of the *Reindeer*?
   a. It didn't have the safe.
   b. It turned around in the storm.
   c. It sank in the ocean.

6. Frisco Kid used oars and
   _____ to make a sail.

7. At the end of the chapter, the *Dazzler* headed for the town of Santa
   _____ .

8. That town is ▆▆ of San Francisco.
   a. north   b. south   c. east   d. west

B CLOZE SENTENCES

Complete each sentence with the correct word.

| afloat | gale | rover |
| destination | hurtle | steamer |

1. The spectators watched the race cars _____ by at 200 miles per hour.

2. The ship sank, but the lifeboat was still _____ .

3. Several trees were blown over during the _____ .

4. Heather packed lightly, even though her _____ was halfway around the world.

C CONTEXT CLUES

For each item, circle the answer that means the same thing as the word in bold type.

1. The **forbidding** cliff loomed over the river.
   a. incorporated   b. threatening
   c. forgotten   d. doubtful

2. Some of the hikers were tired, but others wanted to **forge** ahead.
   a. appreciate   b. sic
   c. move powerfully   d. overtake

Lesson 80 159

D ANAPHORS

Work the items.

Passage A

Frisco Kid said, "We've got to look out for ourselves, I tell you! The sea will kick up worse yet. Lend a hand, and hang on with the other. We've got to bail out the *Dazzler*."

The two boys raced to the cabin. Using a couple of buckets, they flung the water overboard. **It** was heartbreaking work, for the sea flung most of the water back.

1. Write a main-idea sentence that tells what *It* is.

   _____
   _____

Passage B

I flipped on the barn lights and found a welcome sight. The sheep were all bedded down in the dry hay, the lambs curled up against their mamas or standing to fill their bellies with hot milk. The little sheep dogs grinned at me like they'd been having fun, still panting from their wild run. The guard dogs stood in the open side door, preventing any of **their charges** from going back out into the storm.

2. Who are *their charges*?

   _____
   _____

E ELLIPSIS

Write whether *Harumi* or *Yoshi* says each numbered statement.

Harumi, a twelve-year-old girl, was glad to see her brother. "Yoshi," she said, "I can't believe you are finally home." [1] She paused a moment and smiled. "Is college really difficult?" she asked. [2]

"Oh, I think sixth grade was harder, because of Mrs. Ozu." [3]

"Yes, she is a tough teacher. I'm in her class now." [4]

"I know," Yoshi observed. [5] "Does she still give a test every day?" [6]

"Not only that, but she won't give us any recess if we make too much noise." [7]

1. _____
2. _____
3. _____
4. _____
5. _____
6. _____
7. _____

GO TO PART D IN YOUR TEXTBOOK

Name _____

81

A STORY DETAILS

Work the items.

1. Which character was captain on land?
   _____

2. While Joe rode the train, he read a story about the two pirate sloops in a ▨ .
   a. newspaper   b. magazine   c. book

3. Authorities thought the two sloops ▨ during the storm.
   a. escaped   b. sank   c. landed

4. Which company offered a reward for the return of the safe?
   _____

5. Which two characters were entitled to the reward?
   _____

6. How many dollars would each character receive?
   _____

7. Joe's father agreed to ▨ Frisco Kid's money.
   a. give away   b. reject   c. hold

8. At the end, Joe planned to contact Frisco Kid by ▨ .
   a. email   b. telephone   c. telegram

B CLOZE SENTENCES

Complete each sentence with the correct word.

| authorities | previous | property |
| crest | promise | responsibility |

1. The smart student was full of _____ for the future.

2. Picking up litter is everyone's _____ .

3. Tom the piper's son was wanted by the _____ for stealing a pie.

4. They missed the _____ train, so they had to take a later one.

Lesson 81   161

C CONTEXT CLUES

For each item, circle the answer that means the same thing as the word(s) in bold type.

1. Everyone with a winning ticket **is entitled to** a prize.
   a. has the right to   b. loses
   c. doesn't receive   d. incorporates

2. The basketball fans gave the other team an unfriendly **reception.**
   a. destination   b. occupation
   c. response   d. pronunciation

3. Some poems **emphasize** the second syllable of every beat.
   a. poise   b. splutter
   c. give importance to   d. phase out

D MAPS

Work the items.

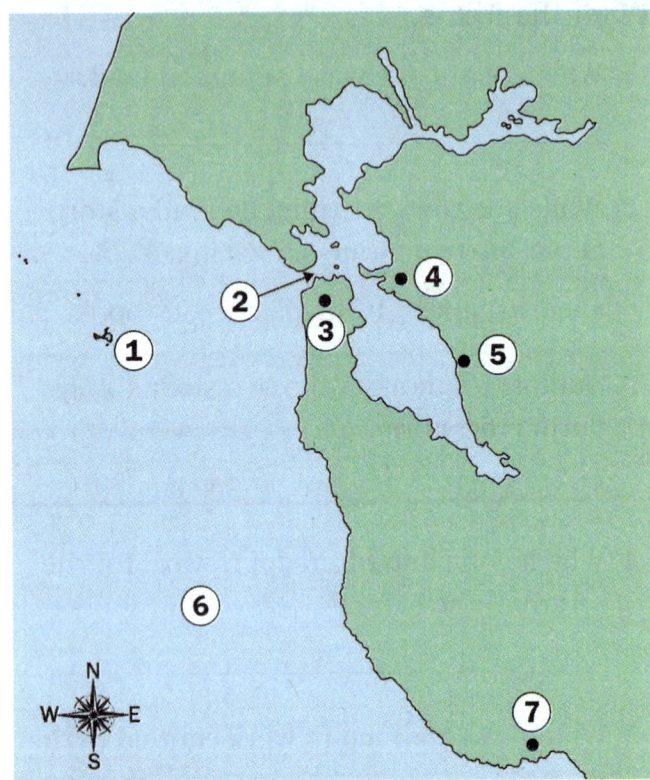

1. Which city does circle **4** show?
   _____

2. Which city does circle **3** show?
   _____

3. Which city does circle **7** show?
   _____

4. The pirates stole a _____ from a factory at circle **5.**

5. Circle ____ shows the Golden Gate.

6. Circle ____ shows the place where the *Reindeer* sank.

7. Circle ____ shows the Farallon Islands.

GO TO PART D IN YOUR TEXTBOOK

Lesson 81

Name _____ **82**

A STORY DETAILS

Work the items.

1. The word *mesa* means _____ in Spanish.

2. A butte is ▓▓ than a mesa.
   a. taller   b. older   c. narrower

3. Mesas and buttes start as part of a ▓▓ .
   a. canyon   b. plateau   c. mountain

4. The Colorado Plateau rose about one from sea level.
   a. kilometer   b. mile   c. league

5. The Grand Canyon is located in the state of ▓▓ .
   a. Nevada   b. Colorado   c. Arizona

6. The Colorado River flows into the ▓▓ .
   a. Gulf of Mexico   b. Persian Gulf
   c. Gulf of California

7. Rock on top of a mesa is called _____ rock.

8. A mesa is surrounded by ▓▓ on all four sides.
   a. canyons   b. buttes   c. the ocean

9. How is a plateau like a sand castle?
   a. They both start in Colorado.
   b. They both rise up and fall down.
   c. They are both made of sand.

B CLOZE SENTENCES

Complete each sentence with the correct word.

| butte | forge | landforms |
| canyon | hurtle | plateau |

1. Mountains, hills, and plains are different types of _____ .

2. A deep cut in the land that usually has a river at the bottom is called a _____ .

3. A tall landform with a narrow flat top and steep sides all the way around is called a _____ .

4. A tall landform with a very large flat top and one steep side is called a _____ .

Lesson 82   163

C CONTEXT CLUES

For each item, circle the answer that means the same thing as the word in bold type.

1. In the Mexican restaurant, customers sat at large **mesas** with colorful tablecloths.

    a. chairs   b. barrels

    c. tables   d. benches

2. Nobody dared to go beyond the **forbidding** entrance to the haunted house.

    a. threatening   b. friendly

    c. afloat   d. breakneck

3. Stella watched the falling star **hurtle** through the sky.

    a. jump over barriers   b. move quickly

    c. doze   d. heave

GO TO PART D IN YOUR TEXTBOOK

Name _____

A STORY DETAILS

Work the items.

1. The Hopi mesas are located in the state of _____ .
   a. Utah   b. Colorado
   c. Arizona   d. Alabama

2. The Hopi have lived in villages on the Black Mesa for about _____ years.
   a. 100   b. 1,000   c. 10,000   d. 100,000

3. The river to the south of Black Mesa is called the Little _____ River.
   a. Arizona   b. Colorado
   c. Utah   d. Alabama

4. Traditional Hopi buildings are made of _____ bricks.
   a. concrete   b. cement
   c. adobe   d. plastic

5. Which type of material do the Hopi use to make bricks?
   a. clay   b. limestone
   c. sandstone   d. plastic

6. What do the Hopi use to move between the different floors of their houses?
   a. stairs   b. elevators
   c. ladders   d. hanging vines

7. The farming that the Hopi use is called _____ farming.

8. Which is the main type of farm animal that the Hopi raise?
   a. sheep   b. cattle
   c. horses   d. donkeys

9. Which main material do the Hopi use to make pots?
   a. wood   b. metal
   c. clay   d. plastic

B CLOZE SENTENCES

Complete each sentence with the correct word.

| adobe | entitled | kachina |
| arid | Hopi | previous |

1. Carving a _____ doll from wood takes a long time.

2. The workers used _____ clay to make bricks.

3. The _____ are famous for their buildings, pottery, jewelry, and weaving.

4. The land was so _____ that nothing could grow there on its own.

Lesson 83   165

C CONTEXT CLUES

For each item, circle the answer that means the same thing as the word in bold type.

1. Some **melons** are as large as basketballs but much tastier.
   a. egg-shaped lemons
   b. circular diagrams
   c. large round fruits
   d. rock fragments

2. The chase was long, but the **authorities** finally caught the bank robber.
   a. authors
   b. law enforcers
   c. conductors
   d. bandits

3. Everyone gets a friendly **reception** at the fancy hotel.
   a. response
   b. promise
   c. emphasis
   d. scowl

D RELATED FACTS

Write the letter of the correct definition next to each landform.

A. wide flat-topped hill with steep sides

B. deep cut in the land that usually has a river at the bottom

C. narrow flat-topped hill with steep sides

D. large piece of land with a flat top and at least one steep side

1. canyon ____

2. plateau ____

3. butte ____

4. mesa ____

GO TO PART D IN YOUR TEXTBOOK

166   Lesson 83

Name _____

A STORY DETAILS

Work the items.

1. In which part of what is now the United States did Lozen grow up?

    a. southeastern   b. northwestern

    c. southwestern   d. northeastern

2. Who led the band of Apache warriors that Lozen joined? _____

3. Which is larger, a band or a tribe?
_____

4. What was the name of Lozen's brother?
_____

5. Lozen's brother said that she was a _____ to her people.

6. What did Lozen use to locate the enemy?

    a. binoculars   b. a hunting dog

    c. supernatural powers   d. a drone

7. The Apache god was named
_____ .

8. Lozen risked her life to save a ▆▆▆ woman from American soldiers.

    a. Hopi   b. pregnant

    c. Seneca   d. very old

9. Lozen died from a lung disease called
_____ .

B CLOZE SENTENCES

Complete each sentence with the correct word.

landform	plateau	status
mesa	secluded	strategy

1. The runaway hid from the police in a _____ spot.

2. Mountains are a main type of _____ .

3. The king wore a crown to show his _____ in the kingdom.

4. To win at sports, you need a winning _____ .

Lesson 84   167

C CONTEXT CLUES

For each item, circle the answer that means the same thing as the word in bold type.

1. The inventor was known for her **ingenuity** in coming up with new ideas.

    a. cleverness   b. accuracy

    c. treachery   d. responsibility

2. You have to take the thorns out of a **nopal** leaf before you can eat the leaf.

    a. supernatural   b. dense

    c. cactus   d. raven

3. Rainwater poured from the mesa into the **canyon**.

    a. butte   b. narrow valley

    c. plateau   d. underbrush

D COMPARING CHARACTERS

Complete each sentence with *Geronimo, Lozen, Ussen,* or *Victoria*.

1. _____ led the last Apache band at war with the United States.

2. To find the enemy, Lozen chanted a prayer to _____ .

3. _____ was in love with a Seneca named Gray Ghost.

4. The warrior who was an expert at stealing enemy horses was named _____ .

E RELATED FACTS

Complete each sentence with the correct word.

| butte | mesa |
| canyon | plateau |

1. A _____ is a *large* piece of land with a flat top and at least one steep side.

2. A _____ is a deep cut in the land that usually has a river at the bottom.

3. A _____ is a *wide* flat-topped hill with steep sides all around.

4. A _____ is a *narrow* flat-topped hill with steep sides all around.

GO TO PART D IN YOUR TEXTBOOK

Name _____

A STORY DETAILS

Work the items.

1. How are baseball, football, and basketball alike?
   a. They're played outside in the winter.
   b. They use the same ball.
   c. They were invented in the United States.
   d. They were played during the 1700s.

2. Circle the letter of the true statement about football teams in the 1880s.
   a. They got four points for a touchdown and five points for a field goal.
   b. They got five points for a touchdown and four points for a field goal.
   c. They got six points for a touchdown and three points for a field goal.

3. The most dangerous type of blocking in 1880s football was the flying _____ .

4. That type of blocking was ▓ by the football rules committee.
   a. encouraged   b. ignored
   c. banned   d. improved

5. James Naismith invented the rules of basketball in about one ▓ .
   a. hour   b. day   c. week   d. month

6. The first game of basketball was played with ▓ baskets.
   a. bread   b. peach   c. net   d. laundry

7. That first game was played with a ▓ ball.
   a. basket   b. hockey   c. soccer   d. soft

8. Rule 3 said that a player cannot ▓ with the ball.
   a. shoot   b. pass   c. run

9. A smart player said he wasn't breaking Rule 3 when he ▓ the ball.
   a. spun   b. dribbled   c. stole   d. shot

B CLOZE SENTENCES

Complete each sentence with the correct word.

| adobe | install | tuberculosis |
| arid | kachina | wedge |

1. The workers needed two hours to _____ the new window.

2. A lung disease that spreads rapidly is called _____ .

3. The land was so _____ that plants could not grow.

4. The football players formed a flying _____ to protect the runner.

Lesson 85

C CONTEXT CLUES

For each item, circle the answer that means the same thing as the word in bold type.

1. The town decided to **ban** leaf blowers because they were too loud.
   - a. burn
   - b. erode
   - c. not allow
   - d. entitle

2. Bad student behavior will **prompt** the teacher to cancel recess.
   - a. cause
   - b. alarm
   - c. emphasize
   - d. forge

3. The children didn't have a soccer ball to play with, so they used a **melon** instead.
   - a. small basketball
   - b. large round fruit
   - c. cauliflower
   - d. diagram

D SPORTS RULES

Work the items.

1. In baseball, how many strikes does a player get before they're out?
   _____

2. In modern football, how many points does a team get for a touchdown?
   _____

3. In modern basketball, players try to shoot the ball through a ▓▓▓ .
   - a. peach basket
   - b. set of goalposts
   - c. hoop and a net
   - d. round clock

4. In baseball, how many players does a team use in the field?
   _____

5. In modern football, how many chances does a team get to move the ball 10 yards?
   _____

GO TO PART D IN YOUR TEXTBOOK

Lesson 85

Name _____ 86

A STORY DETAILS

Work the items.

1. The Mudville baseball team was called the Mudville _____ .

2. The poem says that a _____ silence fell upon the patrons of the game.

3. What did the fans cling to after Cooney and Barrows died at first base?
   _____

4. Flynn was a lulu, but Blake was a _____ .

5. What kind of melancholy sat on the stricken multitude? _____

6. Which player hit a single?
   _____

7. Which player hit a double?
   _____

8. What kind of yell rose from five thousand throats? _____

9. Which player was at bat at the end of Part 1? _____

B CLOZE SENTENCES

Complete each sentence with the correct word.

| doff | ingenuity | secluded |
| eternal | latter | status |

1. I was asked to play either chess or checkers, so I chose the
   _____ .

2. The president's speech was only an hour long, but it seemed _____ .

3. Some people _____ their hats to say hello.

4. The eagle's nest was so _____ that nobody could find it.

Lesson 86

C CONTEXT CLUES

For each item, circle the answer that means the same thing as the word in bold type.

1. Many people **despise** spiders, but they're wonderful animals.
   a. lulu   b. love
   c. hate   d. adopt

2. The cozy **dell** was nestled between two hills.
   a. strategy   b. small valley
   c. nopal   d. tall mountain

3. A **precedes** B and also Z.
   a. happens after   b. prevents
   c. comes before   d. succeeds

D POEM STRUCTURE

Work the items.

Then from five thousand throats and more there rose a lusty yell;

It rumbled through the valley, it rattled in the dell;

It knocked upon the mountain and recoiled upon the flat;

For Casey, mighty Casey, was advancing to the bat.

1. A group of lines in a poem is called a _____ .

2. What is the rhyme scheme for the group of lines above?
   a. ABCD   b. ABAB   c. AABB   d. BABA

3. Each pair of lines in the poem above is called a _____ couplet.

4. Draw slashes between the syllables in the first line.

5. How many syllables are in the first line? _____

GO TO PART E IN YOUR TEXTBOOK

Name _____ 87

A STORY DETAILS

Work the items.

1. What gleamed in Casey's eye when he stepped into the batter's box?
   a. impudence   b. defiance
   c. violence   d. ignorance

2. Casey watched the first pitch in haughty _____ .

3. What did the muffled roar from the audience sound like?
   a. storm waves   b. an echo
   c. sudden stillness d. a sharp crack

4. After the first strike, Casey's face shone with a smile of Christian _____ .

5. What word did the maddened thousands cry after the second strike?
   _____

6. What did Casey pound with cruel violence upon the plate?
   _____

7. What was shattered by the force of Casey's blow?
   a. the ball   b. Casey's bat
   c. the outfield fence d. the air

8. After Casey struck out, there was no _____ in Mudville.

B CLOZE SENTENCES

Complete each sentence with the correct word.

| grandeur | install | wedge |
| haughty | prompt | writhe |

1. After he was tackled, the football player began to _____ in pain.

2. The _____ student thought she was better than everybody else.

3. Few cities can compare with the _____ of Rome.

4. You need to be careful when you _____ a lightbulb.

C CONTEXT CLUES

For each item, circle the answer that means the same thing as the word in bold type.

1. The proud fifth grader cast a **scornful** gaze on the lowly fourth graders.
   a. admiring   b. disrespectful
   c. blinking   d. sorrowful

2. The diners could barely hear each other above the **tumult** of the restaurant.
   a. rapid tumbling   b. dark tunnel
   c. eerie quiet   d. loud noise

3. Preston's **visage** glowed with happiness when he went to the fair.
   a. face   b. vision   c. toes   d. visitors

Lesson 87   173

D RELEVANT INFORMATION

For each item, write *relevant to fact A*, *relevant to fact B*, or *irrelevant*.

Fact A: *Casey was advancing to the bat.*

Fact B: *Cooney died at first.*

1. The game was on television.
   _____

2. The crowd sent up a joyous yell.
   _____

3. A sickly silence fell upon the crowd.
   _____

4. A straggling few got up to go in deep despair.
   _____

5. The team was called the Mudville nine.
   _____

E SEQUENCING

Number the events in the correct sequence.

_____ Casey looked at the first pitch.

_____ Casey struck out.

_____ Two men got on base.

_____ Casey advanced to the batter's box.

_____ Two men were thrown out at first base.

GO TO PART D IN YOUR TEXTBOOK

Lesson 87

Name _____

A STORY DETAILS

Work the items.

1. Before 1776, the 13 colonies were ruled by ▒ .

   a. France   b. Great Britain   c. Spain

2. Which document contains the statement "All men are created equal"?

   a. Bill of Rights   b. Constitution

   c. Declaration of Independence

3. Which document was written last?

   a. Bill of Rights   b. Constitution

   c. Declaration of Independence

4. Which document created a strong federal government?

   a. Bill of Rights   b. Constitution

   c. Declaration of Independence

5. The three branches of the federal government are Congress, the president, and the _____ .

6. Congress consists of the House and the _____ .

7. Which branch of the federal government has the power to write new laws?

   a. the courts   b. the president

   c. Congress

8. Freedom of speech is guaranteed by the First _____ to the Constitution.

9. The only people who had the right to vote when the Constitution was passed were ▒ .

   a. white men   b. white women

   c. slave men   d. slave women

B CLOZE SENTENCES

Complete each sentence with the correct word.

| benefit | dell | lulu |
| congress | latter | veto |

1. The president has the power to _____ new laws.

2. Some tax breaks _____ only rich people.

3. A group of people who make laws for a country is called a _____ .

4. Of the two players, the former is better than the _____ .

Lesson 88

C CONTEXT CLUES

For each item, circle the answer that means the same thing as the word(s) in bold type.

1. The president of the tire company was a **tyrant.**
   a. type of ant
   b. tire expert
   c. cruel leader
   d. retread

2. Some machines **consist of** more than a thousand parts.
   a. despise
   b. precede
   c. doff
   d. are made of

3. Buildings can last a long time, but not a single one **is eternal.**
   a. is beautiful
   b. lasts forever
   c. has grandeur
   d. is internal

D ELLIPSIS

Write whether *Connie* or *Jacob* says each numbered statement.

Connie answered the phone and said, "Hello." [1]

"Hello," said a shaking voice on the other end of the line. [2] "Is this Connie? This is Jacob Drucker calling."

"Oh," said the girl, with an icy tone in her voice. [3] "And what do you want?"

There was a long pause. "Well?" she asked. [4]

"Er, I was wondering, uh, if you, if you want to go to the dance with me." [5]

"You were, were you?" [6]

The ice in her voice began to melt. "Let me think about it. I'll call you back tomorrow." [7]

"Okay." [8]

1. _____
2. _____
3. _____
4. _____
5. _____
6. _____
7. _____
8. _____

GO TO PART D IN YOUR TEXTBOOK

Name _____ 89

A STORY DETAILS

Work the items.

1. Which document says, "All men are created equal"?
   a. The Bill of Rights   b. The Constitution
   c. The Declaration of Independence

2. What were the Northern states called before the Civil War?
   a. Canada   b. free states   c. slave states

3. People who tried to abolish slavery were called _____ .

4. Some slaves escaped to free states on the _____ Railroad.

5. Each state had two ▓▓▓ in Congress.
   a. presidents   b. governors
   c. senators   d. mayors

6. Some Southern states formed a country called the ▓▓▓ States of America.
   a. Confederate   b. Union
   c. United   d. Slave

7. The commander of the Southern army was Robert E. _____ .

8. When the Civil War began, the Northern states were _____ as rich as the Southern states.

9. In 1863, a horrible battle was fought near _____ , Pennsylvania.

B CLOZE SENTENCES

Complete each sentence with the correct word.

abolitionist	revolt	visage
grandeur	scornful	writhe
haughty	tumult	

1. The citizens decided to _____ when the queen took away their freedom.

2. There was such a _____ at the construction site that the workers wore earplugs.

3. When Mr. Barnes was a child, his _____ had no wrinkles.

4. Everyone was impressed by the _____ of the view.

5. The _____ risked her life to free slaves.

Lesson 89   177

C CONTEXT CLUES

For each item, circle the answer that means the same thing as the word(s) in bold type.

1. The **plantation** used slaves to harvest cotton.

    a. factory   b. plant store

    c. amendment   d. large farm

2. The city was so big that its leaders decided to **secede** from the country.

    a. declare   b. withdraw

    c. recoil   d. precede

3. After **one decade** and two years of life, Daniela became a teenager.

    a. five years   b. ten years

    c. twenty years   d. fifty years

4. The new law will **abolish** smoking in city parks.

    a. put an end to b. clench

    c. import   d. respond to

GO TO PART D IN YOUR TEXTBOOK

Name ____

A STORY DETAILS

Work the items.

1. The Gettysburg Address is only ________________ sentences long.
2. Four score and seven years is ________________ years.
3. Lincoln says, "our fathers brought forth on this continent a new nation." Which continent is he referring to?
   a. South America b. Africa
   c. North America d. Antarctica
4. Lincoln says that the United States was conceived in ________.
   a. slavery b. liberty c. poverty
5. What is another word for "final resting place"?
   a. bedroom b. dormitory c. grave
6. The "unfinished work" in the Gettysburg Address is the ________.
   a. Civil War b. cemetery
   c. Battle of Gettysburg
7. The "last full measure of devotion" that the soldiers gave was their ________.
   a. songs b. prayers c. lives
8. The ________________ Amendment says that slavery is not allowed in the United States.

B CLOZE SENTENCES

Complete each sentence with the correct word.

benefit	detract	hallow
congress	engaged	tyrant

1. Gamal and Hana were ________________ to be married.
2. Everyone can ________________ from exercise and a healthy diet.
3. President Lincoln said that we could not ________________ the cemetery.
4. Losing should not ________________ from the fun of playing a game.

C CONTEXT CLUES

For each item, circle the answer that means the same thing as the word(s) in bold type.

1. The police tried to **conceive** a plan for catching the robbers.
   a. devote   b. create
   c. veto   d. overturn

2. Kim was **dedicated** to playing the guitar.
   a. trampled   b. eroded
   c. indicated d. committed

3. The United States government **consists of** three branches: the Congress, the president, and the courts.
   a. is made of   b. declares
   c. consecrates d. grows

D RELATED WORDS

The box shows root words. Use words related to those root words to complete the sentences below the box.

| amend | constitute | propose |
| believe | declare | revolution |

1. The United States began in 1776 with the _____ of Independence.

2. The Americans fought the British in the _____ War.

3. The First _____ in the Bill of Rights guarantees freedom of speech.

4. The first set of rules and laws for the United States is called the _____ .

GO TO PART D IN YOUR TEXTBOOK

A STORY DETAILS

1. Elizabeth Cady Stanton wrote the _____ Falls Declaration.

2. Stanton's declaration was modeled on the Declaration of _____ .

3. Women who asked for the right to vote were called _____ .

4. Stanton and Susan B. Anthony saw a strong connection between giving women the right to vote and ____ .
   a. repealing the Bill of Rights
   b. freeing the slaves
   c. maintaining slavery
   d. the right to bear arms

5. When Anthony tried to vote, she was ____ by the government.
   a. ignored   b. accepted
   c. arrested   d. honored

6. The amendment that would give women the right to vote was nicknamed the _____ Amendment.

7. In 1913, a group of women held a parade in _____ , DC.

8. When Congress failed to act on women's rights, the National Woman's Party started using civil ____ .
   a. disobedience   b. dislocation
   c. display   d. dismay

9. The ____ Amendment gave women the right to vote.
   a. 13th   b. 15th   c. 19th   d. 21st

B CLOZE SENTENCES

Complete each sentence with the correct word.

| abolitionist | plantation | suffrage |
| decades | revolt | suffragette |

1. Adults can vote in elections, but children do not have _____ .

2. Many slaves worked on the cotton _____ .

3. The _____ helped slaves escape to freedom.

4. More than eight _____ passed between the Declaration of Independence and the Gettysburg Address.

Lesson 91

C CONTEXT CLUES

For each item, circle the answer that means the same thing as the word(s) in bold type.

1. Rules for softball **are modeled on** rules for baseball.

    a. consecrate   b. imitate

    c. approve   d. overturn

2. People from all over the country came to the comic-book **convention**.

    a. cemetery   b. constitution

    c. declaration   d. meeting

3. The women would not let the men **abridge** their rights.

    a. secede   b. abolish

    c. reduce   d. portion

D ROOT WORDS

For each word listed below, write the root word.

1. conclusion _____

2. connection _____

3. unequal _____

4. nicknamed _____

5. protester _____

6. devotion _____

7. proposition _____

8. defiance _____

E FILLING OUT FORMS

Use the facts to fill out the form.

Facts: Your name is Juan Martinez. You are signing up with a baseball team. You are sixteen years old, and you have been playing baseball since you were six. You want to be a pitcher, but you can play any position. You can throw three kinds of pitches: a fastball, a slider, and a curveball. You are a student at Roberto Clemente High School, Solarville, Florida.

1. Name (last name first):

    _____

2. Age: _____

3. School name:

    _____

4. School city: _____

5. School state: _____

6. Years of experience playing baseball:

    _____

7. Desired position: _____

8. Positions you can play:

    _____

9. Circle the pitches you know how to throw.

    a. change up   b. curveball

    c. fastball   d. screwball

    e. sinker   f. slider

GO TO PART D IN YOUR TEXTBOOK

Name _____

92

A STORY DETAILS

Work the items.

1. The Civil War took place during the ▨ .
    a. 1760s   b. 1860s   c. 1960s

2. The Southern slave states were part of the _____ .

3. The Northern free states were part of the _____ .

4. Which group of states won the war?
   _____

5. The narrator of the Harriet Tubman biography is named _____ _____ .

6. In which state was the narrator a slave?
   _____

7. How was the woman nicknamed Moses like the man named Moses?
    a. They lived at the same time.
    b. They had the same nickname.
    c. They freed slaves.
    d. They were both in the Bible.

8. The slave girl sang, "Good news, _____ coming!"

B FILLING OUT FORMS

Use the facts to fill out the form.

Facts: Your name is Cindy Hightower. You live at 7594 Lake Street in Minneapolis, Minnesota. You are in the eighth grade, and you want to take a special class in computers. You got an A in mathematics last year, and you got Bs in all your other classes. You want to find out how computers work.

1. Last name:
   _____

2. First name:
   _____

3. Which class are you applying for?
   _____

4. Why do you want to take the class?
   _____
   _____

5. List the grade you received for each class last year:
   - English ____
   - Social Studies ____
   - Mathematics ____

6. Which grade are you in?
   _____

7. Full address:
   _____
   _____

Lesson 92   183

The United States in 1863

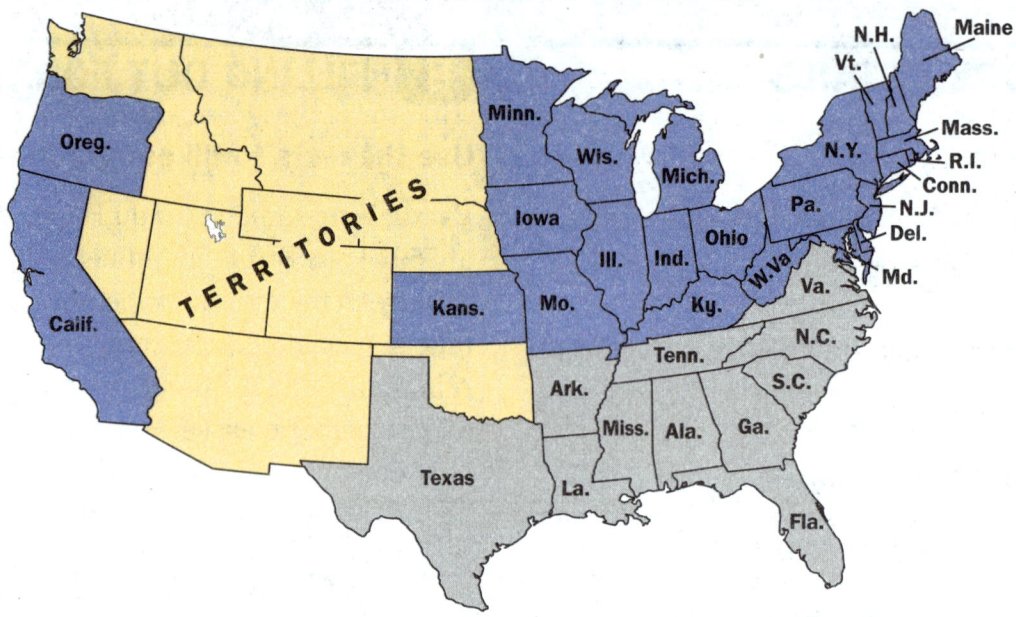

C CONTEXT CLUES

For each item, circle the answer that means the same thing as the word(s) in bold type.

1. The piles of trash **detracted from** the beautiful landscape.
   a. reduced the value of
   b. added to
   c. were absent from
   d. multiplied

2. Teachers are **dedicated** to helping students learn how to read.
   a. abolished
   b. committed
   c. unheeded
   d. straggled

3. It's hard to **conceive of** new ideas.
   a. trample
   b. devote
   c. secede
   d. create

D MAPS

Work the items.

1. The map shows the United States during the ▆▆▆ War.
   a. Mexican
   b. Civil
   c. Vietnam
   d. First World

2. What color are the Union states?
   _____

3. What color are the Confederate states?
   _____

4. What color are the territories?
   _____

5. Which Union state goes farthest north?
   _____

6. Which Confederate state goes farthest west? _____

GO TO PART D IN YOUR TEXTBOOK

Name _____

A STORY DETAILS

Work the items.

1. The system of helping runaway slaves was called the _____ _____ .

2. Slaves would travel from station to station during the ____ .
   a. morning   b. afternoon
   c. early evening   d. night

3. Guides who led the slaves were called _____ .

4. Jim's first hiding place was in ____ .
   a. an attic   b. a living room
   c. a basement   d. a toolshed

5. When Jim asked to go back, Harriet pointed her _____ at him.

6. Mr. Booker had been chased out of town for helping ____ .
   a. slave catchers   b. vagrants
   c. runaway slaves   d. criminals

7. In the swamp, Harriet suddenly ____ .
   a. fired her pistol   b. fell asleep
   c. fell down   d. yelled

8. What mark did Harriet have on her forehead?
   a. tattoo   b. scar
   c. brand   d. insect bite

9. Harriet had received that mark in a ____ .
   a. field   b. cabin
   c. store   d. kitchen

B CLOZE SENTENCES

Complete each sentence with the correct word.

| fits | rickety | suffragette |
| modeled | suffrage | unconscious |

1. Harriet was knocked _____ by the heavy weight.

2. Women in the United States did not have _____ before the Civil War.

3. The new school was _____ on the oldest school in the city.

4. Sleeping _____ can occur at any time.

Lesson 93   185

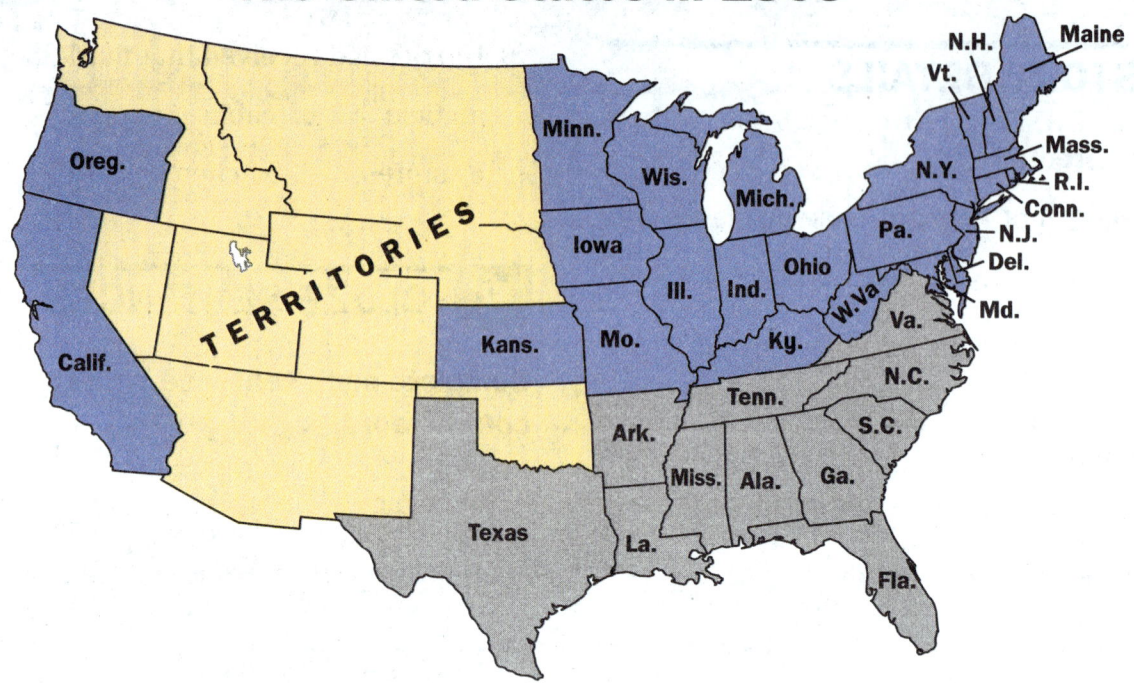

C CONTEXT CLUES

For each item, circle the answer that means the same thing as the word in bold type.

1. The king wanted to **abridge** citizens' rights so he could get more power.

   a. hallow   b. reduce

   c. honor   d. approve

2. It was dangerous to climb the **rickety** ladder.

   a. convention   b. fictional

   c. unstable   d. hallowed

3. When Selena heard a low growl, she **realized** that she was in grave danger.

   a. understood   b. consecrated

   c. detracted   d. engaged

D MAPS

Work the items.

1. The map shows the United States during the ▃▃▃ War.

   a. Mexican   b. Civil

   c. Vietnam   d. First World

2. The gray states belonged to the _____ .

3. The blue states belonged to the _____ .

4. True or false: The territories were already states. _____

5. The two states that go the farthest south are _____ and _____ .

GO TO PART D IN YOUR TEXTBOOK

Lesson 93

Name

A STORY DETAILS

Work the items.

1. Mr. Garrett's hardware store was in the state of _____ .

2. Mr. Garrett belonged to the Society of ▇▇▇ .
   a. Friends
   b. Enemies
   c. Hardware
   d. Storeowners

3. Mr. Still's office was in the state of _____ .

4. To which country did Jim and the others have to travel? _____

5. That country was ▇▇▇ miles from Mr. Still's office.
   a. sixty   b. six hundred   c. six thousand

6. Jim and the others would travel to that country on a ▇▇▇ .
   a. ship   b. plane   c. train   d. wagon

7. The sign behind Jim offered a _____ for Harriet's capture.

8. Harriet and Jim didn't know what was on the sign because they couldn't _____ .

B CLOZE SENTENCES

Complete each sentence with the correct word.

| antislavery | rickety | suspense |
| realize | society | unconscious |

1. People in the bird _____ counted all the bird nests in the park.

2. The scary ride kept Benito in _____ for a long time.

3. It was dangerous to sit in the _____ tree house.

4. The abolitionists belonged to different _____ groups.

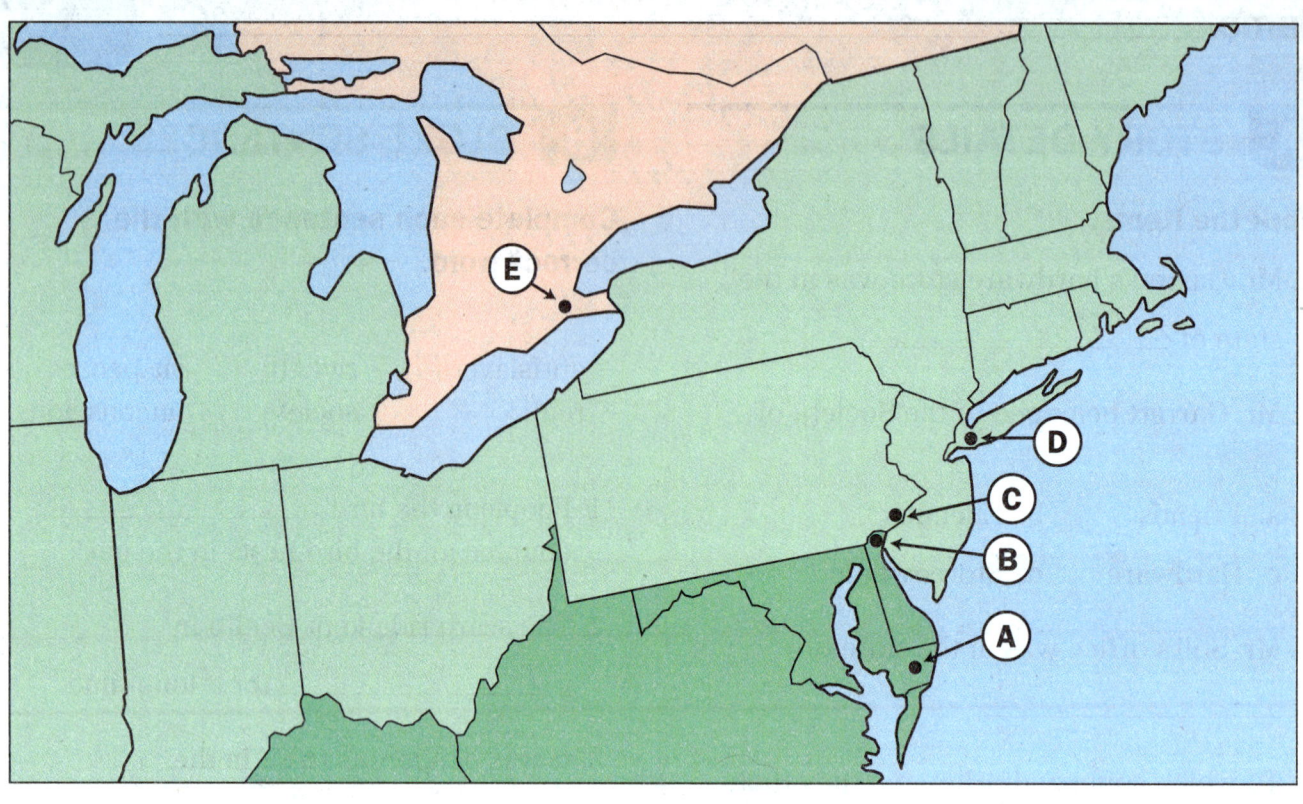

C MAPS

The map shows free states and slave states in 1855.

1. Which color are the free states?
   a. light green   b. dark green   c. tan

2. Which color are the slave states?
   a. light green   b. dark green   c. tan

3. Dot **A** shows Jim's home in the state of _____ .

4. Dot **B** shows where Jim spent the night above a hardware store in the city of _____ , Delaware.

5. Dot **C** shows where Jim met William Still in the city of _____ , Pennsylvania.

6. Dot **D** shows where Jim changed trains in New _____ City.

7. Dot **E** shows the city of Hamilton in ____ .
   a. Canada
   b. Mexico
   c. the United States

GO TO PART D IN YOUR TEXTBOOK

Name

A STORY DETAILS

Work the items.

1. What did Harriet do as the men read the poster?
   a. slept
   b. pretended to read a book
   c. hid under a blanket
   d. walked away

2. The men thought Harriet wasn't the person in the poster because she could _____ .

3. Jim and the others changed trains near _____ _____ City.

4. Jim's last stop in the United States was _____ , New York.

5. In that city, a slave _____ and a police _____ entered Jim's train.

6. The _____ _____ wanted to delay the train.

7. Passengers in the car said Jim had come from ▨ .
   a. Canada
   b. Maryland
   c. New York City
   d. Pennsylvania

8. After the train crossed the bridge, Jim was a ▨ .
   a. slave   b. conductor   c. free man

B RELATED WORDS

The box shows root words. Use words related to the root words to complete the sentences below the box.

| exclaim | realize |
| predict | sense |

1. "Ouch!" is a common _____ that people say.

2. The coach made a _____ that her team would win if they tried harder.

3. A spider crawling up your arm is a creepy _____ .

C CONTEXT CLUES

For each item, circle the answer that means the same thing as the word in bold type.

1. When Kameron opened his wallet, he **realized** that he had no money.
   a. gestured   b. protested
   c. abridged   d. understood

2. The **rickety** and crumbling bridge was the only way across the river.
   a. unstable   b. dull
   c. fictional   d. unequal

Lesson 95

D MAPS

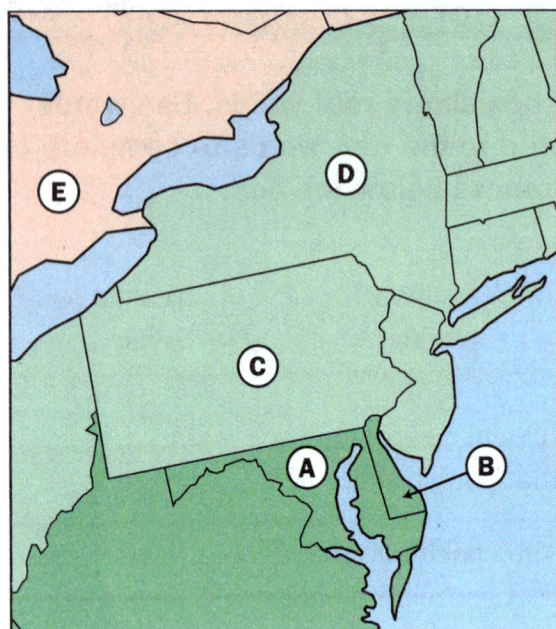

Work the items.

1. State **A** is named ▮▮▮ .
   a. Delaware b. Maryland
   c. Pennsylvania d. New York

2. State **B** is named ▮▮▮ .
   a. Delaware b. Maryland
   c. Pennsylvania d. New York

3. State **C** is named ▮▮▮ .
   a. Delaware b. Maryland
   c. Pennsylvania d. New York

4. State **D** is named ▮▮▮ .
   a. Delaware b. Maryland
   c. Pennsylvania d. New York
   e. Wilmington

5. Country **E** is named ▮▮▮ .
   a. Mexico b. Virginia
   c. Canada d. United States

E CONTRADICTIONS

Work the items.

Freddy Fingerboard plays in a band called The Bums. He is one of the best guitar players in the city. All the bands want Freddy to play with them, but he sticks with The Bums because they pay him the most. It's really something to watch Freddy play. He gets up on that stage, lifts the mouthpiece to his lips, and blows some of the sweetest sounds ever heard on a brass instrument. Freddy has a bright future in the music business. His band has just recorded its first album, *Grungy Tomatoes*.

1. Underline the statement that you assume is true.

2. Draw a wavy line under the statement that contradicts the true statement.

3. Write an *if-then* statement that explains the contradiction.

   _____
   _____
   _____

GO TO PART C IN YOUR TEXTBOOK

190 Lesson 95

Name _____ 96

A STORY DETAILS

Work the items.

1. The incident with Charles Nalle took place during ▨ .

   a. 1855   b. 1857   c. 1860

2. Jim worked for a ▨ in Hamilton, Canada.

   a. shoemaker
   b. toolmaker
   c. cabinetmaker

3. Jim brought a desk to the town of _____ , New York.

4. Why could Jim be arrested in the United States?

   a. He was a runaway slave.
   b. He was from Canada.
   c. He was a conductor on the Underground Railroad.

5. How did Harriet help free Nalle when he left the sheriff's office?

   a. She knocked over all the officers.
   b. She shoved Nalle into the crowd.
   c. She undid his handcuffs.

6. Harriet used her _____ to disguise Nalle.

7. Nalle took a ▨ across the Hudson River.

   a. ferry   b. rowboat   c. life preserver

8. The officers on the other side of the river freed Nalle when they realized that they ▨ .

   a. should help free the slaves
   b. had arrested the wrong man
   c. were surrounded by the mob

B CLOZE SENTENCES

Complete each sentence with the correct word.

| antislavery | dictionary | society |
| atlas | encyclopedia | suspense |

1. The _____ group was connected to the Underground Railroad.

2. The gardeners belonged to the local plant _____ .

3. You can find word definitions in the _____ .

4. The students looked in the _____ to find their town on a map.

Lesson 96

C FILLING OUT FORMS

Use the facts to fill out the form.

Facts: Your name is Rachel Clearwater. You live on a mesa called the Mesa Grande. You do not have a street address. You are looking for work in Bisbee, which is a town thirty miles away from the mesa. You know how to make pottery and how to plaster walls. You have finished high school and two years of college. Because it is such a long drive to the town, you would prefer a full-time job. You are filling out a form at an employment agency.

Note: If any of the following questions do not apply to you, write N/A.

1. Name (last name first):
   _____

2. If you live in Bisbee, what is your street address?
   _____

3. If you live outside of Bisbee, how far away do you live?
   _____

4. List any special skills you have.
   _____
   _____

5. How much college education have you had, if any?
   _____

6. If you want a part-time job, how many hours per week can you work?
   _____

D MAPS

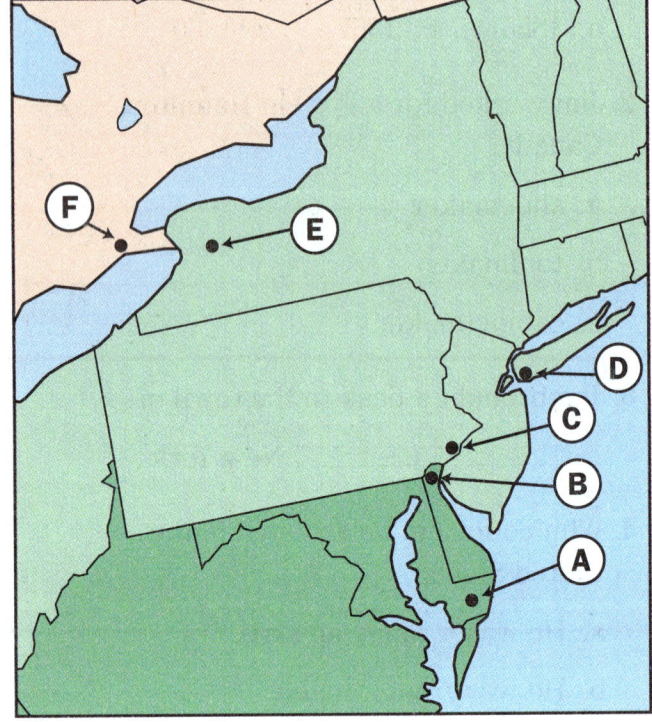

Work the items.

1. Which dot shows New York City?
   ____

2. Which dot shows Philadelphia?
   ____

3. Which dot shows where Jim is living now?
   ____

4. Which dot shows where Jim used to live?
   ____

5. Which dot shows Buffalo?
   ____

GO TO PART C IN YOUR TEXTBOOK

Name _____ 97

A STORY DETAILS

Work the items.

1. The first name of Jim's wife was _____ .

2. In which year did the attack on a Union fort begin the Civil War?
   _____

3. The president of the United States in that year was Abraham _____ .

4. Jim joined the ▒▒▒ army.
   a. Confederate   b. New York   c. Union

5. Fort Wagner was located in South _____ .

6. During the attack on Fort Wagner, Jim was shot in the _____ .

7. Almost ▒▒▒ of the soldiers in Jim's regiment were killed, wounded, or captured during the attack.
   a. one-fourth   b. one-third   c. one-half

8. Harriet compared the battle to a storm over a field of _____ .

9. According to Harriet, what were the crops that were reaped after the battle?
   a. cotton   b. corn   c. dead men

B CLOZE SENTENCES

Complete each sentence with the correct word.

| agony | colonel | reap |
| bombard | groggy | regiment |

1. A military officer who ranks between a major and a general is called a _____ .

2. Gardening is hard work, but then you get to _____ the crops.

3. Anabel was in _____ after she stubbed her toe on the cabinet.

4. Obi was so _____ when he got into bed that he slept with his feet on the pillow.

Lesson 97   193

C RELATED WORDS

The box shows root words. Use *related words* to complete the sentences below the box.

| exclaim | realize |
| predict | sense |

1. After walking for several hours, the hikers came to the _____ that they were lost.

2. When people bet on a horse race, they make a _____ about which horse will win.

3. Everyone turned around after hearing Waldo's loud _____ .

D SEQUENCING

Number the events in the correct sequence.

____ Jim moves to Syracuse, New York.

____ Jim delivers a desk to Troy, New York.

____ Jim is wounded in South Carolina.

____ Jim is a slave in Maryland.

____ Jim escapes to Canada.

E REFERENCE SOURCES

For each item, write whether you would use an *atlas*, a *dictionary*, or an *encyclopedia* to answer the question.

1. Which team won the 1937 World Series? _____

2. Which books did Sylvia Townsend Warner write? _____

3. How many rivers are in the state of Maine? _____

4. How many definitions does the word *for* have? _____

5. How many syllables are in the word *sediment*? _____

GO TO PART D IN YOUR TEXTBOOK

Name _____

A STORY DETAILS

Work the items.

1. Before Jim saw Harriet in Syracuse, he thought his future was ▇ .

   a. bright   b. dark   c. uncertain

2. Harriet told Jim that a cabinetmaker works with his _____ , not with his _____ .

3. The Civil War ended in ▇ .

   a. 1765   b. 1865   c. 1965

4. After the war, Harriet went into debt because ▇ .

   a. she spent money foolishly
   b. the government had no money
   c. the government didn't pay her

5. How did Sarah Bradford help Harriet earn money?

   a. She wrote a book about Harriet's adventures.
   b. She gave Harriet a job.
   c. She organized a charity drive.

6. What big event happened to Harriet in 1867?

   a. The government paid her.
   b. She freed more slaves.
   c. She got married.

7. Harriet died in ▇ .

   a. 1813   b. 1903   c. 1913

8. Jim said Harriet "lived like a ▇ all her life."

   a. free person   b. slave   c. soldier

B CLOZE SENTENCES

Complete each sentence with the correct word.

| deception | society | suspense |
| hobble | staggering | unselfish |

1. After Derrick twisted his ankle, he had to _____ across the floor.

2. The scammer stole money by using _____ .

3. The number of soldiers who died in the Civil War is _____ .

4. Someone who is _____ tries to help other people.

Lesson 98   195

C COMPOUND WORDS

Each sentence includes one part of a compound word. Complete the sentence with the entire compound word.

1. A ground where soldiers fight is called a _____.

2. People who aren't used to the sea can get _____ when they ride on boats.

3. The farmer used a pitchfork to unload hay from the _____.

4. A cannon can fire only one _____ at a time.

D REFERENCE SOURCES

For each item, write whether you would use an *atlas,* a *dictionary,* or an *encyclopedia* to answer the question.

1. How are plants grown?
   _____

2. What does *meander* mean?
   _____

3. How many countries border India?
   _____

4. How is the word *emphatic* pronounced?
   _____

5. How far is it from Chicago to Milwaukee?
   _____

GO TO PART D IN YOUR TEXTBOOK

Name ______________________________

A STORY DETAILS

Work the items.

1. James volunteered to serve in the ____ Army.
   - a. Union
   - b. Northern
   - c. Confederate
   - d. Revolutionary
2. James joined that army in the state of ________________ .
3. The officer who decided to let his troops stay in camp was a ____ .
   - a. general
   - b. colonel
   - c. major
   - d. captain
4. James's leg was hit by a ________________ .
5. The operation the surgeon performed on James's leg is called an ________________ .
6. Because James lost his leg, he was called an ________________ .
7. James's family gave him ____ while he worked on his new leg.
   - a. solitude
   - b. money
   - c. trouble
   - d. ideas
8. The company James started was called the ________________ Company.
9. After James lost his leg, he wrote, "I was the ________________ of despair."

B CLOZE SENTENCES

Complete each sentence with the correct word.

agony	colonel	regiment
bombard	infection	solitude

1. The cut on Selah's finger was red and puffy because she had an ________________ .
2. The ________________ took orders from the general but not from the major.
3. When you live in ________________ , you don't see other people.
4. The army used cannonballs to ________________ the enemy fort.

C CONTEXT CLUES

For each item, circle the answer that means the same thing as the word(s) in bold type.

1. The flimsy wooden shack was **vulnerable to** windy storms.

    a. protected from b. used to
    c. valuable during d. easily harmed by

2. The fire was such a **catastrophe** that the entire town burned to the ground.

    a. disaster b. success
    c. raid d. flood

3. Police officers use many different **techniques** for catching criminals.

    a. reaps b. replacements
    c. ways d. accomplishments

D MULTIPLE ACCOUNTS

Work the items.

Passage A

The battle was like a storm over a field of corn. We saw the lightning and that was the guns. Then we heard the thunder, and that was the big guns. And then we came to get in the crops. It was dead men that we reaped.

Passage B

The Second Battle of Fort Wagner was fought on July 18, 1863. About 5,000 Union soldiers, including an all-black regiment, assaulted the fort, but they were driven back by the 1,800 Confederate soldiers inside the fort. More than 1,600 soldiers on both sides were killed during the daylong battle. Union ships kept shelling the fort for weeks after the battle, and the Confederates finally surrendered on September 7.

1. Which passage is a firsthand account?

    a. A b. B c. both d. neither

2. Which passage is a secondhand account?

    a. A b. B c. both d. neither

3. Which passage was written by someone who may not have experienced the battle?

    a. A b. B c. both d. neither

4. Which passage uses figurative language?

    a. A b. B c. both d. neither

GO TO PART D IN YOUR TEXTBOOK

Name _____ 100

A STORY DETAILS

Work the items.

1. The Senate has 100 senators. How many senators is a majority?

    a. 49   b. 50   c. 51

2. How old do you have to be on Election Day to register to vote?

    a. 16 years old   b. 18 years old

    c. 21 years old

3. The rule for voting is "One _____, one _____."

4. The two main parties in the United States begin with a D and an R. Write their names on the lines below.

    D: _____

    R: _____

5. Who is the president of the United States?

    _____

6. The number of senators in the Senate is based on ____.

    a. the number of people in each state

    b. the number of states

    c. the square miles of the state

7. The number of representatives in the House of Representatives is based on ____.

    a. the number of people in each state

    b. the number of states

    c. the square miles of the state

8. Presidents of the United States are elected for a ____-year term.

    a. two   b. four   c. six

9. Senators are elected for a ____-year term.

    a. two   b. four   c. six

B CLOZE SENTENCES

Complete each sentence with the correct word.

| democracy | presidential | term |
| hobble | representative | unselfish |

1. Each class elected a _____ for the student council.

2. A country controlled by a king or a queen is not a _____ .

3. Hailee was the president, so she had to act _____ at all times.

4. Representatives in Congress are elected for a two-year _____ .

Lesson 100   199

C CONTEXT CLUES

For each item, circle the answer that means the same thing as the word(s) in bold type.

1. You need to get **a majority** of the votes to win an election.

   a. less than half   b. one-half

   c. more than half   d. all

2. The sneaky cardplayer used **deception** to win the poker game.

   a. trickery   b. honesty

   c. reception   d. complaints

3. The cost was so **staggering** that we didn't buy the diamond.

   a. reasonable   b. low

   c. limping   d. astonishing

D REFERENCE SOURCES

Work the items.

Statement A

Carbon dioxide and other greenhouse gases are the main cause of global warming.

1. What kind of reference source would you use to find out if statement A is true?

   a. atlas   b. dictionary   c. encyclopedia

Read the following passage to find out the main cause of global warming.

    The recent rise of the Earth's temperature is called global warming. Gases that trap heat near the surface of the Earth are the main cause of global warming. These gases—which include carbon dioxide, methane, nitrous oxide, and halocarbons—are called *greenhouse gases* because they act like a greenhouse. They take in heat from sunlight but don't let the heat escape. While these gases occur in nature, they are also produced by factories, cars, fireplaces, and other things made by people.

2. Underline the sentence that explains the main cause of global warming.

GO TO PART D IN YOUR TEXTBOOK

Name _____

101

A STORY DETAILS

Work the items.

1. At the beginning of the play, how many kids were in the club?
   _____

2. How many votes did Nancy need to be elected to the club? _____

3. Which other person wanted to be elected to the club? _____

4. Which character came out of the clubhouse? _____

5. That character said that Nancy had ▇ .
   a. been elected unanimously
   b. received the majority of votes
   c. not received a majority of votes
   d. been elected to the club

B CLOZE SENTENCES

Complete each sentence with the correct word.

| beforehand | colonel | rise |
| catastrophe | inflection | unanimously |

1. Questions almost always end with a rising _____ .

2. The instructions said that the play was in a living room at _____ .

3. Amir's mother could tell that he had been eating chocolate _____ because his shirt was covered with dark smears.

4. Everyone voted for Jayda, so she was elected _____ .

C CONTEXT CLUES

For each item, circle the answer that means the same thing as the word(s) in bold type.

1. The fans were **dumbfounded** when the football team scored 96 points before halftime.

    a. really stupid   b. lost

    c. presidential   d. astonished

2. Colten pretended to leave, but he stayed **in earshot of** the party.

    a. far away from

    b. where he could hear

    c. where he could watch

    d. next to

3. The writer enjoyed **solitude** when she worked on her novel.

    a. being vulnerable   b. technique

    c. infection   d. being alone

D VOCABULARY REVIEW

Complete each sentence with the correct word.

> deception   staggering
> hobble   unselfish

1. When you deceive people, you use _____ .

2. People who are _____ put other people first.

3. Rupert earned a _____ amount of money as a singer.

GO TO PART E IN YOUR TEXTBOOK

Name _____ 102

A STORY DETAILS

Work the items.

1. How many votes did Nancy receive for joining the Aces? _____

2. How many votes did Nancy need to be elected to the Aces? _____

3. Sidney said he had voted _____ Nancy.

4. Harriet and Tom said they had voted _____ Nancy.

5. How many people were in Eddie's club when it started? _____

6. To whose club was Nancy elected? _____

7. Why was Nancy elected to Eddie's club?
   a. All five members voted for her.
   b. The only member voted for her.
   c. She received less than a majority of votes.

B CLOZE SENTENCES

Complete each sentence with the correct word.

| democracy | exception | shy |
| dryly | presidential | sulk |

1. The basketball player was one inch _____ of seven feet tall.

2. The bored announcer _____ said who had won the game.

3. Cam began to _____ after she failed the test.

4. The teacher wasn't willing to make an _____ to the rules.

Lesson 102   203

C CONTEXT CLUES

For each item, circle the answer that means the same thing as the word(s) in bold type.

1. More than half a group is **the majority** of the group.
   a. the minority   b. most
   c. every member   d. the representative

2. The crowd was **dumbfounded** by the runner's speed.
   a. hobbled   b. pronounced
   c. astonished   d. announced

3. Senators are elected to a six-year **term** in office.
   a. amount of time b. amount of money
   c. prison sentence d. unit of heat

D COMPARING CHARACTERS

Complete each sentence with *Nancy, Eddie,* or *Sidney.*

1. _____ was certain she would be elected to the club.

2. _____ was too young for the club.

3. _____ had some bad news for another character.

4. _____ thought another character was a pest.

5. _____ was not on stage at the beginning of the play.

GO TO PART D IN YOUR TEXTBOOK

Name _____ 103

A STORY DETAILS

Work the items.

1. When the meeting adjourned, which three club members left the clubhouse first?

   _____

2. Those members invited Nancy to attend a _____ on Saturday night.

3. Nancy replied that she ▬▬▬ .

   a. would be happy to attend
   b. wasn't coming
   c. would think about it

4. Who were the next two members to leave the clubhouse?

   _____

5. Which two members actually voted for Nancy?

   _____

6. Those two members decided to join the club that _____ started.

7. How many votes did each of those two members receive for the new club?

   _____

B CLOZE SENTENCES

Complete each sentence with the correct word.

| beforehand | gavel | treasurer |
| earshot | inflection | unanimously |

1. The club president struck her _____ on a block of wood to begin the meeting.

2. Carmelo was good with money, so he became the _____ for our class.

3. People often use a rising _____ at the end of questions.

4. The father asked his children to stay in _____ when they played outside.

Lesson 103   205

C CONTEXT CLUES

For each item, circle the answer that means the same thing as the word in bold type.

1. The collector paid millions of dollars for the **exquisite** Chinese vase.
   a. unanimous   b. beautiful and delicate
   c. breakable   d. majority

2. Elena wanted to **adjourn** the meeting so she could go home.
   a. end   b. recount
   c. pronounce d. blunder

3. Carlos was **dumbfounded** when his car rose into the air.
   a. mildly surprised   b. annoyed
   c. hasty   d. astonished

D COMPARING CHARACTERS

Complete each sentence with *Alvin, Eddie, Harriet,* or *Nancy.*

1. _____ was betrayed by her friends.

2. _____ did not tell the truth.

3. _____ was president of the new club.

4. _____ quit the old club.

5. _____ became upset.

GO TO PART D IN YOUR TEXTBOOK

Name _____ 104

A POEM DETAILS

Without looking at the poem, complete each line of "Miracles" with the correct word.

1. As to me I know of nothing else but _____,

2. Whether I walk the streets of _____,

3. Or dart my sight over the roofs of houses toward the _____,

4. Or wade with naked feet along the beach just in the edge of the _____,

5. Or stand under trees in the _____,

6. Or watch honeybees busy around the hive of a summer _____,

7. Or animals feeding in the _____,

8. Or birds, or the wonderfulness of insects in the _____,

9. Or the wonderfulness of the sundown, or of the stars shining so quiet and _____,

10. Or the exquisite delicate thin curve of the new moon in _____;

11. These with the rest, one and all, are to me _____,

12. The whole referring, yet each distinct and in its _____.

B CLOZE SENTENCES

Complete each sentence with the correct word.

| cube | distinct | exception |
| cubic | dryly | logic |

1. The giant redwood was _____ from the other trees in the oak forest.

2. Sometimes sugar comes in the shape of a _____.

3. A way of thinking that is based on rules is called _____.

4. The size of a box that is one inch tall, one inch wide, and one inch long is one _____ inch.

Lesson 104   207

C CONTEXT CLUES

For each item, circle the answer that means the same thing as the word(s) in bold type.

1. The cook was **astounded** when the soup turned into liquid gold.
   a. unimpressed   b. hounded
   c. amazed   d. stirring

2. The hawk's wingspan was one inch **shy of** six feet.
   a. less than   b. more than
   c. above   d. with

3. It's best to leave people alone when they're **sulking**.
   a. making silk   b. too friendly
   c. shouting loudly   d. moody and quiet

D READING GRAPHS

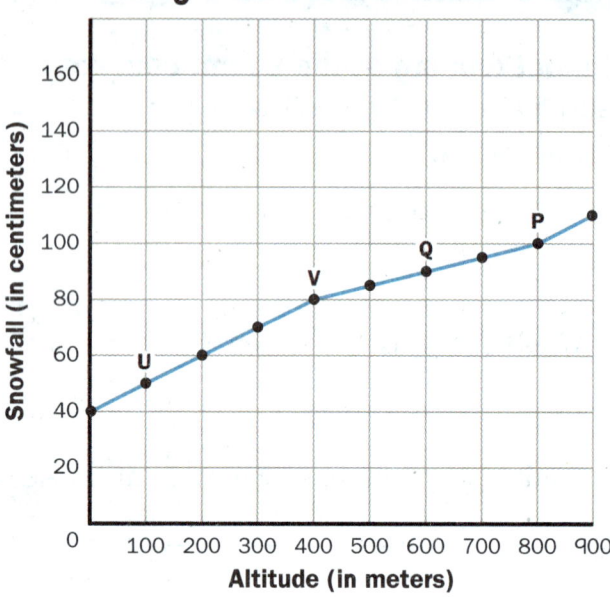

Work the items.

The graph above shows yearly snowfall in the Red Hills. The numbers along the left side tell how many centimeters of snow fall in a year. The numbers along the bottom show the altitude (height) of the hills in meters.

1. How many meters of altitude does dot V show? _____

2. How many centimeters of snow fall at that altitude every year? _____

3. Which altitudes have more snowfall: higher altitudes or lower altitudes?
   _____

4. Which dot shows a higher altitude: U or P?
   _____

GO TO PART D IN YOUR TEXTBOOK

Name _____ 105

A STORY DETAILS

Work the items.

1. Every day, up to a billion ▨ enter the Earth's atmosphere.
   a. meteors   b. meteorites
   c. meteoroids   d. comets

2. Some of those rocks are pulled toward the Earth by the force of _____ .

3. When those rocks begin to melt and create a fiery trail, they are called ▨ .
   a. meteors   b. meteorites
   c. meteoroids   d. comets

4. The rocks that survive the long fall and crash into Earth are called ▨ .
   a. meteors   b. meteorites
   c. meteoroids   d. comets

5. When those rocks crash into Earth, they can make bowl-shaped holes called _____ .

6. When one of those rocks explodes above the ground, the explosion creates a _____ wave that can be felt for miles around.

7. The asteroid belt is located between ▨ .
   a. Venus and Earth
   b. Earth and Mars
   c. Mars and Jupiter
   d. Jupiter and Saturn

8. Sometimes asteroids fall out of orbit and head for the sun as ▨ .
   a. meteors   b. meteorites
   c. meteoroids   d. comets

9. Comets have a _____ made of rocks and dust.

B CLOZE SENTENCES

Complete each sentence with the correct word.

> asteroid   exquisite   orbit
> crater   gavel   treasurer

1. The planets are different in many ways, but they all _____ the sun.

2. The _____ belt is located between two planets.

3. The president pounded a _____ on the table to bring the meeting to order.

4. When the bomb hit the ground, the explosion made a huge _____ .

Lesson 105   209

C CONTEXT CLUES

For each item, circle the answer that means the same thing as the word in bold type.

1. The shiny kitchen sink was made with **nickel.**
   a. bright copper
   b. five-cent coins
   c. stainless steel
   d. silver-white metal

2. We could see **particles** of soot floating in the air.
   a. icicles
   b. small pieces
   c. large chunks
   d. reflections

3. The club decided to **adjourn** their meeting when there was nothing left to say.
   a. end
   b. recount
   c. pronounce
   d. dumbfound

D READING GRAPHS

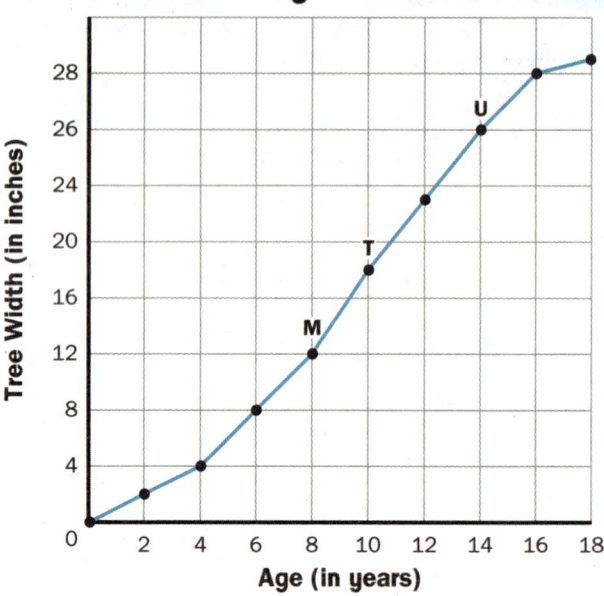

Width and Age of Our Oak Tree

Work the items.

The graph above shows one tree's width at different ages. The numbers along the left side of the graph tell how many inches wide the tree is. The numbers along the bottom tell how many years old the tree is.

1. Dot _____ tells about the tree when it's eight years old.

2. Dot _____ tells about the tree when it's 26 inches wide.

3. As the tree gets older, does it get narrower or wider? _____

4. Which point shows a wider tree, M or T? _____

5. How many inches wide is the tree when it's six years old? _____

GO TO PART D IN YOUR TEXTBOOK

Name _____ 106

A STORY DETAILS

Work the items.

1. The pond David visited was called the _____ Pond.

2. David thought it was amazing that squirrels could run down trees ▭ .
   a. sideways   b. headfirst
   c. feetfirst   d. on their tails

3. David sat under the ▭ tree he'd nicknamed Old Giant.
   a. birch   b. pine
   c. maple   d. oak

4. The ball of fire that roared over David's head was a ▭ .
   a. meteor   b. meteoroid
   c. meteorite   d. comet

5. The crash turned the water of the pond into _____ .

6. The crash turned the pond into a ▭ .
   a. volcano   b. mound
   c. crater   d. dune

7. The water that refilled the pond came from the ▭ .
   a. extraterrestrial rock
   b. sudden rainstorm
   c. water table
   d. nearby stream

8. The place where the earth, the water, and a piece of the sky touched each other was at the _____ of the pond.

B CLOZE SENTENCES

Complete each sentence with the correct word.

| cube | diameter | logic |
| cubic | distinct | scan |

1. The _____ of the round water pipe was two inches across.

2. You need a special machine to _____ drawings to a computer.

3. You can use _____ inches to measure how much space an object takes up.

4. Thinking that follows rules is called _____ .

Lesson 106   211

C CONTEXT CLUES

For each item, circle the answer that means the same thing as the word in bold type.

1. The actor used makeup to **enhance** the color of his eyebrows.
   a. shave   b. improve
   c. reduce   d. eliminate

2. Nobody dared to touch the **searing** pool of molten lead.
   a. heavy   b. screaming
   c. really hot   d. frozen

3. The crowd began to **disperse** after the game was over.
   a. argue   b. thin out
   c. cheer loudly   d. gather

D RELATED FACTS

Complete each sentence with *comet, meteor, meteorite,* or *meteoroid*.

1. An extraterrestrial rock that is falling toward Earth is called a _____.

2. An extraterrestrial rock that has landed on Earth is called a _____.

3. A large ball of ice and rock that orbits the sun is called a _____.

4. An extraterrestrial rock that has not entered Earth's atmosphere is called a _____.

5. The Perseids are one example of a _____ shower.

GO TO PART D IN YOUR TEXTBOOK

Lesson 106

Name _____

A STORY DETAILS

Note: To answer these questions, pretend you live in the same town as Mark Twain during the 1840s.

1. What is the name of your town?
   _____

2. In which state is your town located?
   _____

3. Your town is next to the
   _____ River.

4. Which one of these things does your bedroom have?
   a. heating   b. electricity
   c. furniture d. plumbing

5. You get water for your house from .
   a. a pipe   b. an outside pump
   c. plastic water bottles

6. Which piece of furniture holds the plates and the silverware?
   a. dishwasher   b. sideboard
   c. kitchen drawers

7. Which device does your father want to put on the roof of your house?
   a. water storage tank   b. solar panels
   c. TV antenna

8. You get to school by ___.
   a. walking   b. biking
   c. taking the bus   d. riding in a car

B CLOZE SENTENCES

Complete each sentence with the correct word.

| asteroid | nickel | tradition |
| landing | orbit | weekdays |

1. Some families have a _____ of eating waffles on Sunday.

2. Mika paused on the _____ before climbing the rest of the stairs.

3. The solar system consists of planets that _____ the sun.

4. Students usually go to school on _____ , but not on weekends.

C CONTEXT CLUES

For each item, circle the answer that means the same thing as the word in bold type.

1. The exit sign shone brightly at the end of the long **corridor.**

   a. particles   b. hallway

   c. atmosphere   d. extraterrestrial

2. You can get water out of the pump only by **cranking.**

   a. turning the pump on

   b. spinning the pump

   c. pressing a button

   d. moving the pump handle

3. The ground was covered with **particles** of rock after the meteor landed.

   a. small pieces   b. pictures

   c. big chunks   d. icicles

D MAPS

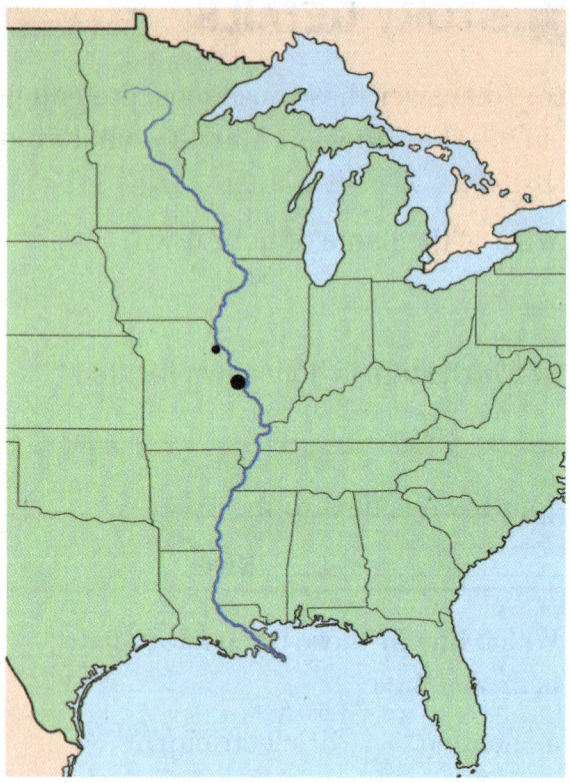

Work the items.

1. The blue line shows the _____ River.

2. In which main direction does that river flow? _____

3. The big dot shows a large city named St. _____ .

4. The small dot shows a town named _____ .

5. In which state are the two dots located? _____

GO TO PART D IN YOUR TEXTBOOK

Name _____

A STORY DETAILS

Work the items.

1. Which animals eat garbage in the streets of Hannibal?
    a. horses   b. pigs
    c. cows   d. goats

2. How many rooms does the school in Hannibal have? _____

3. How many teachers does the school have? _____

4. Most students leave the school when they are _____ years old.

5. The teacher keeps a pile of birch rods in a corner to ▇▇▇ .
    a. whack students who misbehave
    b. use as counting sticks
    c. use for firewood
    d. use in a science experiment

6. The country in "My country, 'tis of thee" is the _____ _____ .

7. Most goods are transported to and from Hannibal on ▇▇▇ .
    a. trains   b. highways
    c. the river d. planes

8. What new form of transportation was being used in the eastern states in the 1840s? _____

B CLOZE SENTENCES

Complete each sentence with the correct word.

| disperse | geography | tradition |
| enhance | legend | unmistakable |

1. The book contained a _____ about King Arthur and the Knights of the Round Table.

2. Nasir heard the _____ wail of a baby from the apartment next door.

3. Eating turkey is a _____ at Thanksgiving.

4. You can use an atlas to study the _____ of a country.

C CONTEXT CLUES

For each item, circle the answer that means the same thing as the word in bold type.

1. The wall was so **rigid** that nothing could bend it.
   a. searing   b. stiff
   c. soft-boiled d. craggy

2. The lion planned to **ambush** the zebra at the edge of the jungle.
   a. scan   b. gather
   c. crank   d. attack

3. The fence builder used a ruler to measure the **diameter** of the round fence post.
   a. width   b. height
   c. atmosphere d. forenoon

D MAPS

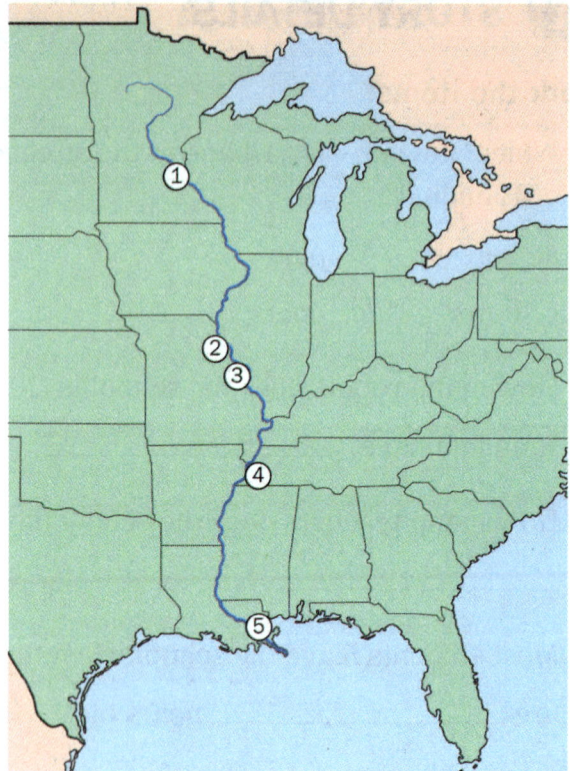

Work the items.

1. The map shows the _____ River.

2. City **1** is named _____.

3. City **5** is named _____.

4. Town **2** is named _____.

5. The city that's closest to town **2** is named _____.

GO TO PART D IN YOUR TEXTBOOK

Name _____ 109

A STORY DETAILS

Work the items.

1. The large boats that came to Hannibal were powered by ▒▒▒ engines.

    a. electric   b. gas

    c. steam   d. diesel

2. Those boats used ▒▒▒ to move through the water.

    a. oars   b. paddlewheels

    c. sails   d. rotors

3. Steamboats were better than sailboats for river travel because steamboats' ▒▒▒ didn't scrape the bottom of the river.

    a. masts   b. smokestacks

    c. hulls   d. forecastles

4. What other advantage did steamboats have over sailboats for river travel?

    a. Steamboats had more power to go upstream.

    b. Steamboats made less noise.

    c. Steamboats could carry passengers.

    d. Steamboats could carry freight.

5. Which direction will the steamboat go when it travels to St. Louis from Hannibal?

    a. upstream   b. downstream

    c. midstream

6. St. Louis has a ▒▒▒ that features a 161-year-old man and a mermaid.

    a. museum   b. play

    c. circus   d. movie

7. Show whether each good was **unloaded** from the steamboat or **loaded** onto the steamboat in Hannibal.

    a. fabrics: loaded   unloaded

    b. pigs: loaded   unloaded

    c. corn: loaded   unloaded

    d. furniture: loaded   unloaded

    e. tools: loaded   unloaded

    f. books: loaded   unloaded

    g. wheat: loaded   unloaded

B CLOZE SENTENCES

Complete each sentence with the correct word.

| bulky | geography | unmistakable |
| dwindle | legend | weekday |

1. The students used an atlas to study _____ .

2. The couch was so _____ that it didn't fit through the door.

3. The backpackers' supplies began to _____ when they hiked an extra day.

4. The story seemed real, but it was really just a _____ .

Lesson 109   217

C CONTEXT CLUES

For each item, circle the answer that means the same thing as the word in bold type.

1. The underwater rock poked a hole in the ship's **hull**.
   a. deck
   b. mast
   c. bottom and sides
   d. ambush

2. Cats loved to sleep on the **plush** chair because it was so soft.
   a. rigid
   b. fancy and expensive
   c. wooden
   d. cheap and flimsy

3. The store's shelves were filled with **merchandise**.
   a. pairs of dice
   b. items that weren't for sale
   c. goods
   d. merchants

D COMPARING CHARACTERS

Complete each sentence with *gambler, lawyer, peddler,* or *settler*.

1. The _____ carried tin boxes filled with goods for sale.

2. The _____ looked lost and bewildered.

3. The _____ carried important papers in a briefcase.

4. The _____ had a deck of cards in her pocket.

5. The _____ planned to start a farm.

E READING GRAPHS

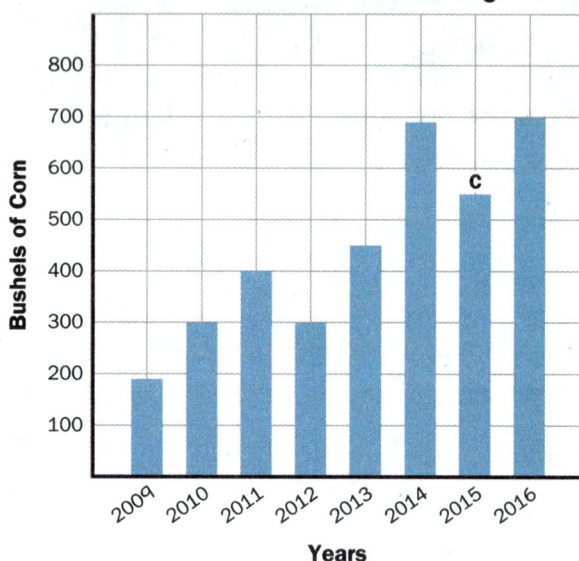

Corn Production on La Grange Farm

Work the items.

The graph above shows how many bushels of corn were produced on La Grange Farm from 2009 to 2016. The numbers along the left side tell how many bushels were produced in a year. The numbers along the bottom name the years.

1. In which year was corn production the lowest? _____

2. Did corn production increase or decrease from 2009 to 2010? _____

3. Corn production increased every year except for two. In which two years did corn production decrease?

   _____

4. Which year does bar C tell about?

   _____

5. How many bushels were produced in 2011? _____

GO TO PART D IN YOUR TEXTBOOK

Name _____ 110

A STORY DETAILS

Work the items.

1. In the article, what was the family's main activity after dinner?
   a. playing board games
   b. surfing the internet
   c. reading
   d. watching television

2. What was the name of the magazine from Philadelphia?
   a. *Better Homes and Gardens*
   b. *Godey's Lady's Book*
   c. *The New Yorker*
   d. *Sports Illustrated*

3. Which disease was common around Hannibal?
   a. yellow fever   b. cholera
   c. malaria   d. dropsy

4. Some doctors robbed graves in the 1840s because they wanted to ▢ .
   a. study dead bodies
   b. find jewelry
   c. bring people back to life
   d. reuse the coffins

5. In the 1840s, some children wore a spider on a necklace to ▢ .
   a. prevent malaria
   b. scare their friends
   c. heal a wound
   d. keep flies away

6. In the 1840s, some children tried to cure a toothache by touching the tooth with ▢ .
   a. a spider on a necklace
   b. the right eye of a wolf
   c. wood from a tree that's been struck by lightning
   d. toothpaste

7. Houses were quiet in the 1840s because they ▢ .
   a. had thicker walls and windows
   b. didn't have electrical appliances
   c. were all in the country
   d. didn't have any windows

B CLOZE SENTENCES

Complete each sentence with the correct word.

> bulky   hull   plush
> dwindle   merchandise   systematically

1. Alannah planted the vegetable garden _____ , moving up one row and down the next.

2. The suitcase was so _____ that it wouldn't fit into the trunk of the car.

3. The captain protected the _____ of the ship by steering clear of the jagged rocks.

4. The crowd began to _____ after the play was over.

Lesson 110

C CONTEXT CLUES

For each item, circle the answer that means the same thing as the word in bold type.

1. The customers were **jabbering** in the crowded restaurant.
   a. talking quickly   b. eating slowly
   c. listening silently   d. waiting

2. The restaurant used social media to **promote** their new menu.
   a. improve   b. criticize
   c. advertise   d. redesign

3. Some companies that were **established** a hundred years ago are still in business.
   a. bankrupt   b. sold
   c. set up   d. dreamed about

D MAPS

Work the items.

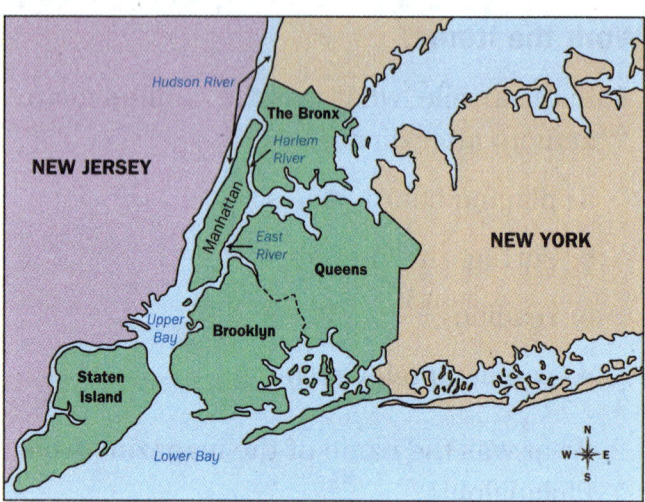

1. Which river runs along the west side of Manhattan?
   _____

2. Which river runs between Manhattan and Brooklyn?
   _____

3. What river runs between Manhattan and The Bronx?
   _____

4. Is Manhattan an island?
   _____

5. What is the name of the bay just south of Manhattan?
   _____

6. Which extends farther north, Manhattan or Queens?
   _____

GO TO PART D IN YOUR TEXTBOOK

Name _____

A STORY DETAILS

Work the items.

1. The story says that Aunt Polly's spectacles were built ▭ .
   a. for service   b. cheaply   c. for style

2. At the beginning of the novel, Tom was hiding ▭ .
   a. in the closet   b. under the bed
   c. outside

3. What had Tom been doing in that hiding place?
   a. eating jam
   b. fighting the Model Boy
   c. getting dressed

4. What did Tom say to escape from Aunt Polly?
   a. "I promise never to eat jam again, Aunt Polly."
   b. "My! Look behind you, Aunt Polly!"
   c. "Will you let me go outside if I wash my hands?"

5. Tom ▭ the Model Boy of the village.
   a. admired   b. hated   c. was

6. The newcomer was wearing a ▭ around his neck.
   a. chain   b. bandana   c. necktie

7. Who won the fight between Tom and the newcomer?

   _____

8. Tom got into his bedroom that night through the ▭ .
   a. front door   b. window   c. back door

9. What ambush was waiting for Tom in his bedroom?
   a. the Model Boy   b. the newcomer
   c. Aunt Polly

B CLOZE SENTENCES

Complete each sentence with the correct word.

| conscience | jabber | systematically |
| imaginary | smug | traitor |

1. You can do the right thing if you listen to your _____ .

2. The winner of the footrace had a _____ expression on her face.

3. Anton sorted the silverware _____ , with forks in one pile, spoons in another, and knives in a third.

4. When the teacher left the room, the students started to _____ with each other.

Lesson 111   221

C CONTEXT CLUES

For each item, circle the answer that means the same thing as the word in bold type.

1. The cake was **smothered** by frosting.
   a. promoted   b. dwindled
   c. covered   d. recited

2. Carlotta had to **sidle** around the other kids at the party.
   a. move sideways   b. take sides
   c. misbehave   d. gather

3. Aubri and Davina decided to **establish** a business selling lemonade on hot days.
   a. table   b. sniffle
   c. set up d. ambush

D READING GRAPHS

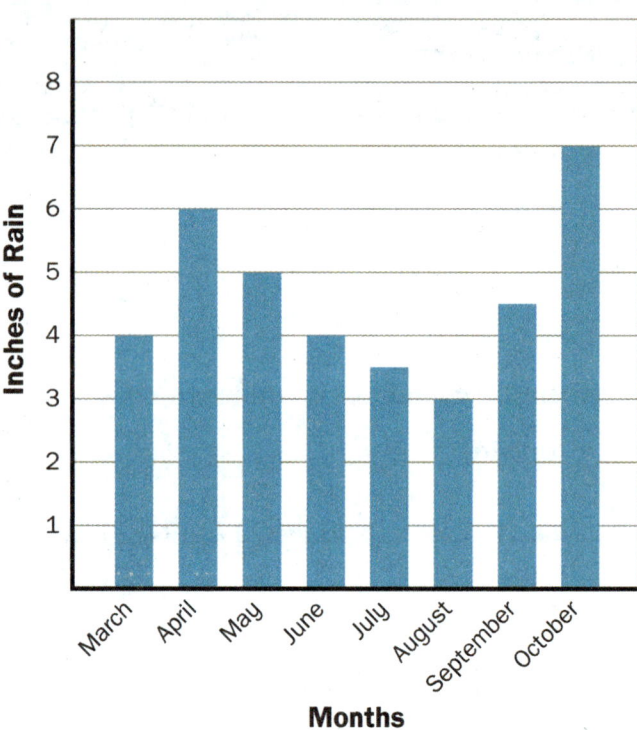

Assume the graph is accurate. Write whether each item *contradicts* or *doesn't contradict* the graph.

1. Seven inches of rain fell in April.

   _____

2. Four inches of rain fell in June.

   _____

3. September was the rainiest month.

   _____

4. The wettest months were during the summer.

   _____

5. Rainfall increased from summer to fall.

   _____

GO TO PART G IN YOUR TEXTBOOK

Name _____

A STORY DETAILS

Work the items.

1. Aunt Polly gave Tom the chore of _____ the fence.

2. What day of the week was it?
   _____

3. Tom's younger brother, _____, came through the gate with a tin pail.

4. That character was taking the pail to the town _____.

5. Who was the first boy to come by after Tom had his inspiration?
   a. Billy Fisher   b. Johnny Miller
   c. Ben Rogers

6. How did Tom actually feel about his chore?
   a. He loved doing it.
   b. He didn't want to do it.
   c. He didn't care one way or the other.

7. How did Tom pretend to feel about his chore?
   a. He loved doing it.
   b. He didn't want to do it.
   c. He didn't care one way or the other.

8. According to Tom's rule, how do you make somebody want something?
   a. Make the thing difficult to get.
   b. Make the thing easy to get.
   c. Offer it at a low price.

B CLOZE SENTENCES

Complete each sentence with the correct word.

| core | philosopher | systematically |
| establish | promote | thimble |

1. The _____ wrote a book about the meaning of life.

2. Nasir forgot to use a _____ when sewing, so his finger was bleeding.

3. Plums, apricots, and other stone fruit have a pit at their _____ .

4. The company used billboards to _____ its products.

Lesson 112   223

C CONTEXT CLUES

For each item, circle the answer that means the same thing as the word in bold type.

1. The pond was **tranquil** on the windless day.
   a. choppy
   b. absorbed
   c. sensational
   d. calm

2. After thinking all day, Emma had a sudden **inspiration** for how to solve the problem.
   a. jabber
   b. conscience
   c. brilliant idea
   d. stomachache

3. You need a telescope to **view** the planets.
   a. look closely at
   b. gimme
   c. perplex
   d. memorize

D LOGIC

Here's a rule of logic: *Just because you know about a part doesn't mean you know about the whole thing.*

The following statement by Liam breaks the rule: "That brown duck can swim underwater. Therefore, all brown birds can swim underwater."

Work the items.

1. Which thing in Liam's statement is the part?
   _____

2. Which thing in Liam's statement is the whole thing?
   _____

3. What conclusion does Liam draw about the whole thing?
   _____
   _____

4. Complete this statement: *Just because you know about a brown duck . . .*
   _____
   _____

GO TO PART E IN YOUR TEXTBOOK

Name _____   **113**

A STORY DETAILS

Work the items.

1. Aunt Polly was ▓▓ when she looked at the whitewashed fence.

   a. absorbed   b. ambushed   c. astonished

2. What game did Tom play in the public square?

   a. baseball   b. soccer   c. soldiers

3. What rank did Tom have in that game?

   a. captain   b. general   c. forward

4. The real first name of the Adored Unknown Girl was _____ .

5. Tom tried to win the girl's admiration by ▓▓ .

   a. calling to her
   b. giving her a present
   c. showing off

6. Before she went in the house, the girl threw a _____ over the fence.

7. Tom put that object next to his ▓▓ .

   a. heart   b. nose   c. belt

8. Who opened the window that Tom was lying underneath?

   a. Becky   b. Jeff   c. a maidservant

9. What did that person throw on Tom?

   a. flowers   b. water   c. trash

B CLOZE SENTENCES

Complete each sentence with the correct word.

| conscience | traitor | vision |
| imaginary | varied | worship |

1. The people traveled to a shrine to _____ a deity.

2. Ethan had a _____ of the future while he was daydreaming.

3. People brought wildly _____ foods to the potluck dinner.

4. Violet's _____ was troubled after she told a lie.

Lesson 113   **225**

C CONTEXT CLUES

For each item, circle the answer that means the same thing as the word in bold type.

1. Everyone laughed at the clown's **absurd** antics.

   a. smug b. ridiculous

   c. worldly d. long-handled

2. The winner of the tennis championship was so overcome with **emotion** that he couldn't speak.

   a. coughing b. sweat

   c. quicklime d. strong feeling

3. The campers **smothered** their fire with dirt before going to sleep.

   a. covered b. crumpled

   c. sidled d. whitewashed

D MAPS

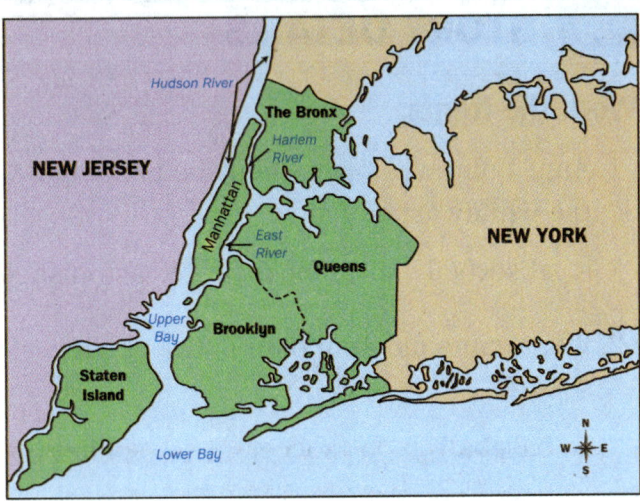

- The map of New York City above is accurate, but some of the statements below contradict the map.

Write whether each statement *contradicts* or *doesn't contradict* the map.

1. The Bronx is south of Queens.

   _____

2. Staten Island is west of Brooklyn.

   _____

3. The Harlem River flows between the East River and the Hudson River.

   _____

4. The Hudson River flows through Queens.

   _____

GO TO PART D IN YOUR TEXTBOOK

Name _____

114

A STORY DETAILS

Work the items.

1. On which day of the week did this chapter take place? _____

2. The Widow Douglas lived in a ▮▮▮ on the hill.
   a. hut   b. trailer   c. mansion

3. After the prayer, Tom captured a _____ with his hand.

4. The only thing Tom knew about the sermon was how many _____ it had.

5. After biting Tom, the pinch bug went into the ▮▮▮ .
   a. aisle   b. pew   c. box

6. A type of dog called a _____ began to play with the pinch bug.

7. That dog finally ▮▮▮ on the pinch bug.
   a. sat down   b. stepped   c. rolled

8. Afterward, the dog looked like a ▮▮▮ .
   a. blazing meteor   b. furry comet
   c. guided missile

B CLOZE SENTENCES

Complete each sentence with the correct word.

| droned | minister | sermon |
| justice | philosopher | view |

1. Carson and Cora were married by a _____ of the peace.

2. After the congregation sang the hymn, the _____ said a prayer.

3. As the speaker _____ on and on, the audience began to yawn and fidget.

4. The priest used a microphone to deliver his _____ in the large church.

Lesson 114   227

C CONTEXT CLUES

For each item, circle the answer that means the same thing as the word in bold type.

1. Molly **lapsed** into a daydream while lying on the grass.
   a. crumpled   b. sweated
   c. sank   d. perplexed

2. People walked **gingerly** because of the broken glass on the pavement.
   a. cautiously   b. sniffling
   c. without looking d. eagerly

3. Several skyscrapers were bunched together in the **core** of the city.
   a. thimble   b. inspiration
   c. choir   d. central part

4. It was hard to find a **tranquil** spot in the busy town.
   a. furry   b. bilious
   c. calm   d. frantic

D LOGIC

Here's a rule of logic: *Just because a person is an expert in one field doesn't mean that person is an expert in another field.*

The following statement breaks the rule: "Nadia Griggs is one of the funniest comedians in the world. She can make you laugh just by looking at you, and after two or three of her jokes, your sides are splitting. So if she recommends Marko jeans, you know they have to be good."

Work the items.

1. Who is the expert in the statement?
   _____

2. In which field is that person an expert?
   _____

3. What product does that person recommend?
   _____

4. Complete this statement: *Just because Nadia Griggs is an expert in comedy . . .*
   _____
   _____

GO TO PART D IN YOUR TEXTBOOK

Name _____ **115**

A STORY DETAILS

Work the items.

1. On which day of the week does this chapter take place? _____

2. Tom dreaded going to _____ .

3. The first ailment Tom considered was his _____ tooth.

4. The next ailment Tom considered was his _____ toe.

5. What word did Tom use to describe his toe to Aunt Polly? _____

6. Aunt Polly tied one end of a silk thread to Tom's tooth and the other end to the _____ .

7. Aunt Polly got Tom to jerk back by thrusting a piece of hot _____ toward his face.

8. Tom discovered that he could ▨ in a new way.
   a. spit   b. whistle   c. smile

B CLOZE SENTENCES

Complete each sentence with the correct word.

| absurd | mortified | vision |
| aggravated | varied | worship |

1. The mountain climber's fingers looked _____ , but she was still alive.

2. The driver got _____ by the traffic, so he began to yell.

3. The mayor had a _____ for how to improve the city.

4. The idea that a cow can jump over the moon is _____ .

Lesson 115

C CONTEXT CLUES

For each item, circle the answer that means the same thing as the word in bold type.

1. The belt was made of **genuine** leather that came from a cow.
   a. fake   b. real
   c. drowsing d. quicklime

2. The most common **ailment** is a cold.
   a. element   b. emotion
   c. experiment d. illness

3. The distance between Atlanta and Seattle is **considerable**.
   a. great   b. furry
   c. short   d. crumpled

D POINT OF VIEW

Tom told several lies in this chapter.

Write *truth* or *lie* for each statement.

1. "Don't move around, Sid, you'll kill me."
   _____

2. "Oh, please, Auntie, don't pull it out."
   _____

3. "I don't want to stay home from school."
   _____

4. "It aches perfectly awful."
   _____

E READING GRAPHS

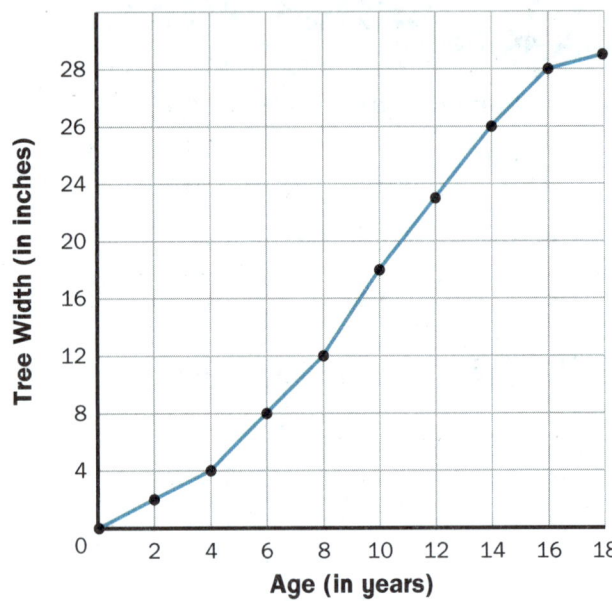

Width and Age of One Tree

Assume the graph is accurate. Write *contradictory* or *not contradictory* for each item.

1. The tree gets narrower as it ages.
   _____

2. When the tree was 12 years old, it was only 12 inches wide.
   _____

3. When the tree was eight years old, it was only eight inches wide.
   _____

4. The tree was wider when it was 12 years old than when it was 10 years old.
   _____

GO TO PART D IN YOUR TEXTBOOK

Name _____

116

A STORY DETAILS

Work the items.

1. All the mothers of the town ▨ Huckleberry Finn.

    a. admired   b. hated   c. avoided

2. The children of the town ▨ Huckleberry Finn.

    a. admired   b. hated   c. avoided

3. Circle one thing Huck had to do.

    a. go to school   b. take a bath

    c. wear clothes

4. Huck said you can use a dead rat to get rid of warts if you take it to a ▨ .

    a. tree stump   b. crossroads

    c. graveyard

5. Huck said you have to go to that place around _____ .

6. Then you have to throw the rat after a ▨ .

    a. witch   b. devil   c. bean

7. Huck said his method wouldn't work on a ▨ .

    a. Friday   b. Sunday   c. Monday

8. Which other animal did Huck have in his hands?

    a. tick   b. spider   c. frog

9. Tom traded his _____ to get Huck's animal.

B CLOZE SENTENCES

Complete each sentence with the correct word.

| enclosed | lapse | wart |
| justice | tick | wistful |

1. Like a spider, a _____ has eight legs.

2. The hungry girl became _____ when she thought about cake.

3. Justin _____ the letter in an envelope.

4. The _____ on Ashley's finger was caused by an infection.

5. The couple got married by a _____ of the peace.

C CONTEXT CLUES

For each item, circle the answer that means the same thing as the word in bold type.

1. Mura was still a **juvenile,** but she acted like an adult.
   a. minister
   b. corpse
   c. young person
   d. sermon

2. The bully was mean and **vulgar,** so nobody liked him.
   a. friendly
   b. vulnerable
   c. likeable
   d. crude

3. We had to step **gingerly** on the floor because of the broken glass.
   a. cautiously
   b. with ginger
   c. loudly
   d. barefoot

D COMPARING CHARACTERS

Complete each sentence with *Tom* or *Huck*.

1. _____ didn't have to go to school.

2. _____ was always the first boy to go barefoot in the spring.

3. _____ traded his tooth for a tick.

4. _____ knew how to get rid of warts with rats.

5. _____ had to go to church.

GO TO PART D IN YOUR TEXTBOOK

Name _____ **117**

A STORY DETAILS

Work the items.

1. Tom was late to school because he had been talking to

   _____ _____ .

2. The only vacant seat on the girls' side of the schoolhouse was next to the Adored

   _____ _____ .

3. The schoolmaster punished Tom for being late by making him sit on the

   _____ side of the room.

4. Tom drew a picture of a ▩ on his slate.
   a. peach   b. house   c. tick

5. The Adored Unknown Girl's real name was

   _____ _____ .

6. What three-word sentence did Tom write on his slate?

   _____

7. The full name of the boy Tom sat next to was

   _____ _____ .

8. Tom removed the _____ from the small box in his pocket.

9. The _____ put an end to the boys' game.

B CLOZE SENTENCES

Complete each sentence with the correct word.

| aggravated | harass | scrawl |
| ailment | mortified | slate |

1. The sheep wouldn't move, so the border collie began to _____ them.

2. Students in the 1800s used chalk to write on a _____ .

3. Other students wrote neatly, but Tom could only _____ a few words on his slate.

4. The doctors couldn't figure out what was causing the mystery _____ .

Lesson 117   233

C CONTEXT CLUES

For each item, circle the answer that means the same thing as the word(s) in bold type.

1. Two boys had a little **scuffle** to get first place in line.
   - a. genuine
   - b. short fight
   - c. scholar
   - d. considerable

2. The teacher **was critical of** the student's sloppy handwriting.
   - a. found fault with
   - b. investigated
   - c. restored
   - d. praised

3. The baker **prodded** the bread with her finger to see if it was fresh.
   - a. sliced
   - b. reddened
   - c. perplexed
   - d. poked

D COMPARING CHARACTERS

Complete each sentence with *Tom, Becky,* or *Joe.*

1. _____ was impressed with a picture on a slate.

2. _____ had better luck with the tick at the end of the game.

3. _____ wrote "I love you" on a slate.

4. _____ sat on both sides of the classroom.

5. _____ finally accepted a peach.

E METAPHORS

Work the items.

A faint wind moaned through the trees.

1. What is something that moans?
   _____
   _____

2. Write a statement that tells what the wind sounded like.
   _____
   _____

GO TO PART E IN YOUR TEXTBOOK

Name

A STORY DETAILS

Work the items.

1. Tom told Becky he wanted to be a ▓▓ when he grew up.
   a. cowboy   b. lawyer   c. clown

2. Tom asked Becky if she had ever been ▓▓.
   a. engaged   b. married   c. single

3. Tom made a blunder when he told Becky that he ▓▓.
   a. had already been engaged
   b. didn't love her
   c. wanted to get married

4. Tom tried to give Becky his brass _____ .

5. What did Becky do with that object?
   a. hit Tom with it
   b. threw it on the floor
   c. put it in her desk

6. What did Huck do to signal Tom later that night?
   a. yelled "Scat! You devil!"
   b. tossed an empty bucket
   c. meowed

7. What was Tom doing when the signal started?
   a. dressing   b. sleeping
   c. waiting impatiently

8. Tom moved along the roof by ▓▓.
   a. walking on two feet
   b. sliding on his stomach
   c. creeping on all fours

9. At the end of the chapter, Tom and Huck were wading through the tall grass of the _____ .

B CLOZE SENTENCES

Complete each sentence with the correct word.

| corpse | engaged | juvenile |
| enclosed | fours | scat |

1. Marina wore a ring on her finger to show that she was _____ to Mario.

2. The soldiers had to crawl on all _____ to get under the fence.

3. The birds decided to _____ when they saw the cat in the yard.

4. Even though Blake was an adult, he acted like a _____ .

C MAPS

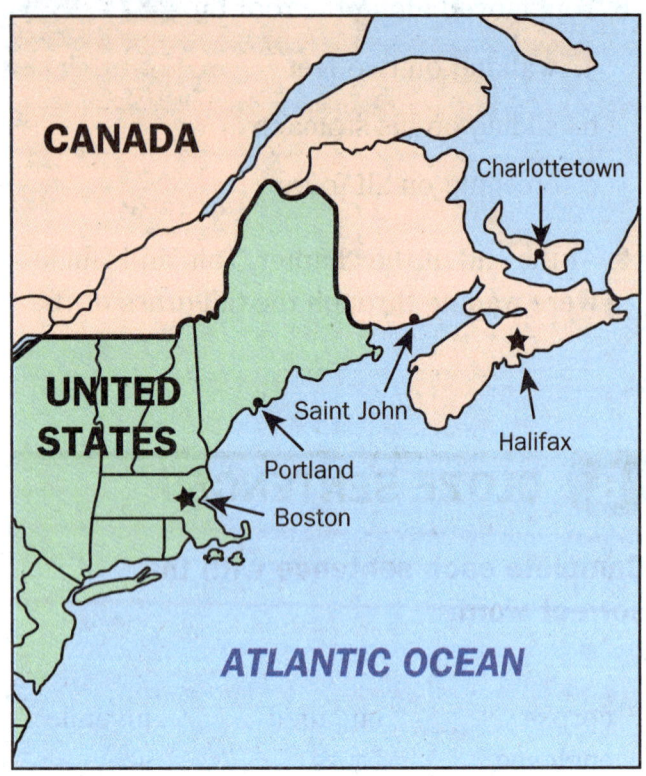

- The map above is accurate.
- Dots show cities with fewer than 100,000 people.
- Stars show cities with more than 100,000 people.

Write whether each item *contradicts* or *doesn't contradict* the map.

1. Saint John is larger than Halifax.
   _____

2. You can go from Charlottetown to Saint John without crossing any water.
   _____

3. Halifax is smaller than Charlottetown.
   _____

4. When you sail from Saint John to Charlottetown, you pass Halifax.
   _____

5. The only way from Boston to Halifax is by water.
   _____

D CONTEXT CLUES

For each item, circle the answer that means the same thing as the word in bold type.

1. Suki made a serious **blunder** on the test, so she failed.
   a. mistake   b. inspection
   c. wart   d. tick

2. The young man on the old bike looked **wistfully** at the fancy car.
   a. impatiently   b. timidly
   c. longingly   d. patiently

3. Burping in public is **vulgar** and unacceptable.
   a. crude   b. fateful
   c. admirable   d. social

GO TO PART D IN YOUR TEXTBOOK

Name _____

119

A STORY DETAILS

Work the items.

1. The grave markers were made of ▓▓ .
   a. stone   b. wood   c. metal

2. At first, Huck thought the approaching figures were ▓▓ .
   a. corpses   b. grave robbers   c. devils

3. What did two of the men do as the third sat by a tree?
   a. dug up a coffin   b. got into a fight
   c. approached through the gloom

4. The man who had sworn to get even with the doctor was named
   _____ _____ .

5. Which weapon was used to kill the doctor?
   a. a shovel   b. a gun   c. a knife

6. Which person thought he had killed the doctor?
   _____ _____

7. Which person really killed the doctor?
   _____ _____

8. The man who didn't kill the doctor began ▓▓ .
   a. blabbing   b. blubbering   c. blinking

B CLOZE SENTENCES

Complete each sentence with the correct word.

| coffin | organs | slate |
| critical | prod | tragedies |

1. The _____ was buried six feet under the ground.

2. Some plays are comedies, but others are _____ .

3. The students were very _____ of the cafeteria food.

4. Many of your _____ are inside your ribs.

Lesson 119   237

C CONTEXT CLUES

For each item, circle the answer that means the same thing as the word in bold type.

1. The toddler started **blubbering** when his mother left for work.
   - a. tiptoeing softly
   - b. idling
   - c. sobbing loudly
   - d. restoring

2. People often have to **grapple** with difficult problems.
   - a. wrestle
   - b. redden
   - c. mortify
   - d. grumble

3. When his arm was in a cast, Oscar could only **scrawl** his name.
   - a. quickly scuffle
   - b. carelessly write
   - c. harass
   - d. inward

D SEQUENCING

Number the events in order from 1 to 5.

____ The doctor argued with Outlaw Joe.

____ Outlaw Joe lied about what had happened.

____ The two boys heard voices approaching.

____ The men hoisted the coffin onto the ground.

____ The doctor was killed.

GO TO PART E IN YOUR TEXTBOOK

Name

A STORY DETAILS

Work the items.

1. Which three characters who were in the graveyard know who killed the doctor?

   _____

2. Which character who was in the graveyard doesn't know who killed the doctor?

   _____

3. Why doesn't that person know who killed the doctor?
   a. He's dead.   b. He was knocked out.
   c. He was looking the other way.

4. Tom and Huck's oath said they would ▇ if they ever told about what they saw.
   a. be quiet   b. run away
   c. drop down dead

5. Tom and Huck used their own _____ to sign their names to the oath.

6. According to Tom and Huck, what does it mean if a howling stray dog faces a person?
   a. The dog belongs to the person.
   b. The person will get rid of their warts.
   c. The person will die.

7. What sound did Tom and Huck hear from the other end of the building?
   a. snoring   b. howling   c. talking

B CLOZE SENTENCES

Complete each sentence with the correct word.

> blunder   initials   swear
> hooky   superstitious   whereabouts

1. Nobody knew the _____ of the missing children.

2. High school seniors play _____ on Senior Skip Day.

3. The judge made everyone _____ to tell the truth.

4. Londyn put her _____ on the basketball so people would know it belonged to her.

5. People who are _____ have many strange beliefs.

C CONTEXT CLUES

For each item, circle the answer that means the same thing as the word(s) in bold type.

1. The president made **an oath** to lead the country.
   a. a blubber   b. a scrawl
   c. a solemn promise   d. a temptation

2. The farmer told the wild turkeys to **scat** from her cornfield.
   a. eat the grain   b. go away
   c. take the eggs   d. clean the dirt

Lesson 120   239

D SUPERSTITIONS

The statements below show what Tom and Huck believed. For each statement, write *superstitious* or *not superstitious*.

1. You can get rid of warts with a dead rat.
   _____

2. Outlaw Joe is someone to fear.
   _____

3. You can wake somebody by meowing.
   _____

4. A howling dog means death.
   _____

5. Devils don't visit graveyards on Sunday.
   _____

E MAP READING

San Francisco Bay Area
- **LARGE CITIES**
- **Small cities**
- *Towns*

Assume the map is accurate. For each statement, write *contradictory* or *not contradictory*.

1. Oakland has more people than Santa Cruz.
   _____

2. San Francisco is west of Oakland.
   _____

3. Fremont is north of Oakland.
   _____

4. Santa Cruz has more people than San Jose. _____

5. San Jose has more people than Fremont.
   _____

GO TO PART D IN YOUR TEXTBOOK

Name _____   121

A STORY DETAILS

Work the items.

1. Which character was the stray dog facing when it howled? _____

2. Tom believed that character would ▓▓▓ because of the dog.
   a. wake up   b. get fleas   c. die

3. Tom discovered his brass _____ at his school desk.

4. The village was suddenly ▓▓▓ with the ghastly news of the murder.
   a. electrified   b. nailed   c. plumbed

5. All the village residents drifted toward the ▓▓▓ that afternoon.
   a. tannery   b. schoolhouse
   c. graveyard

6. The _____ led Muff Potter by the arm.

7. Tom and Huck thought _____ would strike Outlaw Joe for telling a lie.

8. Tom and Huck thought Joe had sold himself to the ▓▓▓ .
   a. doctor   b. sheriff   c. devil

B CLOZE SENTENCES

Complete each sentence with the correct word.

> coffin   grapple   tragedy
> forgiveness   organs   worm

1. Evangeline had to _____ her way through the dancers to get to the other side of the room.

2. Griffin begged for his mom's _____ after he forgot to wash the dishes.

3. Football players can hurt their _____ when they get tackled.

4. The airplane crash was a horrible _____ that killed many people.

Lesson 121   241

C CONTEXT CLUES

For each item, circle the answer that means the same thing as the word in bold type.

1. Everyone was frightened by the **ghastly** monster.
   - a. blubber
   - b. friendly
   - c. gas-filled
   - d. horrible

2. The crowd was **electrified** by the amazing circus.
   - a. excited
   - b. shocked
   - c. plugged in
   - d. sworn

3. The stray cat gave such a **pathetic** look that Jamal let it into the house.
   - a. lordly
   - b. downward
   - c. pitiful
   - d. worm-eaten

D FILLING OUT FORMS

Use the facts to fill out the form.

Facts: Your name is Kesia Andache. You live in Kenya, which is a country in Africa. You are applying for a passport so you can visit the United States, where your cousins live. You plan to visit for one month. Because you have so much time, you may visit other parts of the country after you see your cousins. You work for the Kenyan Computer Company, where you install memory boards in computers. This is the first time you have applied for a passport.

PRINT ALL ANSWERS IN CAPITAL LETTERS.

1. Write the first five letters of your last name.
   _____

2. Write the first three letters of your first name.
   _____

3. Which country do you desire to visit?
   _____

4. About how many weeks do you plan to stay?
   _____

5. What is the full name of your employer?
   _____
   _____

6. In which country do you reside?
   _____

GO TO PART D IN YOUR TEXTBOOK

Name _____

A STORY DETAILS

Work the items.

1. Tom's ▨ disturbed his sleep for as much as a week.

   a. snoring   b. sleepwalking   c. secret

2. In his sleep, Tom said, "Don't ▨ me so—I'll tell."

   a. resent   b. prevent   c. torment

3. How did Tom keep himself from talking in his sleep?

   a. He tied up his jaws.
   b. He stuffed his mouth with cotton.
   c. He put a pillow over his head.

4. The gifts that Tom gave to Muff Potter helped ease Tom's ▨.

   a. confidence   b. conscience
   c. consciousness

5. When Becky stopped coming to school, there was nothing but ▨ for Tom.

   a. dreariness   b. happiness
   c. cleanliness

6. Tom tried to get news of Becky from ▨.

   a. Huck   b. Jeff   c. Sid

7. Tom did all the ▨ things he could think of to get Becky's attention.

   a. heroic   b. pathetic   c. organic

8. At the end of the chapter, Tom was crushed and ▨.

   a. crestfallen   b. triumphant   c. ghastly

B CLOZE SENTENCES

Complete each sentence with the correct word.

> crestfallen   heroic   swear
> handspring   superstitious   whereabouts

1. Odysseus is known for his many _____ actions.

2. Imena was _____ when Jamal didn't return her phone call.

3. The police can track your cell phone to figure out your _____ .

4. The gymnast did a cartwheel and then a _____ .

Lesson 122

C CONTEXT CLUES

For each item, circle the answer that means the same thing as the word(s) in bold type.

1. People at the zoo loved to watch the monkey's **antics**.
   a. ants and ticks
   b. aunts
   c. initials
   d. funny actions

2. Doctors make **an oath** to do no harm.
   a. a checkup
   b. a solemn promise
   c. a hooky
   d. an oaf

3. Amina's full name was Amina Barnes Cooley, so **her initials** were ABC.
   a. the last letters of her full name
   b. the first letters of her last name
   c. the first letters of her full name
   d. her nickname

D SEQUENCING

Number the events in order from 1 to 5.

____ Becky found out Tom had been engaged before.

____ Tom was ordered to sit next to Becky in school.

____ Tom was crestfallen when Becky ignored his antics.

____ Becky returned Tom's brass doorknob.

____ Tom and Becky became engaged to be married.

E MAPS

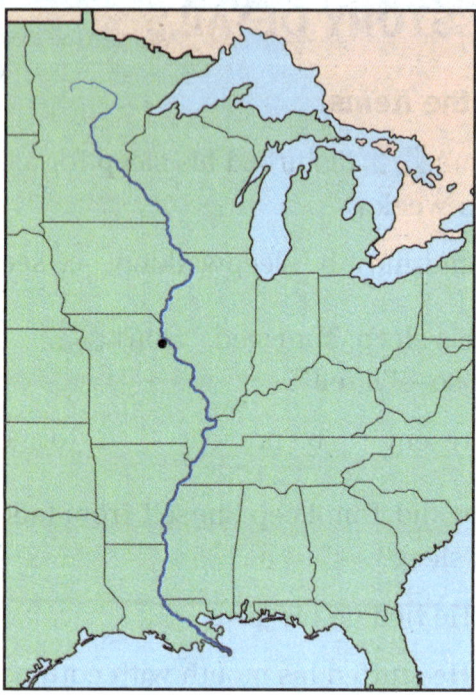

Work the items.

1. The map shows the _____ River in blue.

2. In which main direction does the river flow? _____

3. The big paddlewheel boats that used the river in the 1840s were called _____.

4. The dot shows a town. The real name of that town is _____.

5. In the novel *Tom Sawyer*, that town is called St. _____.

GO TO PART D IN YOUR TEXTBOOK

Name

A STORY DETAILS

Work the items.

1. Tom flirted with _____ Lawrence.

2. Becky invited the other students to a _____ .

3. Which male character did not ask for an invitation to that event?
   _____ _____

4. Becky looked at a _____ book with Alfred Temple.

5. When Tom saw Alfred and Becky sitting together, Tom burned with ▓▓▓ .
   a. pity   b. jealousy
   c. a high temperature

6. How were Becky and Tom the same in this chapter?
   a. They flirted to get revenge.
   b. They made up with each other.
   c. They fell in love with somebody else.

7. What did Alfred do to spite Tom?
   a. spilled ink on Tom's spelling book
   b. got into a fight with Tom
   c. convinced Amy to leave Tom

8. Becky decided to let Tom get punished because she ▓▓▓ .
   a. wanted the brass doorknob back
   b. was still in love with him
   c. remembered how he had ignored her invitation to the picnic

B CLOZE SENTENCES

Complete each sentence with the correct word.

| electrified | forgiveness | intolerable |
| flirt | ghastly | random |

1. The hot weather was _____ for the polar bear.

2. Kata began to _____ with Karl, even though she didn't like him.

3. Vanessa begged for Leroy's _____ after she stepped on his toes.

4. The teacher chose students at _____ to answer questions.

Lesson 123

C CONTEXT CLUES

For each item, circle the answer that means the same thing as the word(s) in bold type.

1. Vani ate too much dinner, so she **was indifferent** about dessert.
   - a. differed
   - b. didn't care
   - c. inquired
   - d. was anxious

2. The poor man **was jealous of** his rich neighbor's fancy car.
   - a. envied
   - b. forgave
   - c. purchased
   - d. borrowed

3. Everybody screamed when the **ghastly** monster appeared on the movie screen.
   - a. pathetic
   - b. worm-like
   - c. horrid
   - d. watchdog

D COMPARING CHARACTERS

Complete each sentence with *Tom, Becky,* or *Tom and Becky*.

1. _____ flirted with another character.

2. _____ looked at pictures with another character.

3. _____ had an imaginary fight with another character.

4. _____ acted one way but felt another way.

GO TO PART D IN YOUR TEXTBOOK

Name _____

A STORY DETAILS

Work the items.

1. The schoolmaster, Mr. Dobbins, had always wanted to be a _____.

2. Mr. Dobbins kept an _____ book in his desk.

3. The book had a picture of a _____ man.

4. Which character tore the picture?
   a. Tom   b. Alfred   c. Becky

5. Tom received two punishments that afternoon. What was Tom punished for the first time?
   a. being late to school
   b. spilling ink on his spelling book
   c. tearing the picture

6. What was Tom punished for the second time?
   a. being late to school
   b. spilling ink on his spelling book
   c. tearing the picture

7. What was Tom's punishment for the second incident?
   a. staying after school
   b. sitting with the girls
   c. standing in the corner

8. After Tom took Becky's punishment, she said, "Tom, how *could* you be so _____!"

B CLOZE SENTENCES

Complete each sentence with the correct word.

anatomy   frustration   heroic
antics   handspring   proceedings

1. The trial began with long and formal _____.

2. Obi made faces, walked backwards, wiggled his ears, and performed many other _____.

3. The _____ lifeguard saved a boy from drowning.

4. Doctors spend a lot of time studying the _____ of the human body.

Lesson 124   247

C CONTEXT CLUES

For each item, circle the answer that means the same thing as the word in bold type.

1. Taking a test without studying is **folly**.
   a. funny   b. intent
   c. grating   d. a foolish act

2. The soldiers lined up in **ranks** across the field.
   a. tanks   b. rows
   c. circles   d. random groups

3. Ricardo was **crestfallen** after his team lost the game.
   a. disappointed   b. lighthearted
   c. absentminded   d. sorer

D POINT OF VIEW

Write whether each statement by Tom is *true* or *false*.

1. "I tore the anatomy book."
   _____

2. "I didn't spill ink on my spelling book."
   _____

3. "I stopped to talk to Huckleberry Finn."
   _____

4. "Amy, I love you more than I love Becky."
   _____

5. "Becky, I've never been engaged before."
   _____

GO TO PART D IN YOUR TEXTBOOK

Name _____

A STORY DETAILS

Work the items.

1. Tom started to write a _____ but abandoned it after three days.

2. Which one of these events was cancelled?
   a. minstrel show   b. circus
   c. Fourth of July parade

3. Muff Potter's trial stirred the sleepy ▓▓ of the town.
   a. electricity b. atmosphere c. circus

4. Huck and Tom knew Muff Potter was ▓▓ of the murder.
   a. guilty   b. innocent   c. unaware

5. The boys had made an oath to ▓▓ .
   a. keep quiet   b. tell the truth
   c. forgive Joe

6. How had Muff Potter helped Tom in the past?
   a. He gave Tom half a fish.
   b. He mended Tom's kites.
   c. He stood by Tom when Tom was out of luck.

7. What feeling did Muff Potter have for the boys?
   a. contempt   b. indifference
   c. gratitude

8. Some people said that Muff was the bloodiest-looking ▓▓ in the country.
   a. fisherman   b. butcher   c. villain

B CLOZE SENTENCES

Complete each sentence with the correct word.

| diary | indifferent | isolated |
| flirt | intolerable | lynch |

1. Kareem wrote in his _____ every night.

2. The mob wanted to _____ the suspect without giving him a trial.

3. Their house is so _____ that nobody visits them.

4. Dafna's pain was _____ , so she began to scream.

Lesson 125   249

C CONTEXT CLUES

For each item, circle the answer that means the same thing as the word in bold type.

1. In January, the Super Bowl is a frequent **topic** of discussion.
   a. abuse   b. captive
   c. pang   d. subject

2. In the movie, everyone feared the **villain** from outer space.
   a. villager   b. evil person
   c. sufferer   d. random person

3. The courtroom had a tense **atmosphere** that made everyone nervous.
   a. mood   b. jealousy
   c. difficulty d. greatness

D COMPARING CHARACTERS

Complete each sentence with *keep* or *break*.

1. Muff Potter may be hanged if Tom and Huck _____ their oath to remain silent.

2. Huck and Tom may be in serious danger from Outlaw Joe if they _____ their oath.

3. Outlaw Joe may go free if Tom and Huck _____ their oath.

4. Huck and Tom will feel cowardly and treacherous if they _____ their oath.

GO TO PART D IN YOUR TEXTBOOK

E READING GRAPHS

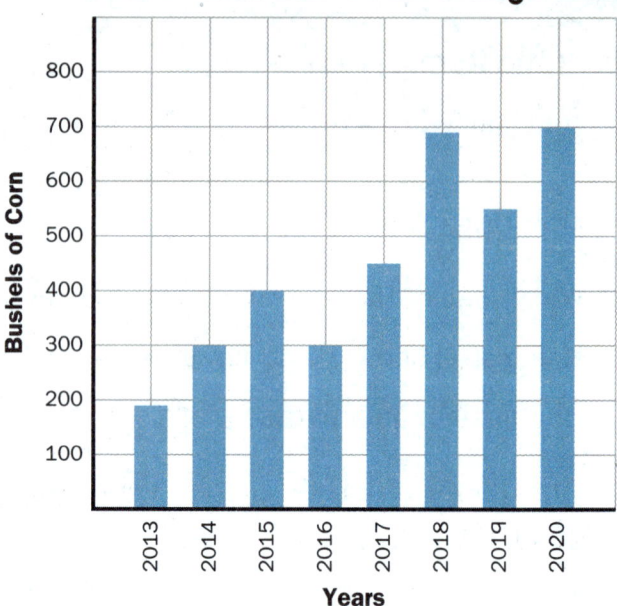

Corn Production on La Grange Farm

Assume the graph is accurate. Write *contradictory* or *not contradictory* for each item.

1. The year 2019 was the least productive year for corn. _____

2. The farm produced more corn in 2018 than in 2016. _____

3. Four hundred bushels of corn were produced in 2015. _____

4. Corn production decreased from 2013 to 2015. _____

Name

A STORY DETAILS

- Pretend you are Tom Sawyer.

Work the items.

1. On the seventeenth of June, about the hour of midnight, you were in the _____.

2. Were you anywhere near Horse Williams's grave? _____

3. You were hiding behind the ▇ trees on the edge of the grave.
   a. oak   b. birch   c. elm

4. Was anybody with you?
   _____

5. You were carrying a dead _____.

6. You thought that dead object would cure _____.

7. Who killed the doctor?
   _____ _____

8. Why didn't you tell your story before?
   a. Outlaw Joe said he would kill me if I told.
   b. I was afraid to tell.
   c. I didn't see what happened.

B CLOZE SENTENCES

Complete each sentence with the correct word.

| anatomy | elms | haggard |
| climax | folly | ranks |

1. The detective found the killer at the _____ of the story.

2. The city planted _____ along its streets to give shade.

3. Medical students spend a lot of time learning about human _____.

4. The players arranged their pieces in _____ across the game board.

Lesson 126   251

C CONTEXT CLUES

For each item, circle the answer that means the same thing as the word(s) in bold type.

1. The red car was **a trifle** bigger than the blue car.

    a. much b. sorely

    c. slightly d. scornfully

2. The judge asked the jury if they had reached a **verdict.**

    a. proceeding b. frustration

    c. decision d. denial

3. Troy looked **haggard** after three days without sleep.

    a. absent b. sick and tired

    c. immortal d. unshaken

D CONTRADICTIONS

Work the items.

Grady was testifying at Muff Potter's trial. He said, "Yes, I saw Muff Potter commit the murder. I remember it as if it were yesterday. I happened to be out for a late-night walk. The air was calm, and the whole town was asleep. Suddenly, I heard men arguing. I ran toward the sound and arrived just in time to see Muff Potter commit the fatal deed. Unfortunately, I was unable to see where he went afterward because the sun got in my eyes. However, I have no doubt he was the one who did it."

1. Underline the statement you assume to be true.

2. Draw a wavy line below the contradiction.

3. Write an *if-then* statement that explains the contradiction.

   _____

   _____

   _____

GO TO PART E IN YOUR TEXTBOOK

Name _____

A STORY DETAILS

Work the items.

1. Tom had ▉▉ desire to dig for hidden treasure.
   a. an indifferent   b. a raging
   c. a lack of

2. Which boy didn't plan to save his share of the treasure? _____

3. What was that boy's reason for not saving the treasure?
   a. His father would spend it.
   b. He didn't have a bank account.
   c. He didn't want any treasure.

4. The boys dug for treasure near a ▉▉ tree.
   a. healthy   b. freshly planted
   c. dead-limb

5. Tom said they didn't find treasure near the tree because _____ might have interfered.

6. The boys agreed to find a spot ▉▉ .
   a. where the shadow of the limb falls at midnight
   b. under the floor of a haunted house
   c. on an island

7. Huck planned to signal Tom that night by ▉▉ .
   a. barking
   b. throwing pebbles at his window
   c. meowing

B CLOZE SENTENCES

Complete each sentence with the correct word.

| confidentially | interfere | pick |
| diary | lynch | yonder |

1. The miner used a _____ to dig the tunnel.

2. The president spoke _____ with her top advisers about state secrets.

3. You can see my house _____ , at the end of the field.

4. You can get a foul if you _____ with another player's shot in basketball.

C CONTEXT CLUES

For each item, circle the answer that means the same thing as the word in bold type.

1. The hat covered the boy's hair and **brow**.
   a. ears
   b. forehead
   c. neck
   d. chin

2. Funeral homes have a gloomy **atmosphere**.
   a. isolation
   b. detective
   c. secrecy
   d. mood

3. Tee shirts cost ten dollars **apiece** at the clothing store.
   a. each
   b. for each sleeve
   c. a dozen
   d. per foot

4. The pirate was a well-known **villain** who terrified people.
   a. clown
   b. evil person
   c. sailor
   d. actor

D COMPARING CHARACTERS

Complete each sentence with *Tom*, *Huck*, or *Tom and Huck*.

1. _____ wanted to get married.

2. _____ knew where to dig for treasure.

3. _____ thought all girls were the same.

4. _____ had superstitious beliefs.

5. _____ feared Outlaw Joe.

GO TO PART D IN YOUR TEXTBOOK

Name _____ 128

A STORY DETAILS

Work the items.

1. Huck and Tom started digging when they judged that ▓▓ had come.
   a. ghosts   b. midnight   c. noon

2. They dug where the ▓▓ of the limb fell.
   a. leaves   b. bark   c. shadow

3. The next place they decided to try was the _____ house.

4. The boys thought the blue lights inside that place were caused by _____ .

5. Which day of the week did the boys think was unlucky? _____

6. What was the full name of the Englishman who robbed the rich and gave to the poor?
   _____ _____

7. On which day of the week did the boys climb up a ruined staircase?
   _____

8. Why did the boys lie down on the floor at the end of the chapter?
   a. They were tired from digging.
   b. They wanted to look downstairs.
   c. They didn't want to be seen.

B CLOZE SENTENCES

Complete each sentence with the correct word.

| climax | intruder | verdict |
| interfere | trifle | whiten |

1. The _____ in the rich person's home was a jewel thief.

2. Mister Granger used bleach to _____ his family's dirty sheets.

3. The criminal was taken to jail after receiving a guilty _____ .

4. The soccer player tried to _____ with the other team's passes.

Lesson 128   255

C CONTEXT CLUES

For each item, circle the answer that means the same thing as the word in bold type.

1. The blue team was **utterly** defeated by the red team.
   a. scornfully   b. absently
   c. completely   d. dreamily

2. At midnight, the stray dog began **baying** at the full moon.
   a. circusing   b. lingering
   c. grating   d. howling

3. Everyone took pity on the **haggard** child.
   a. sick and tired   b. healthy and wise
   c. isolated   d. distressing

D SUPERSTITIONS

Write whether each statement is *superstitious* or *not superstitious*.

1. Friday is an unlucky day.
   _____

2. Ghosts live in haunted houses.
   _____

3. Houses should be kept clean.
   _____

4. A dead man might say something.
   _____

5. Friday is just like any other day.
   _____

GO TO PART D IN YOUR TEXTBOOK

Name _____ 129

A STORY DETAILS

Work the items.

1. Outlaw Joe disguised himself as a deaf and _____ person.

2. Joe planned to do a dangerous job in St. _____ .

3. The men planned to travel to the state of _____ after Joe finished the dangerous job.

4. When Tom tried to leave, he brought a ▮ creak from the floor.
   a. hilarious   b. hideous   c. hidden

5. What type of metal did Joe and his friend have in their bag?
   a. bronze   b. silver   c. gold

6. The box that Joe discovered was made of ▮ .
   a. steel   b. gold   c. iron

7. The coins inside the box were made of ▮ .
   a. copper   b. silver   c. gold

8. The men agreed to put the treasure in hiding place Number _____ .

9. That hiding place was under a _____ .

B CLOZE SENTENCES

Complete each sentence with the correct word.

| apiece | eternity | pick |
| brow | interfere | yonder |

1. Sailing across the ocean seemed to take an _____ .

2. At the ballpark, the hot dogs cost five dollars _____ .

3. The mountain over _____ is ten thousand feet high.

4. You have to use a _____ to break up hard soil.

Lesson 129   257

C CONTEXT CLUES

For each item, circle the answer that means the same thing as the word in bold type.

1. The travelers felt **blissful** when they reached their destination at last.
   a. confidential   b. distressing
   c. joyful   d. insecure

2. The grave robbers used shovels to **unearth** the coffin.
   a. bury   b. dig up
   c. secure   d. abuse

3. Rosemary couldn't sleep because of the **infernal** howling of the coyotes.
   a. brightly moonlit
   b. somewhat suspect
   c. very annoying
   d. mortal

D SEQUENCING

Number the events in order from 1 to 4.

____ Outlaw Joe did a job "up the river."

____ Outlaw Joe ran away from the murder trial.

____ Outlaw Joe found a box full of gold.

____ Outlaw Joe killed the doctor.

E MAPS

- The map above is accurate, but some of the statements contradict what is shown on the map.

Circle *contradictory* or *not contradictory* for each statement.

1. New Orleans is south of Memphis.
   contradictory   not contradictory

2. The Mississippi River flows into the Gulf of Mexico.
   contradictory   not contradictory

3. St. Louis is in the state of Missouri.
   contradictory   not contradictory

4. The Mississippi River touches twelve states.
   contradictory   not contradictory

5. Arkansas is north of Iowa.
   contradictory   not contradictory

GO TO PART D IN YOUR TEXTBOOK

Name _____ 130

A STORY DETAILS

Work the items.

1. Why didn't Outlaw Joe reach the second floor of the haunted house?
   a. He never tried to reach it.
   b. He couldn't unlock the door to the stairs.
   c. He fell through the stairs.

2. The boys thought that Outlaw Joe wanted to get revenge on ▨ .
   a. Huck and Tom   b. Muff Potter
   c. the sheriff

3. Tom thought that all references to "hundreds" and "thousands" were ▨ .
   a. exaggerations   b. completely untrue
   c. understated

4. What kind of boat was Huck sitting on when Tom found him?
   a. steamboat   b. sailboat   c. flatboat

5. Tom thought Number Two was a house number. What was wrong with that idea?
   a. Houses in St. Petersburg had bigger numbers.
   b. There were no house numbers in St. Petersburg.
   c. Several houses were Number Two.

6. Because of the problem with house numbers, the boys thought Number Two might be a _____ room.

7. Why did that room seem like a good hiding place?
   a. It was underground.
   b. It had no doors.
   c. It was locked at all times.

8. What objects did the boys plan to use to enter Number Two?
   a. keys   b. sledgehammers   c. saws

B CLOZE SENTENCES

Complete each sentence with the correct word.

| baying | intruder | one-horse |
| flatboat | namely | whiten |

1. Some types of toothpaste claim they can _____ your teeth.

2. The sailors used a _____ to take barrels across the shallow river.

3. Nothing ever happens in this _____ town.

4. There are three parts to every day, _____ , morning, afternoon, and night.

Lesson 130   259

C CONTEXT CLUES

For each item, circle the answer that means the same thing as the word(s) in bold type.

1. The campers were **utterly** scared when the rattlesnake entered their tent.
   a. deepening
   b. critically
   c. barely
   d. completely

2. Ruben was untidy, and his room was filled with **clutter**.
   a. rough estimates
   b. a confused mess
   c. deep misery
   d. a shanty

3. The teacher **made a reference to** tomorrow's test.
   a. mentioned
   b. studied for
   c. recalled
   d. suspected

D COMPARING CHARACTERS

Complete each sentence with *Tom*, *Huck*, or *Outlaw Joe*.

1. "I have to do that revenge job," said _____.

2. "My adventure yesterday must have been a dream," said _____.

3. "I'll take this treasure to Number Two," said _____.

4. "I guess I'll sleep in this barrel tonight," said _____.

GO TO PART D IN YOUR TEXTBOOK

Name _____

A STORY DETAILS

Work the items.

1. While Tom tried to enter the hotel room, Huck ▨ .
   a. stood sentry
   b. went back to his barrel
   c. lay down to rest

2. Why was Tom able to get into the room?
   a. One of the keys opened the door.
   b. He crawled through a window.
   c. The door was not locked.

3. Outlaw Joe was sleeping on the ▨ inside the room.
   a. bed   b. couch   c. floor

4. Why did the boys need to go back to the room?
   a. They wanted to find the treasure.
   b. They needed to get the towel back.
   c. They needed to wake up Outlaw Joe.

5. Which friend of Tom's returned to the village on Friday? _____

6. Which day of the week was the picnic scheduled for? _____

7. Tom planned to visit the Widow _____ after the picnic.

8. For Tom, the sure fun of the evening at the widow's outweighed the ▨ .
   a. children's picnic
   b. uncertain treasure
   c. good night's sleep

B CLOZE SENTENCES

Complete each sentence with the correct word.

> charter   infernal   rollick
> eternity   profound   slaughterhouse

1. The butcher bought meat from a _____ .

2. The school had to _____ a bus for the field trip.

3. The silence was so _____ that Toshi couldn't hear a thing.

4. Children like to _____ in playgrounds.

Lesson 131   261

C CONTEXT CLUES

For each item, circle the answer that means the same thing as the word in bold type.

1. After many months of courtship, Poloma finally **consented** to marry Saleem.
   a. agreed   b. estimated
   c. interfered d. reflected

2. The sisters **resembled** each other in their height and hair color.
   a. rejected   b. suspected
   c. were like   d. unearthed

3. The castle was protected by a **sentry** who stood at the gate.
   a. moat   b. dragon
   c. guard   d. blissful

4. It was hard to walk in the **throng** of people downtown.
   a. absence   b. uncertainty
   c. secrecy   d. crowd

D STORY REVIEW

Complete each sentence with *novel, short story, poem,* or *play.*

1. "Earth and Water and Sky" is a _____.

2. *All in Favor* is a _____.

3. "Miracles" is a _____.

4. *The Adventures of Tom Sawyer* is a _____.

5. "Casey at the Bat" is a _____.

GO TO PART E IN YOUR TEXTBOOK

Name _____

A STORY DETAILS

Work the items.

1. What type of boat took the children to the picnic?

    a. flatboat   b. sailboat   c. steamboat

2. After eating, the children played in ▨ Cave.

    a. McDonald's   b. McDougal's

    c. McCormick's

3. The cave was like ▨ .

    a. a racetrack   b. a maze   c. an open pit

4. The sky was almost _____ when the children returned to the mouth of the cave.

5. What was Huck doing when the children returned to the village?

    a. watching the hotel

    b. walking past the quarry

    c. stepping on a twig

6. Huck followed the two men to the _____ Douglas's house.

7. Huck ran to the ▨ house for help.

    a. Englishman's   b. Irishman's

    c. Welshman's

8. At the end of the chapter, Huck heard an explosion of ▨ .

    a. firecrackers   b. fire alarms

    c. firearms

B CLOZE SENTENCES

Complete each sentence with the correct word.

| clutter | flatboat | one-horse |
| elude | namely | quarry |

1. The robber ran down an alley to _____ the police.

2. All the limestone in the courthouse came from the same _____ .

3. There are two parts to every screwdriver, _____ , the handle and the blade.

4. There wasn't even a stoplight in the _____ town.

Lesson 132 263

C CONTEXT CLUES

For each item, circle the answer that means the same thing as the word(s) in bold type.

1. The softball coach told Karina not to **flinch** when it was her turn at bat.
   a. romp gaily
   b. show fear
   c. drag bunt
   d. slumber loudly

2. The kayakers pulled into **an inlet** on the south side of the lake.
   a. a reference
   b. a large outlet
   c. an estate
   d. a small bay

3. The old watch was so **intricate** that no one could fix it.
   a. inaccurate
   b. complex
   c. catlike
   d. dogged

D STORY STRUCTURE

Write whether the events in each item take place *at the same time* or *at different times.*

1. The steamboat goes past the wharf.

   Huck watches the hotel.

   _____

2. The children play in the cave.

   Huck follows the two men.

   _____

3. Huck runs to the Welshman's house.

   Outlaw Joe waits for the lights to go out at the Widow Douglas's house.

   _____

GO TO PART D IN YOUR TEXTBOOK

Name _____ 133

A STORY DETAILS

Work the items.

1. On what day of the week does this chapter take place? _____

2. As the Welshman was sneaking up on the scoundrels, he ▨ .
   a. coughed   b. slipped   c. sneezed

3. The Welshman stopped chasing the scoundrels when he lost the _____ of their feet.

4. Huck made a mistake when he said the "deaf and silent" man could _____ .

5. Who was the "deaf and silent" man?
   _____ _____

6. The scoundrels left a bundle of _____ tools behind.

7. Huck thought the treasure was still in the ▨ .
   a. hotel   b. bundle   c. haunted house

8. The Welshman's eyes kept ▨ deeper and deeper into Huck.
   a. blinking   b. staring   c. boring

B CLOZE SENTENCES

Complete each sentence with the correct word.

| consent | relieve | scoundrel |
| profound | resemble | slaughterhouse |

1. Big Al was the only _____ daring enough to steal the police car.

2. Using a flashlight can _____ your fear of the dark.

3. The silence was so _____ that no one dared to say a word.

4. It's not wise to _____ to an agreement you don't understand.

Lesson 133   265

C CONTEXT CLUES

For each item, circle the answer that means the same thing as the word in bold type.

1. The boss asked Natasha to be her **deputy**.
   a. charter   b. sentry
   c. throng   d. assistant

2. Four strong **chaps** carried the giant box on their shoulders.
   a. oxen   b. men
   c. couples   d. firearms

3. Kara needed time to **reflect** about the company's job offer.
   a. think carefully   b. rollick
   c. be upset   d. tell everyone

D COMPARING CHARACTERS

Complete each sentence with *Huck* or *Tom*.

1. _____ was not good at telling lies.

2. _____ was very good at telling lies.

3. _____ planned to spend the night at the Widow Douglas's.

4. _____ did not go to the picnic.

5. _____ saved the Widow Douglas's life.

GO TO PART D IN YOUR TEXTBOOK

Name _____

A STORY DETAILS

- The main characters in *Tom Sawyer* were at several different locations at the end of this chapter.

Complete each sentence with *the cave*, *Tom Sawyer's house*, *the Welshman's house*, or *unknown*.

1. Huck's location was
   _____.

2. Tom's location was
   _____.

3. Aunt Polly's location was
   _____.

4. Outlaw Joe's location was
   _____.

5. Becky's location was
   _____.

6. The Widow Douglas's location was
   _____.

7. Judge Thatcher's location was
   _____.

8. Sid's location was
   _____.

B CLOZE SENTENCES

Complete each sentence with the correct word.

| elude | intricate | relic |
| flinch | quarry | whiskey |

1. You have to be an adult to buy
   _____.

2. The windup watch was a
   _____ from the 1950s.

3. The poor mouse was unable to
   _____ the wily cat.

4. The silver necklace was so
   _____ that it looked like a spiderweb.

C SETTINGS

Complete each sentence with *Hannibal*, *Ithaca*, *London*, or *Oakland*.

1. Odysseus lived on the island of
   _____.

2. *The Cruise of the Dazzler* takes place near
   _____.

3. The St. Petersburg in *Tom Sawyer* is really a town called _____.

4. Sara Crewe lived in the city of
   _____.

5. St. Louis is in the same state as
   _____.

Lesson 134

D CONTEXT CLUES

For each item, circle the answer that means the same thing as the word in bold type.

1. The fancy party had a **lavish** amount of food.
   a. considerable b. dreadful
   c. crazed d. breezy

2. The island was so **remote** that only a few people had been there.
   a. inlet b. manned
   c. pale d. far away

3. Some people prefer to walk ahead of a group, but others prefer to **straggle** behind.
   a. romp b. walk slowly
   c. slumber d. yield

E FILLING OUT FORMS

Use the facts to fill out the form.

Facts: Your name is Tom Sawyer, and you live in St. Petersburg, Missouri. You are 22 years old and are applying to the University of Missouri Law School. You once testified at a murder trial, where you were the most important witness. You are good with words and can make people believe almost anything you say. Although people think you are smart, you have been a poor student. Your grade-school teacher, Mr. Dobbins, thought you were a naughty boy and often punished you.

1. Write your full name (last name first).
   _____

2. In which state do you reside?
   _____

3. Describe your experience with the legal system in one or two sentences.
   _____
   _____
   _____

4. What qualities do you have that might make you a good lawyer?
   _____
   _____
   _____

5. Did you get good grades in school?
   _____

6. What was the name of your grade-school teacher?
   _____

GO TO PART D IN YOUR TEXTBOOK

Name

A STORY DETAILS

Work the items.

1. At the beginning of this chapter, Tom and Becky scarcely noticed they were in a part of the cave without any _____ on the walls.

2. Tom and Becky found a narrow stairway behind a _____ .

3. The ceiling of one cavern was covered with animals called _____ .

4. Those animals were disturbed by ▨ .
   a. light   b. movement   c. sound

5. The story says, "the deep stillness of the place laid a ▨ hand upon the spirits of the children."
   a. comforting   b. gloved   c. clammy

6. When Tom and Becky realized they were lost, why didn't they go back the way they came?
   a. They forgot to bring a map.
   b. They knew another way.
   c. They wanted to avoid the animals.

7. What did Tom forget to make as he and Becky walked through the cave?
   a. piles of rocks   b. marks on the walls
   c. sandwiches

B CLOZE SENTENCES

Complete each sentence with the correct word.

| apprehensive | chap | influence |
| burglar | deputy | revived |

1. After getting lots of water and sun, the plant finally _____ .

2. Everyone felt _____ about the massive storm.

3. The lawyer used words carefully to _____ the jury.

4. Baylee was a _____ sheriff, but she really wanted to be a sheriff.

Lesson 135   269

C CONTEXT CLUES

For each item, circle the answer that means the same thing as the word(s) in bold type.

1. The hairs on a human head are too **numerous** to count.
   a. thin
   b. light
   c. many
   d. long

2. The patient **felt relieved** after talking to the doctor.
   a. came back to life
   b. worried less
   c. felt sicker
   d. was angry

3. The smiling banker turned out to be a **scoundrel** who stole everyone's money and left town.
   a. dishonest person
   b. jolly baker
   c. slunk
   d. sentry

D POEM REVIEW

Write whether each line comes from "Miracles," "The Tide Rises," or "Written in March."

1. The little waves, with their soft white hands
   _____

2. To me, the sea is a continual miracle
   _____

3. Or the exquisite delicate thin curve of the new moon in spring
   _____

4. The rain is over and gone!
   _____

5. The twilight dampens, the curlew calls
   _____

E COMPARING CHARACTERS

Complete each sentence with *Tom*, *Becky*, or *Outlaw Joe*.

1. "I escaped from the Welshman," said _____ .

2. "I decided to go to the picnic instead of helping Huck," said _____ .

3. "I saw a beautiful country in my dream," said _____ .

4. "I was unable to get my revenge," said _____ .

5. "I forgot to make marks on the wall," said _____ .

GO TO PART D IN YOUR TEXTBOOK

Name ____________________

136

A STORY DETAILS

Work the items.

1. Tom wanted to stay by the spring so he and Becky could ____ .

   a. go swimming b. drink water

   c. write their names

2. Tom and Becky watched the candle burn away until only a half-inch of ____ remained.

   a. flame b. smoke c. wick

3. What sound gave hope to Tom and Becky?

   a. dripping water b. a shout c. a siren

4. Tom and Becky couldn't tell how deep or wide the ____________________ were.

5. Tom unwound a line of ____________________ as he groped along a passage.

6. Who was holding a candle not twenty yards from Tom? ____________________
____

7. The story says that hunger is greater than ____ .

   a. fear b. pride c. thirst

B CLOZE SENTENCES

Complete each sentence with the correct word.

lavish	paralyzed	relic
overwhelmed	pitfall	remote

1. Nasir was ____________________ by the number of text messages on his cell phone.

2. Missing your flight is a classic ____________________ of air travel.

3. It's hard to get more ____________________ than the South Pole.

C CONTEXT CLUES

For each item, circle the answer that means the same thing as the word in bold type.

1. Fala **proposed** taking a shortcut to the store.

    a. suggested   b. straggled

    c. disagreed about   d. dreaded

2. The wolf was **famished** because there was nothing to eat.

    a. overhanging   b. half-crazed

    c. pale   d. very hungry

3. Many people fell asleep during the **tedious** sermon.

    a. bygone   b. boring

    c. clammy   d. pleasant

GO TO PART D IN YOUR TEXTBOOK

Name _____ 137

A STORY DETAILS

Work the items.

1. While Tom was missing, Aunt Polly dropped into ▓▓▓ .
   a. melancholy   b. a pitfall   c. rejoicing

2. When Tom explored the third passage, he noticed a speck of ▓▓▓ .
   a. dust   b. gold   c. light

3. On what day of the week were the children found? _____

4. After the children were found, a throng of people swept ▓▓▓ up the main street.
   a. magnificently   b. ordinarily
   c. securely

5. After the children were found, Judge Thatcher ▓▓▓ the cave door.
   a. repaired   b. sealed   c. removed

6. Tom turned as ▓▓▓ when Judge Thatcher told him about the cave door.
   a. red as a beet   b. white as a sheet
   c. green as a lime

7. Outlaw Joe tried to hack through the cave door with his _____ .

8. Outlaw Joe drank the water that dripped into a ▓▓▓ .
   a. stalactite   b. bowl   c. stalagmite

B CLOZE SENTENCES

Complete each sentence with the correct word.

| apprehensive | influence | revive |
| funeral | provisions | sill |

1. Their _____ for the long hike included lots of water.

2. All the people at the _____ wore black clothes.

3. The children were _____ when they entered the haunted house.

4. My cats love to sleep on the sunny _____ at the bottom of the window.

Lesson 137   273

C CONTEXT CLUES

For each item, circle the answer that means the same thing as the word in bold type.

1. There were only nine houses in the **hamlet** at the end of the road.

   a. boatload   b. short wick

   c. small village   d. overhang

2. The church bells began to **peal** when it was time for the celebration.

   a. disagree   b. ring loudly

   c. pity   d. clam

3. Tom and Huck have **numerous** adventures in several books.

   a. many   b. whichever

   c. filing   d. dogged

D SEQUENCING

Number the events in the correct sequence.

____ Tom saw Outlaw Joe in the cave.

____ Tom and Becky got lost in the cave.

____ Tom crawled out of the cave.

____ Tom and Becky entered the cave.

____ Outlaw Joe starved to death.

GO TO PART D IN YOUR TEXTBOOK

Name _____

A STORY DETAILS

Work the items.

1. Tom and Huck traveled down the river in a small boat called a _____ .

2. The secret entrance to the cave was in a thick clump of _____ .

3. Tom wanted his gang of _____ to use the cave.

4. The gang would capture people and hold them for ▇▇▇ .
   a. ever   b. arrest   c. ransom

5. What had Tom and Becky left at the spring?
   a. a fragment of candle
   b. a cup of water
   c. a smoke mark on the wall

6. Outlaw Joe had said that Hiding Place Number Two was under the _____ .

7. Huck was afraid that Outlaw Joe's _____ would be near Hiding Place Number Two.

B CLOZE SENTENCES

Complete each sentence with the correct word.

| amounted | overwhelming | ransom |
| foundry | paralyzed | tedious |

1. The movie was so boring and _____ that everyone fell asleep.

2. The government refused to pay a _____ for the captured soldier.

3. Sasha took the old metal posts to the _____ to be melted down.

4. The bill for the wedding _____ to twenty thousand dollars.

C CONTEXT CLUES

For each item, circle the answer that means the same thing as the word in bold type.

1. The **bluffs** got steeper as the kayakers traveled down the stream.
   a. landslides b. water-drips
   c. riverbanks d. pitfalls

2. Roy felt **famished** after a day without food.
   a. very hungry b. very thirsty
   c. very thin d. famous

3. It's easy to **propose** a plan, but it's hard to carry out a plan.
   a. secure b. influence
   c. revive d. suggest

D COMPARE AND CONTRAST

Complete each sentence with *Tom*, *Huck*, or *Tom and Huck*.

1. _____
   learned about things by reading books.

2. _____
   had superstitious beliefs.

3. _____
   made a plan for finding the treasure.

4. _____
   didn't want anybody to know that he saved the widow.

5. _____
   wanted to name a gang after himself.

GO TO PART D IN YOUR TEXTBOOK

A STORY DETAILS

Work the items.

1. What is one piece of evidence that Tom used to figure out where the treasure box was?

    a. a map   b. footprints   c. an arrow

2. The treasure box weighed about _____ pounds.

3. Why did the boys put the treasure in bags?

    a. The treasure box was falling apart.
    b. The treasure box was screwed into the ground.
    c. They couldn't carry the treasure box.

4. The Welshman thought that Tom and Huck were carrying old ▬▬ in the wagon.

    a. silver   b. iron   c. tin

5. The Widow Douglas told the guests that she was _____ Huck.

6. Huck almost forgot the discomfort of his new clothes in the _____ of the widow's praise.

7. Huck and Tom's treasure amounted to a little over _____ thousand dollars.

8. A little over _____ thousand dollars of the treasure belonged to Huck.

B CLOZE SENTENCES

Complete each sentence with the correct word.

| adopt | interrupted | provisions |
| funeral | occupied | skimmed |

1. The huge chest of drawers _____ about one-fourth of the bedroom.

2. Many people wanted to _____ the cute puppy.

3. The rude boy _____ Betty right after she started speaking.

4. The quickly moving flat stone _____ across the surface of the pond.

C CONTEXT CLUES

For each item, circle the answer that means the same thing as the word in bold type.

1. Taka hadn't studied, so she **fretted** about taking the test.
   a. dampened   b. straggled
   c. worried   d. slunk

2. Mario could **furnish** an excuse for everything he did wrong.
   a. supply   b. educate
   c. clad   d. secure

3. When the clock struck midnight, the bells began to **peal**.
   a. peel   b. rind
   c. gnaw   d. ring

D COMPARING CHARACTERS

Complete each sentence about Huck with *Aunt Polly, Tom, the Welshman,* or *the Widow Douglas.*

1. "He signals me by meowing like a cat," said _____.

2. "I won't allow my nephews to play with that filthy young man," said _____.

3. "I could tell he was lying about what happened at the Widow Douglas's," said _____.

4. "I found out how good he was when I took care of him," said _____.

GO TO PART D IN YOUR TEXTBOOK

Name ______________________________

A STORY DETAILS

Work the items.

1. The Widow Douglas put Huck's share of the treasure in the ________________ .
2. How many dollars a day did Huck get from the treasure? ________________
3. The Widow Douglas introduced Huck into ____ .

   a. savagery b. robbery c. society
4. Huck complained that the Widow Douglas eats, goes to bed, and gets up by a ________________ .
5. Tom found Huck sleeping in a ________________ .
6. Tom said Huck had to be ____ to join the gang.

   a. famished b. respectable c. wealthy
7. Why couldn't the boys have their initiation ceremonies in a haunted house?

   a. All the haunted houses had been ripped apart.

   b. They had to hold the ceremonies in a cave.

   c. They were afraid of ghosts.
8. Huck thought the Widow Douglas would be proud of him if he became a famous ________________ .

B CLOZE SENTENCES

Complete each sentence with the correct word.

actual	civilization	ransom
amount	foundry	visible

1. The estimated cost for the project was much lower than the ________________ cost.
2. The tall tower was ________________ for miles around.
3. Some people don't want to join modern ________________ .
4. The temperature inside the ________________ was very high.

C CONTEXT CLUES

For each item, circle the answer that means the same thing as the word in bold type.

1. Nothing could **quench** the raging fire.
   - a. glorify
   - b. put out
   - c. wick
   - d. edit

2. The speaker's bad jokes had little **impact** on the crowd.
   - a. effect
   - b. interrupt
   - c. fret
   - d. captive

3. Cassandra had to scale the **bluff** to escape the rapidly rising river.
   - a. joke
   - b. rind
   - c. boatload
   - d. cliff

D COMPARE AND CONTRAST

Complete each sentence with *Tom* or *Huck*.

1. "Being rich ain't what it's cracked up to be," said _____.

2. "I got to wear them blamed clothes that just smothers me," said _____.

3. "We can't let you into the gang if you ain't respectable," said _____.

4. "We'll do it just like they do in the books," said _____.

5. "I like the woods and the river and the barrels, and I'll stick to them," said _____.

GO TO PART D IN YOUR TEXTBOOK

280   Lesson 140